Faith to Finish

By

Karen Faith McGowan

"...let us run with patience the race that is set before us. Looking unto Jesus the author and finisher of our faith"
(Hebrews 12:1-2).

Faith to Finish

ISBN10: 0-9795782-8-0
ISBN13: 978-0-9795782-8-1

For book ordering information or to schedule a speaking engagement, please contact:

Karen Faith McGowan
P.O. Box 204534
Augusta, Georgia 30917-4534
706-449-2863

Email FTF@knology.net

Published By:
Christian Writers Network
4104-C Colben Blvd.
Evans, Georgia 30809
(706) 210-1000

Dedication

I dedicate this book to my dad, Joe Dismuke, who taught me the most valuable lesson of my life, which was how to love "unconditionally." Because of his example, I have been able to accept God's unconditional love for me, I am able to forgive and love others, and I am able to enjoy an intimate relationship with my Heavenly Father, the One who first loved me. Thank you, Dad.

I also dedicate this book to my nephew, Jeffrey John Cason, and his mother, Ann Jacobs. Only God was aware of the fact that as she was reading this book on July 3, 2007, she was about to become the first person to benefit from the words on its pages.

While God was preparing her heart for loss, He was preparing Jeffrey for his finish line and the completion of his life's race. Jeffrey's death gives completion, explanation, and closure to this book.

All our days are numbered, and it is not for us to know how long our race will be. It is our faith in God and our relationship with Him that sustains us through the storms of life, allows us to keep running with patience, and gives us the faith to finish our race with the anticipation of reaching our eternal reward in Heaven.

Jeffrey John Cason sustained fatal injuries
in an automobile accident on
July 4th, 2007

3

Acknowledgements

First of all, I would like to thank my Heavenly Father for answering my prayer. Seven years ago, I asked God for a story to share that would minister to the hearts of people who were searching for an up close and personal relationship with Him, as I was.

God's ways are not our ways, and though He didn't answer my prayer quite like I would have imagined, the remarkable story He placed on my lips and in my heart will resonate how His power and glory were revealed to me from now to eternity.

I would also like to thank Him for allowing me the privilege to print my story in order that you too could learn that God continues to perform miracles in the lives of His children.

I thank Him for demonstrating His love for me through His Son, Jesus Christ. I also thank Him for loving me enough to want to spend eighteen days in fellowship with me. He held me, comforted me, revealed things to me, taught me, and sustained me. I praise Him for an up close and personal "Close Encounter" with God the Father, God the Son, and God the Holy Spirit. I thank Him for never giving up on me and for seeing me worthy of perfecting my faith.

To the churches who allowed me the first opportunities to share my story, I thank you. Each opportunity allowed me to grow in the realization of the need in our world for people to grow deeper in their relationship with God. We live in a society that is searching for love and acceptance. People everywhere are trying to find purpose and fulfillment in their lives. The problem is, they are looking everywhere except right where they can find it, in the arms of God.

To the many congregations who prayed for me; I hope that one day I will have the opportunity of visiting you and letting your people see a miracle. I believe one of God's reasons for leaving me in the race was to allow my story to give hope and to build faith in those who are witnesses to His marvelous works. How blessed I am that He chose me to endure the pain in order to obtain the gain. I am humbled that He saw me worthy of His call and that He trusted me to obey. In the world's eyes I may be a "nobody," but to God I am a "somebody" who loves Him with all her heart.

I could never have completed this book without the encouragement and supportive assistance of my family.

To my husband, Charles:
You have always believed in me, even when I didn't believe in myself. You have been the wind beneath my wings that raised me up to be the person I am today, with God's help and guidance. You are my best friend, my confidant, and the foundation for our family. You walked with me through the most difficult time in my life and you never let go of me. You sacrificially gave of yourself to care for my every need, even though you had needs of your own. I will be forever grateful to God for your presence in my life. For forty years you have been my best friend and I thank God for the blessing of being your wife and the mother of your children.

You have stood by me when members of my own family rejected me. You have rejoiced with me in the good times and shared my sorrow in the bad times.

You worked to provide for our needs and you bore the financial burden of my illness with never so much as one complaint. What would I have done without you to care for me, pray for me, and love me through this experience? I cannot imagine.

You have watched over me and shared in my pain. You shed tears of joy with me in the victories and shared my grief in the disappointments. Through it all, we both have learned to trust God more. We have also learned what it really means to walk by faith, not by sight. I will love you always with every fiber of my being. I know that you were created just for me. In your humble, meek spirit lies a giant of a man.

To my sons Paul and Nathan:

The two of you have always been my joy. You are my greatest gifts from Heaven, next to Jesus Christ. I cannot imagine my life without the two of you in it. You have always made me so proud to be your mother. You needed me and I needed you. I cherish the memories of times past and I look forward to making many more.

I will never forget Christmas 2005. For the first time in either of your lives I couldn't wish you a Merry Christmas. It was so hard not to be able to hold you in my arms, hug you, or thank you for just being "you." How it broke my heart to feel separated from you by a lack of consciousness. I was aware of your presence and I was aware of your encouraging words to keep fighting for life; however, I knew that I could do nothing to ease your pain. At that time, I had no way of knowing if there would ever be another Christmas to celebrate together.

I prayed that God would see me worthy of continuing my race here on earth. I wanted to be able to do more for His kingdom and it was your words of comfort and your need that helped me to keep pressing on. You helped me to maintain my position in the race as I trusted God, in faith, for the outcome.

I was totally dependent on family, friends, and my Heavenly Father to give you the comfort that I could not give you. This was one time Mom could not kiss you and make the hurt go away. My illness was a trial that we all had to endure. Though I was helpless and unable to comfort you, God was there to do that for me.

As I drew near death's door there were so many things I wanted another chance to say to you. I never told you enough how much I love you, appreciate you, and how proud I am of the strong men the two of you have become. I never told you enough the things about you that made you special in my eyes. I prayed for another chance to do so and according to His will, God answered my prayer.

This is my chance to permanently write my love letter to you, but there is nothing more important for me to say than to encourage you to run your race with patience and a determination to know God intimately. Let your lives be a walk of faith and dependence on God to lead, guide, and direct your paths. Seek always to walk in obedience to His will for your lives and you will forever be blessed.

Know that His presence is with you always, even when the time comes that I am not. I trust that this experience was His opportunity to allow you to feel His presence in your lives, as I have felt Him in mine. I am so grateful that you both know Him as your Savior and for that reason we will be together for all eternity. I tell you once more, "I will love you always and forever."

You not only stood by me, but you also stood by your father to support him during a time when he was so distraught. This brought me great comfort when I was unable to do so myself. I knew that if God chose to take me home to Heaven you would take care of him for me.

To all those who read this book:

I pray that you will benefit from the lessons I have learned through this experience and I hope you will be able to incorporate these things into your own lives so that you can also know God more intimately.

May you see me as a person who trusted God and learned to walk by faith. Through the power of the Holy Spirit living within you may you find the faith, the determination, the persistence, and the endurance to complete your own life's race as you walk in obedience to His will. You can and you will if you seek to know Him with all your heart. I am blessed to know that He would use me as an example to help you find the "Faith to Finish." In doing so He has given my life its purpose.

To my husband, children, family, and friends:

Thank you for never letting me give up. I was ready to say goodbye to this old world and all its troubles, but I clung to life from a bed in ICU because I didn't want to say goodbye to you. In fact, because I love you so much, I could hardly stand the thought of never being able to share with you my experience of being in the presence of Jehovah. I was so anxious to tell you how He gave me such peace and comfort as He walked with me through the valley of the shadow of death. I pray that in this book I have given you just a glimpse of what it was like to be surrounded and protected by the presence of God.

To my daughters-in-law, Suzanne and Sharon:

I feel so blessed to have you in our family. Our prayer for our sons was always that they would find a mate that would love them as much as we did and that would take care of them as we had always tried to do. I am confident that God created you both for our sons.

I love you for taking such good care of my husband while I was in a coma and for doing the many things you did to make sure he was cared for, like helping him choose his clothes!

I thank you for taking such good care of me during and after my hospitalization. From keeping the nurses straight, to pedicures, from grocery shopping, to hairdressing, from transporting me to and from appointments, to laundry, from paying bills, to words of encouragement - you did it all! I thank you for loving me so much.

To those who cared for me professionally:

I would be negligent if I failed to also recognize the doctors, nurses, and therapists who cared for me during my illness and rehabilitation. You allowed God's wisdom to permeate your decisions for treatment. When it seemed there was nothing more you could do, God gave you an alternative and you listened.

May you always know that because you cared for me with hands skilled by God's grace and because God chose to heal me and spare me for His purpose, you will be a part of every good thing I do for the rest of my life. Every person whose life I am able to touch will also be touched by you. I thank you from the bottom of my heart.

To the many family members, friends, and acquaintances who have asked for a written account of my story:

I thank you for the encouragement to complete this daunting task. For all those who kept me focused by asking me the status of this book, I thank you. You too will have a part in touching lives through this endeavor.

To my sisters-in-law, Ann and Melba:

I thank you for being so willing to give of your time, wisdom, and knowledge in order to make this book a blessing for others. I will always be grateful to you for your sacrificial effort, even in the midst of your own personal pain.

To my many friends and family:

Thank you for your prayers. They drew you closer to God. Though they weren't prayed to change His will, He used your prayers to prepare you to accept His will.

God knew that my work on earth was not complete, but still He tested my faith, my trust, and my patience. He tested my belief in His ability to heal me and He proved to me that there is no peace like being totally surrendered to Him and obedient to His purpose. In my dependent state, He transported me to a higher level in my spiritual walk. I will forever be grateful to Him for His mercy and healing.

May you all find joy in knowing that God always has our best interest in mind and He will work His will and way in our lives in order to perfect our faith and give us the strength to keep running to the finish line. It is a faith that is found only in knowing Him. God will use whatever it takes to prove His love for us as He draws us closer and closer to His heart. May He bless you all, as He has blessed me.

My tribute:
May all honor, glory, and praise be to God for the things He has done and continues to do in my life.

"I thank my God upon every remembrance of you" (*Philippians 1:3*).

Karen

Table of Contents

Preface

"Let the words of my mouth, and the meditation of my heart, be acceptable in thy sight, O Lord, my strength, and my redeemer." (Psalm 19:14)

You are about to read a compelling story about a journey of faith, belief, hope, deliverance, and obedience, based on my true life experiences. I pray that your hearts will be blessed by the reading of how God used the events in my life, the longing of my heart, His miraculous healing of my body, and the restoration of my soul to mold me into a vessel of service for His honor and glory.

He used my circumstances to draw me closer to Himself and He established my faith in Him so that I would be able to run with patience the race that was set before me. Because my faith is in Him, I know that I will be able to keep running, even through the storms of life. I will always be looking to Jesus who will continue to perfect my faith until I reach my finish line.

I pray that God will quicken your heart and that you will realize that He wants to have a "Close Encounter" with you, just as He did with me. His heart is bent on an intimate relationship with you and He is looking for a life that is moldable and surrendered to His will. It is in the intimacy of your relationship with your Heavenly Father that you will find the peace that surpasses all understanding.

I pray that your life will take on a new meaning and a new purpose as the Holy Spirit uses the words He has given me to prick your heart and get your attention.

It is my goal to share with you the incredible experience that changed my life by bringing me face to face with my Heavenly Father, His Son, Jesus Christ, and His Holy Spirit.

Most importantly, it is my goal to help you realize that I am just "a nobody" in the eyes of the world, but I have been given a story by "a somebody" to share with "anybody" who will read and listen. This "somebody" is the answer to your doubt and confusion. He is the answer to your troubles and difficulties. He is the answer to your discouragement, doubt, and disbelief. He is the answer to your pain and despair. He is the One who loves you with an everlasting love. He is Holy God.

I pray that by the time you reach the end of this book you will know for certain that His promises are true and that He does work all things for the good of those who love Him and who are called according to His purpose (Romans 8:28). But, I don't want to leave you there. In order for my life to produce fruit, I want to lead you through a pathway of getting to know God more intimately, which will help you find His purpose for your own life.

"Finding Faith to Finish" is a handbook that will introduce you to the Triune God. By getting to know Him more you will gain insight into how He works in your life through each of His three persons; Father, Son, and Holy Spirit. In this handbook I share with you:

- Things I have learned about having faith in Him
- How to seek His wisdom and understanding
- How to become like Him in humility
- Why we need to obey Him
- How to understand the purpose of your sufferings
- How to let go of the past
- What it means to have your life produce abundant fruit

I pray that you learn from my experiences and that within the pages of the handbook, you will find the faith to finish your own race, while walking hand-in-hand with God.

How seriously are you taking your pursuit of a relationship with Him? How much are you longing to find your life's purpose? How is your walk of faith and obedience? If you will seek God as I did, you will find what you are looking for, because He is longing to share His love with you.

If reading my account gives you some direction and insight, then I will know that my suffering was not in vain. I have made an attempt to record the most precious days of my life....my journey through the valley of the shadow of death. I pray that my experience will help you find your place in the race and that you will pursue a position in first place.

God's word says that we have a race to run. This race is different from the world's view because it is not about competition and it's not about being the winner. It's about having the "Faith to Finish;" no matter the call, no matter the circumstances, no matter the obstacles, and no matter the tests.

Oh yes, it's a race that tests our faith because without a test, there is no grade and without a grade, there is no promotion. God wants to promote us to a new level in our faith walk with Him. Our reward for this promotion will not be a medal; it will be joy on earth and in Heaven a crown of righteousness.

It is my goal, and should be that of every Christian, to cross the finish line knowing that I did my best and I ran my race to please God. My heart's desire is to be able to stand before my Lord in Heaven and hear Him say, "Well done, My good and faithful servant."

The theme of my story is based on Hebrews 12:1-2.

"Wherefore seeing we also are compassed about with so great a cloud of witnesses, let us lay aside every weight, and the sin which doth so easily beset us, and let us run with patience the race that is set before us. Looking unto Jesus the author and finisher of our faith."

As believers, we belong to God. We have been bought with a price, which was the blood of Jesus Christ shed on Calvary. He came to earth to redeem us from our sins and to save us from an eternity in hell.

Christ came to earth to complete His Father's will and He did it out of love. His love is so unfathomable that we will never be able to grasp the magnitude of it. He was willing to suffer agony in order to provide a way for us to spend eternity

14

in Heaven with Him. It is not God's will that any should perish, but that all men would come to know Christ as a Savior who died and rose again to sit at the right hand of God to intercede on our behalf.

It is with a grateful heart that I accept my challenge. With the world looking on, I will run my race with faith, grace, and dignity. I know that with God's help, I will have faith to finish the race He has set before me and that I will have the patience and perseverance to pursue the victory which comes from knowing Him. I will not be a victim of my circumstances; but instead, with God fighting my battles for me, I will reach the finish line victorious.

God has a plan for your life, as He does for mine. His plan is "to give you hope and a future," as His word tells us in Jeremiah 29:11. The many bumps in the road, the crooked paths, the trials and tribulations, the problems, and even the times of crisis that occur in our lives are merely tools in God's hands. They strengthen our faith, teach us more of who He is, and make us more dependent on Him.

God molds us and refines us for His service. It is through the fire that the impurities are removed, shackles are broken, and we come forth as gold. All He asks for is our availability to be molded, not our ability to withstand the heat. He doesn't call the equipped, He equips the called. He doesn't want our excuses. All He wants is a heart that is willing to follow Him, no matter the cost.

God's desire is that we accept His greatest gift to us, which is His Son, Jesus Christ. By this acceptance, we become connected to Him and we are forever privileged to have fellowship with Him. The decision doesn't stop there. He also wants us to make a conscious decision to have an ongoing, intimate relationship with Him. He wants us to walk in fellowship with the Holy Spirit who connects us to God forever and who leads and guides us on our journey through life.

In His word God says that if we will draw near to Him He will show us great and mighty things that we are not aware of.

15

He is drawing you towards Himself right at this very moment and you are taking the first step in following Him by continuing to read this book.

I encourage you to seek Him because He cares for you. God knows your every weakness. He knows your struggles and He also knows your heart. Even though we sin against Him, He still loves us with an unconditional, everlasting love.

What is it that made you want to read this book? Did someone suggest it to you? Was it the title that caught your eye or did the Holy Spirit guide you to leaf through its pages in anticipation of hearing from God?

Are you passionately running to finish your life's race for God's kingdom and for eternity or are you running to keep from losing? Are you running on a treadmill headed nowhere or are you running the race with an eternal purpose in mind? Are your eyes fixed on the finish line or are you focused on the trivial matters of life which leave you confused and without direction? Are you trying to run, but finding that your race is encumbered by obstacles and detours? Have you been running so long in the race that you have run out of steam?

I pray that your faith will be awakened, re-energized, reaffirmed, and redirected as you seek to hear from God. Trust Him when to simply trust Him is the hardest thing of all. He will guide you along the journey as you surrender your heart and will to His control.

If you're feeling lonely, unworthy, and unloved, allow God to wrap His arms around you and cradle you with an everlasting, unconditional love that surpasses all human comprehension. He will use the scriptures quoted in this book to speak to you, as He did to me.

This is my first endeavor to capture my thoughts, translate them, and put them on paper. It is my desire that all the glory and honor goes to God Almighty, my Savior Jesus Christ, and the Holy Spirit who lives within me. It is He who has given me a story to tell and then equipped me for the call.

All my life I have wanted to be used by God to make a difference in "your" life. The explicit instruction from God to write this book has given purpose to my life. Within its pages God may give you the direction you are looking for in order to find your purpose as well. Nothing would please me more!

Thank you for taking the time to read my first literary accomplishment. If it changes your life, I would love to hear about it. But if it changes yours, chances are there is someone you know who needs to deepen their relationship with God too. All I ask of you is to join me in the race. See the world as your mission field and never be ashamed to share the gospel. Pick up the baton of faith and "pass it on."

God bless you,
Karen Faith McGowan

Introduction

The Race

"...let us run with patience the race that is set before us. Looking unto Jesus, the author and finisher of our faith (Hebrews 12:1-2).

God has given each of us a race to run. He expects us to run it with patience and perseverance. It is our responsibility to run with one focus and that is to glorify God. If we are running in obedience to Him, our lives will glorify Him.

Let's break this scripture down to see if we can understand a little more about why the writer of Hebrews compared our lives to a race.

Verse 1:

The *"...large crowd of witnesses"* gives reference to heroes of the past who ran their race with endurance and faith. Such heroes would be men of God such as Noah. He obeyed God and endured the scorn of unbelievers, but built an ark as God instructed him, even though he didn't know what a flood was and there wasn't a storm cloud in the sky.

Then there was Sarah, preparing for childbirth at one hundred years of age because she believed God and His promise that she would bear a son.

How could we not mention Abraham who lifted a blade to slay his only son, still believing and trusting that God would provide a sacrifice, and He did. These heroes walked in faith, along with so many, many more.

If a Bible study group was going to study heroes of faith, would your name be mentioned as one of the most faithful? I believe that our faith is one of the most rewarded aspects of our Christian lives.

If you were to find yourself in a time of testing, how firm would you stand in your faith?

The true test of our faith is our "testimony." God's grace will see us through our tests. We learn from the experience and we grow in the process. We testify of God's faithfulness as we wait on His instruction and His timing. We testify of His love and mercy that sustains us and prepares us for what He has called us to do. The faithful will testify.

The heroes of faith that I have briefly mentioned, have been escorted off the track and into the grandstands, but their legacy remains to encourage those of us who are still in the arena to keep the "Faith to Finish."

I am not a theologian or Bible scholar, but I believe the crowd of witnesses could also mean the world that is always watching to see how we are going to run our race. We testify of our faith every time we fall and get back up. With our eyes fixed on the author and finisher of our faith, we show the world where we put our faith and trust by maintaining our position in the race.

No runner would ever think of adding excess weight that would impede his progress. Therefore we must "...*lay aside every weight and the sin which doth so easily beset us.*" This means all the things that get in our way of serving God and those that prevent our fellowship with Him. For a Christian, this would mean anything that would slow our pace or impair our progression of growing in faith.

This could be things like a lack of discipline, lack of obedience, unconfessed sin, procrastination, lack of perseverance, fear, guilt, lack of humility, pride, relationships, and a host of other things.

To "...*run with patience (endurance) the race that is set before us*" refers to the shedding of unnecessary burdens. "Endurance" in the Greek implies to press on to the end despite obstacles or difficulties. It also implies refusing to be deterred. The word "race" refers to the path God has pre-ordained for us.

19

Verse 2: In this verse the author instructs us to keep "...*looking unto Jesus.*" This means to keep our focus on Him because Jesus is the source and perfecter of our faith. In other words, He is the One who initiated and will finish our faith.

Many times in the New Testament joy is linked with suffering. Jesus endured suffering on a cross in exchange for the "*joy*" of providing a way of escape for sinners. "...*endured the cross*" means that nothing mattered more to Him than doing His Father's will. "I have come that you may have life and have it more abundantly."

He, "...*despising the shame,*" held it of little importance compared to the joy of persevering to the end. His joy was found in fulfilling His Father's will and for doing so He now sits "...*at the right hand of the throne of God.*"

Verse 3: "*Consider*" means to think about, compare, and weigh Christ's endurance against any of our sufferings. No matter what we will ever have to endure, it will never compare to the suffering Christ did for us on Calvary. The shame and weight of the whole world's sins were upon Him.

The writer of Hebrews wanted us to see our difficulties both as discipline and opportunities for growth because the Lord chastens those whom He loves and He demands repentance for our sins. What a blessing is God's love.

Some pain is included in God's course for His children. Our Heavenly Father's main interest is in building our character into the likeness of Christ. God's discipline provides us with a sense of security and assures us of our relationship with Him. The ultimate goal of His discipline is "inner healing".

He also wants us to see our trials as opportunities for promotion. God tests our devotion to Him by allowing us decisions which show Him where our devotion lies. He will not promote us until we are ready to handle the assignment.

"*Lest ye be wearied and faint in your minds*" refers to keeping our eyes fixed on Jesus so that we will not lose heart.

The way to prevent our weariness is to have a determined plan to finish the race God has for us, regardless of the handicaps or obstacles. By God's grace (unmerited favor), we will endure, we will walk in faith, we will trust in His provision, and we will never walk alone.

Obviously, God wants us to see our lives through His eyes and that is, as a race. Our race began the day we were born and it will end the day we die. What we do with the years, months, and days between birth and death is a choice given to us by God, our Creator. One day every man will give account for what he did with his life and how he ran his race.

The key to running this race is endurance. This doesn't mean that we look for an easy way to finish or an easy way out of trials. Instead, it means deciding to grit our teeth, put our face to the wind, and ask for strength, through the power of the Holy Spirit, to contend in the race, endure it, and finish. To endure is the only way to finish successfully.

Our challenge is to end well so that God's glory will be made manifest and His grace will be evident in our lives. As we run with patience it will be our faith that sustains us. With each victory our faith will grow and our belief in the outcome of the race will strengthen us.

Only God knows who may hear of our faithfulness to keep running. Through our testimony others will become believers by accepting Christ as the leader of their race. Therefore, we will have passed the torch to another follower. This is God's command (Matthew 28).

In Romans 14:12 we read, *"...every one of us will give account of himself to God."* The Holy Spirit is our accountability partner. He will help us make sure we run our race with integrity, even when the odds are against us.

There is no way for us to know where our race will take us. There will be times when we find ourselves running in a marathon and other times it may be a one-hundred-yard dash. Some days we may be in a sprint or maybe we'll be in a steady jog. No matter how we are running, it is up to us to move step by step with the Savior while allowing Him to live

21

in and through us that we may be a beacon of light to a sinful world. The testimony of our faith will illuminate their paths and show them the way to salvation.

The testimony of our faith and obedience should be, *"I am crucified with Christ: nevertheless I live; yet not I, but Christ liveth in me: and the life which I now live in the flesh I live by the faith of the Son of God, who loved me, and gave Himself for me." Galatians 2:20.*

One of life's undeniable truths is that the path we choose will ultimately determine our future. Fueled by the desire to find our course, our restlessness will keep us in the race. We then have a choice: to follow Christ and find peace and purpose, or go our own way and find confusion and discontent.

The greatest blessing of my life has been to be a walking miracle of God and to be able to give hope and encouragement to others because of God's amazing grace. It was His mercy and grace that sustained me during the most difficult portion of my race, thus far. No doubt, before my life is over there will be other opportunities for God to use His refining fire to purify me and prepare me. I pray that it will be my unwavering faith in Him that again brings about an even greater testimony.

God will never shortchange us. He is patiently waiting to give us all the instruction, training, and guidance we need so that we will be equipped to not only run our race, but run successfully.

With God we get what we pay for. "Give, and it shall be given unto you; good measure, pressed down, and shaken together, and running over…" When we give Him our life, the reward is so worth the price (Luke 6:38).

Our sense of purpose will cause us to work with a sense of excellence. This doesn't mean we will always be the best at everything, but it will insure that we maintain our feelings of self-worth by giving Him our best. Knowing our purpose will also help us take responsibility for our actions, realizing that there are consequences for not following the leader of our race, Jesus Christ.

When we give our best we will give of ourselves in love to others, just as Christ loved us. Give your best and God will bless you. There is no better feeling than walking away from a race knowing that, even if you weren't the winner, you trusted God by faith, ran your best, and you finished.

*"The Race"...*is the foundation for everything we will talk about in this book. I will give you my best effort, though feeble as it may seem. I will share with you my testimony of how God answered my prayer and drew me nearer to Himself. It was a "Close Encounter" that placed me in the presence of Jehovah God.

I will give you examples of my humanness, frailty, and weaknesses in order that I may show you that God can use anyone who has a willing and submissive heart. I will attempt to portray my life in such transparency that I pray you will see yourself in my circumstances and question your own response to the urging of the Holy Spirit when He says, "Follow me."

I will give you an introduction to a Heavenly Father who longs for you to know Him intimately as Father, Son, and Holy Spirit. Knowing Him is the reason we are in this race and how well we know Him will determine how we finish.

My goal will be to portray the mighty hand of God as the "author and finisher of my faith." My prayer is that you will find direction for your own path, a light to lead, a footprint to follow, and a purpose for doing so.

I am confident that I have done my best to complete the task that God commissioned me to do. He instructed me to share with you what He has done in my life through a relationship that I found in Him. He said, "Tell My people how much I love them, tell them what it is like to be in My presence, and tell them how much I long to have an intimate relationship with them."

Before you were born, God was creating a master plan for your life. He equipped you with the skills and talents that He knew would be necessary for you to use in running your race. By finding out who you are in Him and through developing a personal relationship with Him, you will find the direction you are looking for in your life, just as I did.

May the Holy Spirit open the eyes of your heart and reveal to you God's plan for your race as we take a final look at what it means to run our race and to have the "Faith to Finish."

In order to finish our RACE well, we will need to:

R-elease control to the One and only One who is in control
A-ccept our divine "Coach," Jesus Christ
C-ommit to a life of humility and obedience to God
E-xpect the blessing of eternal life that will be awaiting us when we cross the finish line.

I pray, through the inspiration of the Holy Spirit, God will use me as a vessel to provide you with the equipment you will need to run your race successfully. His instructions are included in His rule book, the Bible. I am just one of His **messengers.**

Are you ready to run? If so, ask God to reveal Himself as never before. Ask Him what Hew would have you to do. He longs to hear your prayers and through them you will find the courage to start your race and the *"Faith to Finish."*

Chapter 1
To Know Him, My Heart's Desire

I will never forget the day or the words that pierced my heart and caused me to begin a process of healing, wisdom, and restoration. I will share these with you a little later on.

Before I do, I want to tell you that this process has taken over ten years and is ongoing. It included many stops along the way, including a walk through the valley of the shadow of death. Every circumstance that has happened in my life has helped to mold me and make me into the image of Christ and I continue in my pursuit of knowing Him. It is and always has been my heart's desire.

I see His face in every aspect of my life, the trials and the triumphs. Putting it all together was the key. Only God could have orchestrated the events that came together as *"A Close Encounter of Three Kinds."*

My story begins and ends with a passionate desire to know who God is and to have a relationship with Him that allows me to know Him personally and intimately. The more I began to know Him, the more I began to understand His direction and purpose for my life. The more I understood Him, the more I enjoyed fellowship with Him. The deeper our relationship grew, the more my heart longed to follow Him and the more I followed Him, the more faith He bestowed.

All my life I knew there was more to a relationship with God than just knowing Christ as my Savior. He is a Triune God which means He has three persons: God the Father, God the Son, and God the Holy Spirit. I would often ask myself this question? Why was it necessary for God to become three in one? I knew Christ as my Savior, but the purpose of knowing God intimately as my Father and the Holy Spirit as my Comforter, Teacher, and Guide eluded me.

It took God revealing Himself to me at a time of great need as my *Heavenly Father*, my *Friend*, and my *Comforter* for me to understand His purposes.

I didn't want to neglect any part of a relationship with God, but because I didn't completely understand the role of each of His persons there was an empty feeling in my heart for many years that I knew only He could fill.

God used this void to create a yearning and restlessness in my heart to know Him more. All my life I wanted to please God and I wanted my life to count for Him. I wanted to be able to stand before Him complete and unashamed. I wanted Him to work through me and to use me to help others. I spent many years searching in all the wrong places to find that the whole time He had been pursuing me as much as I was pursuing Him. My longing to have a relationship with Him has been a life long journey of faith. I guess you could say I am appropriately named, "Faith."

We read from the words of Moses,"...*if you seek the Lord your God, you will find Him, if you look for Him with all your heart and with all your soul*" (Deuteronomy 4:29).

In the book of James we read, *"Draw nigh to God, and He will draw nigh to you"* (James 4:8).

This is my story. It is about the ensuing personal, intimate relationship that has transpired because of my willingness to seek after Him. My search for God led me to a bed in an Intensive Care Unit where He came to me and changed my heart. He freed me from the chains of my past and removed obstacles that were hindering my fellowship with Him. He revealed His love to me and showed me that the only thing that mattered in my life was obeying Him. He showed me that I needed to run my race with a goal of fulfilling "His" eternal purposes, not my own.

It didn't take some deep theological knowledge of the scriptures for me to find Him. Knowing "about" Him is a good thing, but knowing the facts about Him did not bring about my relationship "with" Him. I had spent decades trying to accumulate a wealth of information about Him, when all it took to deepen my relationship with Him was a desire to spend time getting to know Him.

Any relationship has to be pursued, but especially one that you want to grow deeper. Think about any new relationship in your life. You could listen to what others have to say about this person all day long, but you would never develop an intimate relationship with them unless you spent time in their presence. By fellowshipping with them you would; learn their ways, you would understand their thoughts, and you would learn their likes and dislikes. The more you got to know them the more you would trust them, believe them, and follow them. It is the same way with our relationship with God.

Let me stop right here to say, when I refer to having an intimate relationship with God, I am not referring to the way the world many times interprets the word "intimate." I am talking about knowing Him so deeply that you "connect at the heart." Having an intimate relationship means you are comfortable sharing even the innermost parts of who you are. It is a relationship built on faith and trust. God longs to have this kind of relationship with every one of His children.

The way I got to know God more was by spending time with Him. This can be accomplished in many ways, but for me it was through prayer and reading His love letter to me, the Bible. God's thoughts are not our thoughts and I will never be able to think as He does, but the more I got to know Him, the more I began to understand how He was using my circumstances, the good and the bad, to deepen my relationship with Him, to develop my faith, and to build my trust in Him.

In order for me to know God intimately, I had to remove any known sin in my life by asking for His forgiveness. Sometimes my sin was obvious, like a bad attitude. But sometimes my sins were more subtle like pride, selfishness, greed, unforgiveness, or the need to ask for forgiveness. My sin separated me from fellowship with God, but not from the love of God. He had to get my attention to show me that sin was hindering my fellowship with Him, but nothing I could ever do would cause Him not to love me. I thank God that in His mercy, He is faithful and just to forgive us of our sins when we repent and ask for His forgiveness.

The intimacy of our relationship grew deeper when I was able to accept His immeasurable, matchless love.

Again, He used events in my life to teach me that His love is unconditional. Not only was this true, but He expected me to love others unconditionally too, even those who are sometimes more difficult to love. He taught me that the way I would show Him how much I loved Him was in how much I loved others. I had to learn the difference between conditional and unconditional love.

In order for our relationship to deepen, I also had to learn to walk in humility, meaning that I put God's plan for my life ahead of my own. He also taught me to put the needs of others before my own. The lesson of humility came with a price.

God taught me that the closer I walked in obedience to His will for my life, the closer our relationship would be. I had to give up selfish ambition to realize the joy and blessing of abiding in His will, even during the times when I didn't understand what He was doing. In order for me to walk in obedience, I had to learn to trust Him with every aspect of my life as I walked by faith, not by sight. As I sought to know Him more, He showed me that my life was to bring honor and glory to Him and that by walking in faith, by being obedient, and by walking humbly before Him and others, this would be accomplished.

The proof of our relationship with God lies in the fruit that is produced in our lives. As I yielded to His control, my passion and my desire became producing "abundant fruit." The most important thing in my life is to continue to grow in my relationship with the Lord. The second most important thing in my life is to help others come to know Him as Savior and then to help them continue to grow in their relationship with Him. By following the path He has given me to run, God can now take my willing heart, my past failures, and my desire to bring honor and glory to His name and make it fruitful.

I pray that through my experience and my attempts to record the courtship between my God and me, you will realize your need to grow in your own relationship with Him as well, by getting to know Him in His three persons.

He can take our lives and turn them into something beautiful, no matter our past. He has a plan and He will give us hope for our future. Trust Him, for God "makes all things beautiful in His time."

I have discovered the joy of building my relationship with God and how it has had an impact on every area of my life. Knowing Him is the most important relationship I have and the fellowship we share is not to be compared with any other.

It takes faith and perseverance to finish our race. In building my relationship with God I have found the encouragement to keep pressing on, knowing that He always has my best interest in mind.

The path has not always been easy. There have been obstacles along my way and hurdles I've had to cross. I have met with boulders and I have climbed high mountains. There have been deserts to cross and rivers to forge. There have been times in my life that I was a victim and there have been times that I was a victor. I have had some hard tests to take, just as I have had some that I didn't pass. There have been times that God's voice was audible and there have times that His voice has been silent. But that's what life is all about. It's about how God builds our foundation of faith in Him, one step at a time. The testing of our faith is how He discovers the strength of our faith.

I could have stopped and fallen to defeat at the first challenge, but I have run with endurance, even in the hard times, because my heart's desire is to honor Him with my faithfulness. God never promised me that my life would be a bed of roses, but He did promise me that He would give me the grace and mercy to help me get through whatever came my way. He has never let me down, even when my faith wavered and I deserved it. God has always been right there to pick me up, dust me off, redirect my path, and put me back on track so that I could keep running.

Because of my "Close Encounter" with Him, I now have my eyes fixed on an eternal goal. Through His eyes I can see more clearly than ever that this life He calls a vapor, will soon be passed. Only what's done for Christ will last through eternity.

God in His Holy Spirit is the One who impressed upon my heart to write this book. He is the One who answered my prayer and gave me a story to write about. But there is one thing we are all called to do as His children and that is to share His love and story of salvation with the world.

Our mission field may be in our home, our workplace, our school or our church. Wherever it is God has planted us, He expects us to grow, bloom, and produce fruit. He has gifted each of us with unique qualities that equip us for the harvest.

I want to be a fruit bearer, how about you? This is the longing of my heart and it came from a deep desire to know God more. He is a "...rewarder of those who diligently seek Him." I am anxiously awaiting my reward in Heaven. Not for the deeds I have done, but in hopes of seeing the faces of those whose lives were changed because God chose to use me. He perfected my faith by allowing me a glimpse of who He is and He gave me a burning desire to know Him even more.

Through glimpses of Heaven He showed me what I would be enjoying at my victory celebration. Through His love He taught me that He would be with me until the end of my race here on earth and for eternity thereafter. He created in me a longing for my eternal home. He introduced me to the Holy Spirit who would sustain me during a very dry, barren land.

By His grace He chose me, singled me out, sanctified me, and anointed me. He daily gives me just enough strength to find the "Faith to Finish" the race He has set before me.

Building My Faith

I praise God that I am not who I used to be and I praise Him for who I am yet to become. I don't believe in dwelling on the past, but I do believe in learning from it. Sometimes in retrospect God allows us to see how far we have come in our relationship with Him by reminding us of His faithfulness to us.

Looking back I can see God's handiwork as He wove together a tapestry of beautiful threads to create a picture of His glory in my life. The many different colors and textures of the threads exemplify the life I live today. They are what make me beautiful in the eyes of God because I am His creation. I was fashioned in His image.

An Awakening

Now I will tell you how this process of spiritual growth began.

About ten years ago, I was sitting in church listening intently to the sermon being preached by a wonderful expositor of the word of God. He also had a reputation of being very thorough in his presentations and rarely added anything to his sermon that he had not already prepared to say.

On this particular day, however, the Holy Spirit had other plans. God used this pastor to open my eyes to His gift of unconditional love. It was the beginning of a relationship of trust and dependence on Him for every aspect of my life. I want to share with you his profound statements for they have truly changed my life. It allowed me to begin not only a healing process from years of conditional love, but of learning how to accept His "unconditional love."

During the sermon, which this pastor had so skillfully prepared, he spoke these words as if they were only to be said for me. I know it was of the Holy Spirit's leading that he said,

"I had not planned on saying this, but obviously there is someone in this service who needs to hear it and needs to know God loves them unconditionally. So I just want to say, if you are an adult who has been living your entire life trying to earn the love and blessing of another person, even someone who is dear to you. I am going to release you of a burden that is weighing you down. It's because this burden is keeping you from God's best.

If you haven't earned their love by now, it is not likely that you ever will. However, God will not leave you empty hearted for He will provide other ways and other people to bless you and fill the void that remains in your life."

This was a harsh realization for me and it hit me like a ton of bricks because I had always held on to the hope that one day I would be "good enough" to be accepted and deserving of love from someone who I later realized didn't know how to express it.

It is usually during our childhood and formative years that we receive the encouragement, praise, and blessing that allows us to grow into adulthood with the confidence to pass this blessing on to our own children.

But sometimes these things are withheld because of a "conditional love." Rigid expectations and criticism replace love and acceptance. Judgment and pride replace worthiness and forgiveness.

The damaging thing is that instead of growing up confident and secure, we grow up ashamed and feeling guilty for not being perfect, and unloved. The criticism that we have known gets internalized as we become very critical of ourselves and even sometimes others. The scars that are left behind are doubt, confusion, lack of trust, low self-esteem, and insecurity.

Our defense mechanism becomes a wall we build around ourselves that dares anyone to hurt us again. That is, until God enters the picture and proves to us His "unconditional love." We cannot earn it, there is nothing we can do to deserve it, no one can take it away from us, and it will always be. Once we can accept God's love, we can learn to walk in freedom and victory over our past. More than I had ever realized before, I was searching for that freedom.

His next statement was the one I want you to hear loud and clear. He went on to say:

"True love does not have to be earned; it is freely given, just as your Heavenly Father in Heaven has given His love to you. His love is eternal and everlasting. He longs to hold you in His arms and love you as you have never been loved before. He will always be there for you. He doesn't demand perfection, only your will to be submissive. He knows your weaknesses and loves you anyway. He knows you will fail, yet allows you these opportunities to let your failures be avenues of spiritual growth. He loved you before you were born. He has a plan for your life and He will draw you into a lifetime of an intimate, personal relationship with Himself. If you will seek Him, He is all you need. He is the only One in this world that you have to please and all you have to do is accept His gift of love.

First you have to learn to love yourself as He loves you. Then accept the fact that you are worthy of His grace. He is a King. As His child, you are a joint heir."

I will never forget his words for they touched my heart as if they had come from the Holy Spirit Himself. I am so glad for the opportunity to record them on the pages of this book because I know there are millions of others who are longing to be freed from the same chains of hopelessness and despair.

Words cannot express the peace and joy that was expressed in my life through the power of the Holy Spirit. I am not going to tell you that immediately I was set free, but what I do want to say is that the healing process began. Instead of seeking approval, I began to seek God. As I sought Him, I found his unconditional love. I began to see that I had allowed my circumstances to be a stronghold on my life; one that had held me captive way too long. It was time to break free.

God started chipping away the wall of stone that one day was going to reveal His masterpiece. With each new challenge, I saw opportunities to deepen my relationship with Him. I knew that He was fighting my battles for me and He was developing my dependence on Him with each step towards my independent will to accept His love for me. I wanted God to mold me and make me into a useable vessel of service for Him. I wanted Him to know how much I longed to serve Him with all my heart. I was willing to separate myself from all else in order to follow Him and I made these things known to Him. I had no idea at the time of the cost.

Until that time, I had spent my whole life feeling like I had to earn God's love in order to become acceptable in His sight. A past "conditional" relationship had affected my ability to accept His love. Because I had not accepted God's love, it was hard for me to share His love with others. My service to Him became more of an obligation instead of an act of love. I thank Him for revealing this to me. No longer did I want to serve Him out of obligation. I wanted to serve out of obedience.

Because of my heart's desire to know Him and serve Him, I was constantly examining my life and asking Him, "God, am I doing what You want me to do?" I became so absorbed with seeking God's will that I got caught up in acts "of" service, while neglecting to consistently nurture my motivation "for" service, which was my love and desire to know Him more. I wanted to please God so much that I became a "yes" person. You know what I mean, "Ask Karen, she will do anything!" This sometimes only created resentment.

Hosea 6:6 says, *"For I delight in loyalty rather than sacrifice, and in the knowledge of God rather than burnt offerings."* God reminds His people throughout scripture to present their service out of a love for Him, not out of duty, not out of sacrifice, and not because someone expects you to. Instead, He wants us to serve Him out of a heart of love. There are a lot of good things we can do, but sometimes the good things get in the way of the best things God wants us to do.

I wanted God to know that I trusted Him with every aspect of my life. In anticipation I waited for His direction. I wanted to witness the power of prayer and I wanted my life to bring Him glory. I wanted to be His servant. I wanted to be under the leadership, power, and protection of His Holy Spirit.

I also knew that I had to be content with the plan that God had already prepared for me, knowing that He would reveal it in His time. I was mature enough as a Christian to know that a desire for spiritual growth sometimes means pain, but I also knew that God would never allow me to be tempted above that which I was able to bear.

I wanted my life to exhibit the fruits of the spirit and one of these is patience. This has never been one of my virtues and God knew better than me that it was an area of my life that needed improvement. His work in me was going to require a period of waiting in order to produce this fruit in me.

The scriptures talk about growing in the grace and knowledge of our Lord Jesus Christ (II Peter 3:18). I knew I wasn't satisfied with what I knew about God. I needed to study in order to show myself approved. I wanted to strengthen the relationship between us and I wanted to know more about His word. I was developing an insatiable hunger and thirst for more of Him.

Even though my relationship with Him was not where I wanted it to be and even though I was in the midst of the growing process, I still found peace and contentment as I yearned to know and understand more and more of His ways. He was always patient with me.

If only I had realized how much God had been longing to have this kind of relationship with me all my life. He had orchestrated events that caused my faith to be tested and He had allowed these events to deepen my trust in His word. I know now how much He wanted me to trust Him and believe in His overflowing, omniscient, "unconditional" love. Instead of trusting in His love, I had lived in fear of rejection. How deceived I was.

I Thessalonians 5:24 promises, *"Faithful is He who calls you, and He also will bring it to pass."* The broken vessel of my life was being mended by the Potter's hand. I knew in my heart that He would somehow honor my desire to live for Him. I just had no idea how, when, or where.

In Philippians 3:12 Paul says, "...I count not myself to have apprehended: but this one thing I do, forgetting those things which are behind, and reaching forth unto those things which are before, I press toward the prize of the high calling of God in Christ Jesus."

The phrase "press on" means "to pursue." I was committed and pursuing God. I wanted to know Him not just as my Savior, but in all of His three persons.

No matter what the world teaches, God's love story is written on the pages of His Word, the Bible. With a foundation of scripture in my heart, I started to build a relationship with my Heavenly Father. It was a journey of faith, hope, and deliverance.

I had no idea that in finding Him, I would also find myself and all that matters in this life. Everything I had been looking for in my relationship with God was to be expressed through His divine appointment with me. An encounter that would take place on a hospital bed in ICU.

A New Place of Growth

In 1998, God led us to a little country church in our community. This new place of growth truly proved to be one of God's miracles in my life. This part of my race took me to a place of continued spiritual growth, as God placed people in my path who taught me about His love. I will never forget our first Sunday there. As soon as we sat down, a very friendly lady sitting behind us introduced herself and welcomed us to the service. In fact, the whole church was friendly! I had never seen so many people hugging each other and shaking hands. I had never felt so welcomed in a church service before..

Another thing that impressed me about this church was that when the time came for the invitation, the alter was full of people gathering around one another to pray. It didn't take me long to realize that God had lead me to a place where He was going to teach me about what real love is and He was going to do it through His people. He was answering my prayer to know Him more and He was doing it one step at a time. I was seeking Him and He was leading me.

The lady I met that day was a leader in the women's ministry of this church. I wanted to get to know these people who seemed so happy in the Lord because I wanted more of what they had. The church we had previously attended had no such ministry. In fact, there was hardly any outreach. The first thing I did when we sat down that day was open the bulletin to see what ministries were available. I wanted to see how seriously this church took Christ's commandment to "…Go ye therefore." She invited me to come to their next women's ministry meeting and I told her I would.

My longing was so deep and so sincere that it pulled me out of my comfort zone and placed me among strangers. Only God could have given me the courage to attend the meeting that night because in my shyness I would never have done so on my own. I knew that I would find what I was looking for if I kept following God.

Jeanne became my mentor and I began to grow. I could see that she was a person I could trust. One day while we were talking, she started telling me about some things that had happened in her family. The more she talked, the more I thought to myself, we must be sisters!

The difference was, she had learned to trust God through prayer and seeking wisdom. She had found a way to overcome rejection. For the first time in my life I felt comfortable and I began to share with her the similarities of our pasts. It was the first time I had ever opened up my heart not only to release past hurts, but to accept what God was teaching me about His love.

I had never known anyone so real and transparent as Jeanne. She made it comfortable to just be myself. I never felt I had to explain how I felt about anything to her. It was as if she already knew.

But what I did see was that she wasn't bitter because of her past, she was better. I didn't want to be bitter either because I had lived with seeing that emotion expressed and I didn't want to allow my circumstances to influence my emotions anymore. I wanted to be just like Jeanne. She was a God-send... my angel sent to deliver God's message of "unconditional love."

Little by little the baggage I had carried for so long began to fall off as I started growing in the knowledge of God's love. The weight of guilt and fear of having done something to deserve my plight began to lighten. The more I learned, the more I craved. The more I craved, the more God freely gave. He used this godly woman as the vehicle to teach me what it meant to be loved unconditionally. It was awesome!

We joined the congregation and it was good to feel like I was part of a family. I became the church pianist the following year and considered it such a blessing to be able to give back to the people the love that they had bestowed on me. I loved being a part of leading them in worship.

I also started to realize that I was not the only person who needed to know more about God's love and that I was not any different from the rest of the world. We all need to know how much God cares for us and how much He wants to fellowship with us.

My faith grew as I experienced visible answers to my prayers. I asked for wisdom and discernment and God continued to teach me. I began to see things from a different perspective as though God was making His way more clear. His ways are not our ways, so I knew I would never be able to fully understand Him and how He was working all things for my good, even my past. However, I was growing in the grace and knowledge of my Lord Jesus Christ and I was finding joy.

I felt God's hand on my life, though I still lacked His clear direction and purpose. I was content to keep a steady pace in my race until I heard his voice telling me to change courses. At least I knew I was finally on the right track.

God continued to nurture the seed He had planted in my heart many years before and that was to help others along the journey to knowing Him personally, passionately, and intimately, even though I was so desperately searching for Him myself. I knew I was not the only person with a deep, passionate desire for a relationship with Him. My heart longed to find those people who wanted to join the journey with me. Together we would come to know Him more. I was willing to share what I had learned and I would teach them how to pass it on. I just didn't know at the time how God was going to prepare me to deliver this message.

I think most people who have walked through God's preparation would agree that it is a good thing that we don't always know how God is going to use our circumstances to prepare us. God's plan was to begin with me. I couldn't empty my cup on others until He had completely emptied me of myself, reshaped me, mended my broken parts, and filled me with His love.

God's Pruning Shears

There is a song that I have sung off and on for many years called, "Whatever It Takes." I always had to do some very deep soul searching prior to singing this song because of the words. They always make me stop and ask myself, "Am I willing to go through "whatever it takes" in order for God to draw me closer to Himself?" I don't sing a song that I don't mean the words with all my heart. For me, singing is not a performance, it is a ministry. It is a way for the Holy Spirit to use the words of the songs I sing to speak to the hearts of His people. It's not so much about skill as it is about being willing to use a God-given talent and allow Him to work through it.

The first time I ever heard this song was when our youngest son, Nathan, had been diagnosed with a very serious blood disorder. He was two years old at the time and even then, twenty-eight years ago, God was checking out my willingness to give up whatever it took to serve Him. It was another valley He had walked me through, another test of my faith, another way for Him to show me His love because in His grace and mercy, He miraculously healed him.

"Yes Lord, whatever it takes to draw me closer to You, that's what I'd be willing to do." That doesn't mean that because I am submissive there will only be good times. What it does mean is that I can expect God's pruning shears to cut away the dead branches of my life that are useless to Him and it means I can expect Him to remove any hindrances that are keeping my focus off of His will and purpose. If I am to be truly surrendered to Him, it means willing to bear pain, suffering, and loss. If I am to obey, it means to follow Christ.

I am grafted into Your perfect plan as You gently call me into Your presence.
I am guided by Your Holy Spirit as You teach me to live my life through Your plan.
I am humbled by Your holy calling as You set me apart and prepare me.
I am drawn to You Lord. Lead me I pray.
Take me, mold me, use me, and fill me. I give my life to You.

As I began to think about the many Christians I had known throughout my life, I thought about their complacency towards developing their relationship with God. It seemed that so many people thought that once their eternity was sealed by salvation the accountability was over. Many times there was a lack of commitment and dedication to continue growing the relationship. I am not excluding myself from this list by any means, I just knew that there had to be more. I knew my salvation was just the beginning, but where and how was I to start building a deeper relationship and understanding of God, the scriptures, or even life?

Why is it that we claim the title of Christian yet walk around unhappy, defeated, fearful, and without direction? If you were to look at the faces of those sitting in some of the congregations I have stood before you may wonder, as I have, where's the joy? Where is the contentment one finds in a relationship with God? I can't help but question the level of commitment in a life without joy…a commitment to deepen the relationship. Once I was one of these faces.

Why do we accept the gift (Jesus) and forget the thank you note (a life of obedience)? Could it be that we are deceived? Oh how Satan would love to keep us in this pit! But, if you want to get out of a pit, you must quit digging!

Salvation ends the courtship, but it's the beginning of the relationship. Everyday we should be on our knees thanking God for the privilege of being able to walk in fellowship with Him.

41

Even late into my adult years I was still very critical of myself and my abilities. I was always trying to be perfect so that I would be accepted. One Sunday morning as my husband and I were leaving church several people stopped to intentionally let me know how much they were blessed by my music. I made light of the compliment (my lack of self-esteem and knowing how to accept a compliment) and said something demeaning like, "Oh, you just need hearing aids because I made all kinds of mistakes!"

My husband (the man with the keen insight) was very quiet all the way to the car, but when we were in private he said, "Do you realize how much you hurt people's feelings and how much you take away their joy of thanking you when you shoot down their compliments?"

Now, he never meant to hurt my feelings by saying this, but God used what he said to help me realize how to accept the gift of praise. I realized it was a blessing I had lacked as a child and obviously it left me not knowing how to accept it.

God was using these people to give me a blessing and I needed to learn to be grateful to them and not so self-critical. I also needed to be more grateful to God for giving me the talent that He had given me. I had never thought so seriously about the consequences of my behavior. The last thing I would ever have wanted to do was hurt somebody's feelings. God showed me that it was okay to accept a gift of love and simply say "Thank you, I am blessed."

I was often accused of being prideful when I was growing up just because when I did something I tried to do it well. Actually, I felt the opposite of prideful. All my life I had been very critical of myself, which caused me to be an overachiever who was always working to prove myself worthy of recognition.

I must tell you this little story. I was rather chubby as a youth and was teased alot by my two brothers. Of course, I forgave them long ago because we were just children, but I still like to remind them of one particular remark that they used to make. I was about ten years old at the time and at an age often indicated as "pre-teen." They got a big kick out of calling me an "overgrown protein."

I guess it was kind of funny when you stop to think about it. In a way, I suppose it added to my self-esteem issues, but trust me I love my brothers to death. This was my problem, not theirs!

You know how we tend to run ahead of God sometimes instead of waiting on Him to show us His plan? Well, that was me! I was so anxious to serve God that I tried to create His plan instead of follow it. I offered to help in the ladies ministry, but didn't find my niche there. I tried to open several other doors, but I knew in my heart that they were not what God desired for me at that time either. Sometimes I think we get the idea that if we run ahead of Him we might be able to eliminate some of the trials that produce our patience. WRONG! He was still working on me and I still had a lot to learn.

I knew that God was continuing to prepare me for His service, but He was also teaching me to wait on His timing. I wasn't looking for vain glory, I just wanted to find out what His plans were and I guess I thought I could help Him out by offering suggestions. WRONG again! Praise God, at least I had matured enough in Him to know when He was leading me and when He was not.

I'm going to throw this next part in for free.

In my opinion, one of the worst things we can do as servants of God is to take a position that we know is not in His will for us, just because someone else thinks we would be good at it. When we do, we are not only going to be miserable, but we will be cheating another person out of a position God had prepared for them. Worse than either of these things is that when we are busy doing the wrong thing, we miss out on the right thing. Be sure of God's call and then proceed in confidence with your obedience and faith in Him to give you what you need in order to complete the task. After all, He doesn't call us to do something "we" think we are good at. He just calls and then enables us to use the gifts "He" has given us. We can rest assured, if He brings us to it, He will bring us through it.

In other words, don't ever be afraid to say "no" to man unless you are willing to say "no" to God! If you have prayed earnestly for God's direction and you know that what you are being asked to do is not in His will for you, remember, "No" is a complete sentence and doesn't require an explanation. Just be absolutely sure and confident that you are walking in obedience and not preference because the last thing you want to do is say no to God! Don't say "no" until you "know!"

A Stirring in My Soul

In July of 1999, I attended a Women of Faith Conference in Atlanta, Georgia with a group of ladies from our church. It was my first time to be exposed to the speakers of the Women of Faith. I sat in awe listening to them share their stories in order to encourage and help others, like me. They shared how God had delivered them from things like rejection, depression, relationships, and low self-esteem.

Wow! I sat there wondering; if God could deliver these powerful women and still use them despite their past, could He possibly use me too to do something of this magnitude? I couldn't see how, but it sure was a blissful thought!

It seemed everything they were saying was just for me, even though there were approximately twenty-eight thousand women in attendance. My heart was overwhelmed. I was sitting there with my heart aching to know God the way these women knew Him and I so wanted for Him to use me to help others as they had helped me. God was continuing to open the door of my heart and pour in His love and I was absorbing all that I could hold.

Being at that conference was exactly where God wanted me to be. It was a place where He was nurturing the seed that He had planted in my heart to know Him more and now He was also showing me that my life could make a difference. He was continuing to heal my soul and I needed to learn to give Him complete control.

A little water and a lot of fertilizer had taken place over time and now God was about to shed some light on the seed He had previously planted. A new revelation was taking place and the seed was about to resurrect and come forth as part of God's plan. His "Son-light" had been warming my soul for so many years as He was preparing it for the acceptance of a vision of my future. Right there in the middle of a stadium in Atlanta, Georgia, God was painting a picture of possibilities. He was showing me that in His plan, nothing is impossible.

I was unaware of the fact that He was loving me right into submission by opening my eyes to His power to free me from the chains that held me fast. I was amazed at the thought that He could possibly consider me worthy of the responsibility of being His mouthpiece of hope and encouragement. I felt so humbled to even think that He loved me that much. I sat there in tears.

One of the women who attended this conference with me was my sister-in-law, Dale. I will never forget our conversation as we sat quietly during one of the intermissions. I was trying to savor the words that had been spoken. I wanted to remember every line and every illustration because it seemed that every speaker had prepared her speech just for me.

They were so confident, but it wasn't in themselves. It was in the God who enabled them. They were confident in what God had already done in their lives and what He was able to continue to do "through" them. I couldn't help but think how awesome that must feel. Each one was so poised. They all had a background of trials and struggles that validated their testimony and that was what gave them credibility. But now they were living a victorious life; the kind that I wanted so badly myself. It was obvious that they had an intimate relationship with God.

They spoke of assurance, of God's abundant grace, and of His deliverance. I sat there thinking, could this be me one

45

day? I felt the nudge of God on my heart telling me that one day my story would make a difference in lives too. I said to Him, "Lord I want to make a difference in as many lives as possible in my lifetime, but could You possibly think I am capable of doing something like public speaking?" I thought, surely He must be thinking of someone else because I would be much better at doing something behind the scenes. The greater vision kind of made me sick to my stomach. You know, the kind that feels like anxiety versus anticipation.

I opened my Bible and there in front of me was *Psalm 22:25* which says, *"My praise shall be of thee in the great congregation."* I read a little further to *Psalm 26:12, "...in the congregation will I bless the Lord."* I said, "Oh God, could You be giving me a hint, a preview of a coming attraction?"

There are only a few people in my life that I would have felt comfortable sharing such a thought with, but Dale was one of them. She had always believed in me through all my transitions and many, if not most times, had more faith in me than I had in myself. So I turned to her and said, "You know Dale, I would give just about anything to be like those women...strong in their faith, bold in their belief, and able to encourage so many women with their stories of victory."

She smiled at me as if to reassure me that she didn't think I was crazy for thinking such a thought and quickly responded, "Karen, you could do anything those women are doing. You sing, you play the piano, and you could be a speaker too."

(Read this slowly) My next response was one I am sure was heard throughout the Heavens because God had been waiting on me to realize my inability, so that He could prove to me His ability. He had waited patiently until I was able to see myself worthy of His call. I could hardly contain my emotions as I realized that only His unconditional love would look beyond my faults and see my needs. And then I said it...the statement that made this book a reality:

"But Dale, I want to believe that God could use me like He is using them, but there is one huge thing that is missing that they have and I don't." She said, *"What could that possibly be?"* I said,

"I don't have a story!"

Friend, I am here to tell you that God knows and delights in giving us the desires of our heart. We never know how He is going to fulfill that desire, but our job is to be willing to accept the preparation. I left that conference with a grateful heart for receiving a vision from God of the plans He had for me, but I was also overwhelmed at the thought. All the way home I kept saying to myself, "I wonder how God is going to fulfill His plan?"

God had been waiting and planning for this occasion for a long time. I believe that once He heard my request for a story, He started to put into place a myriad of events that were going to take place in my life over the next five years. They would be the things that would give me the story that I had said my life was missing.

I had no idea of the magnitude of His plan, but to whom much is given much is required. In order for God to entrust me with His fruit-bearing, I was going to have to prove myself worthy and capable of bearing fruit by walking in faith. Little did I know of the circumstances that would bring about spiritual growth and an increase in my faith like I had never known before. He would teach me through trials that my relationship with Him would give me the faith that I was going to need to finish my life's race and He did it by revealing Himself to me in a "Close Encounter of Three Kinds."

On the ride home from Atlanta, we were asked to share specific things about the conference that had touched our hearts. I realized that it wasn't just one thing I was taking away, there were many things. There was hope for answered prayer, healing, and restoration. There was faith and a desire to move forward, even though I didn't know what lay in store. There was reassurance that God really did love me enough to want to work with me and make me worthy of His call.

In fact, I believe when Heaven heard what I said about not having a story, the angels began to assemble in order to witness the transformation of a willing heart into a servant of God. It was "my" heart!

It's a good thing they knew and I didn't because the train of events that were about to transpire were going to be the most difficult days of my life. They would also become the answer to my prayer to know God more and they would create a story of profound proportions.

For the next seven years, God was going to keep me on His "things to do list." He never stopped working on me and He never gave up on the process of creating in me a clean and pure heart.

Since the age of five I had known Christ as my Savior. When I accepted Him, I was introduced to my Heavenly Father and His Holy Spirit, but like many other acquaintances in my life, I had never really developed the "relationship."

My years of searching for an intimate relationship with God would climax on a bed in an Intensive Care Unit, clinging to life in my earthly realm and to my Savior's hand in His Heavenly realm.

The last chapter of my search for unconditional love included a "Close Encounter" with God Himself in His three persons: God the Father, who was to be my Healer and Great Physician; God the Son, who stood by His promise to never leave or forsake me; and God the Holy Spirit, who gave me comfort and guided me through the most difficult trial of my personal life.

I hope you realize that I did not reach this point overnight and I have not, nor will I ever reach a point of perfection, but I will keep striving for excellence as I press towards the prize. I hope my story encourages you, especially if you are going through a time of preparation in your own life. Trust God because it is through the refiner's fire that we are brought forth as gold.

I spent many years designing and creating wedding gowns. Making the gown itself takes a lot of time and patience, but it's the fine detailed beading that gives each gown its beauty. It's the time-consuming special touches that make each gown unique.

I like to compare my life to a wedding gown, especially at this point. God had designed and created a beautiful gown and it was made of fine fabric. The fit was perfect and the style was just for me. It was radiant white to signify my pure heart and motives, but it lacked the detail work. Plain and simple was my gown before. Now the master seamstress's hand was about to add the details that would make my life one of distinction. His design would be what made my gown (my life) special.

As I share with you my heart and my story, please know that my intention would never be to grumble or complain, but instead, to bring honor and glory to God for His goodness to me. I could never be angry at Him for allowing me the privilege and honor of being in His presence. I could never thank Him enough for revealing to me His heart and His love. I praise Him all the day long for choosing me to share this story because I am sure He had many likely candidates, but He chose me.

Romans 11:29 says, *"For God's gifts and His call are irrevocable."* He never withdraws them once they are given and He does not change His mind about those to whom He gives His grace or to whom He sends His call.

I want you to see that I am no different from you or anyone else. I have endured obstacles and I have been challenged in my walk with God. What I do want you to see is that everything we go through in life is part of building our relationship with Him. With each opportunity we have a choice to draw closer to Him or turn away. When we turn to face the Son (Jesus Christ), our Heavenly Father (God) is right beside Him and the One who tells us which way to turn (Holy Spirit) is standing right beside us. Awesome isn't it?

I want you to realize that this story is about a God who loved me so much that He heard my plea to know Him intimately and He wanted the same kind of relationship and fellowship with me. He wanted me to depend on Him, instead of trying to do things on my own. He knew my longing to experience His love and my desire to share it with others. He knew my heart and my desire to be set free from feelings and emotions that had held me captive far too long, while hindering my ability to be His devoted servant. He was about to give my life its direction.

He gave me a story of profound proportion. It started the moment I was born, but God breathed new life into it the moment I spoke the desires of my heart at the Women of Faith Conference. It was when I said, "I don't have a story." By giving me a story, He has also given me a way to make a difference in your life.

God revealed Himself to me in ways that drew me so close to Him that nothing could ever separate me from His love. Nothing in my life is more important to me than serving God. My heart is overwhelmed with thanksgiving for all He has allowed me to experience. I am so grateful for our relationship because it is built on faith and trust. I know that He has great plans for me (Jeremiah 29:11). I know that whatever comes my way it will be for my good and for His purpose because I love him and want to obey Him.

There is nothing too difficult for God. I am learning to let Him fight all my battles and I am learning to receive His grace as unmerited favor. I did not deserve what His Son did for me on Calvary, but I understand the reason He had to come as my Redeemer. In light of Christ's suffering, nothing we will ever endure will surpass it. He gave His all for you and me.

A Christian life is not about doom and gloom, bitterness, grudges, condemnation, guilt, or despair. It's about living in victory through Christ and celebrating what He has done for us. It's about living to bring honor and glory to His name.

All the things that we have experienced in our lives become part of our story. It's who we are, it's what makes us unique and special and it's what we are called to share in order to give hope to a hopeless world. It's what God will use to work through us to accomplish His purpose.

God singled me out and called me by name that day in Atlanta, Georgia and I surrendered. I didn't know the consequences, but they didn't matter anyway. My submission was not complete until my will had been broken and everything in me had been spilled out for Jesus.

My search for God had been the builder of my faith. I had been studying for this test of faith for many years and now God said it was time to finish the exam. When He felt I was prepared to accept His call, He asked this question, "Are you willing to follow Me, whatever it takes?"

On this test, I would be required to make the highest score in faith that I had ever made. Faith would become more than just my middle name; it would become my connection with God. It would be necessary for me to make many sacrifices in order to achieve my score. I also had no idea how long the test would take, but it didn't matter because God was teaching me patience.

There is a quote that was given to me by a missionary friend many years ago when our son, Nathan was very ill. It has stood the test of time and it has brought me such comfort and reassurance whenever I felt my faith was being tested. I hope it encourages you too. It says:

"God often encourages the weak in faith with speedy answers to prayer, but the strong in faith are often tested by God's delays."

Whenever I have felt that God was delaying my answer to prayer or delaying my progression through a difficult time, I knew that it was my faith that He was testing. It wasn't necessarily His punishment or judgment against me, though I had to make sure that I repented of any known sin. Many times, He was simply taking my faith to the next level. I am humbled and grateful to Him.

From Gas Man to Grass Man

Two months had passed since my trip to the Women of Faith Conference. The first thing God tested was my faith in His ability to provide in every circumstance of our lives, including our finances.

My husband is a hard-working man and he spent most of his life building a business for someone else. For over thirty-four years he had worked for a large natural gas company. I guess you could say he attended the school of "hard-knocks" because with no more than a high school education he had advanced the corporate ladder through hard work and dedication. He loved his job. I believe that he was undoubtedly, the most loyal person in the company. Even when he obtained a management position and was salaried, he devoted twelve to fourteen hours a day to doing his job the best he knew how. In all his years as an employee he had never called in a day sick and never had any accidents or reprimands.

Yet, in October of 1999, Charles was called out of a training class to answer a phone call. On the other end of the line was his boss who told him that he no longer had a job. He was crushed. The company called it a downsize, but his position wasn't eliminated; there was just a restructuring of employee positions.

Charles is very humble and he never wanted much more out of life than to be comfortable and take care of his family. The fact that he was no longer needed in a position that brought him fulfillment and satisfaction was quite a blow to his ego, as it would be to most any person. No doubt you know of someone yourself who has been through this very common occurrence in our society today.

There were days when we were so overwhelmed by decisions that our lives seemed to have turned upside down. There was retirement, but he was too young; there was insurance, but it was so expensive; and there was uncertainty about his future employment because he had no idea where, when, or if he would find a job.

Even though we tried not to doubt, there was uncertainty and insecurity about our finances. With his loss of income we had no idea how we would survive, let alone maintain our current lifestyle. We had always been faithful in our tithes and offerings and we knew that God would take care of us, but in our humanity, we couldn't see how God could possibly work things out when, at that time, we had only my income as a registered nurse to live on.

Oddly enough, a few months before his layoff we had done some fairly serious financial planning with a professional to see where we needed to be in preparation for our retirement years. Little did we know that all this planning was about to go down the drain. I will always believe that God wanted us to see that He is the only financial planner that we really need. He took out of our hands what we could control and put into our hands what we could not. His plan was to teach us dependence on Him.

Charles had difficulty securing a job, but finally he was hired by a local cable company, making a salary about one-third of his previous pay. Humbled, but willing to do whatever he needed to do to support his family, he endured what was a not so pleasant atmosphere in order to provide some income. Even in this circumstance, God was working. He placed Charles in a situation where his Christian testimony was really needed.

I was working as a registered nurse so it was easy for me to pick up extra hours at the hospital. But working twelve-hour shifts made it increasingly more difficult to keep a positive attitude. I stayed exhausted and rarely did anything in my off time except sleep.

On the days I was be having a hard time dealing with the pressures, Charles would lift me up. Then on the days when he was having difficulty with self-esteem and insecurity, I would raise him up. It was a grieving process that we had to walk through, just as if a member of our family had died.

I will always remember what he would say to encourage me: "God has always taken care of us and we've just got to keep believing that He will not forsake us now."

This was not the time to turn our backs on God. It was the time to turn our hearts to Him. Though I will admit it was very difficult at times to hold on to our faith, in our hearts we knew that God had a reason for allowing this to happen. We promised Him that we would keep trusting Him and we did. As we were praying for continued direction in our lives, God was turning this "gas" man into a "grass man."

It would have been simple to question God. It would have been easy to become bitter and turn away, but we knew that our trials only come to make us stronger and to build our faith.

Personally, I knew it was part of my answer to God's last question, "Are you willing to follow Me, whatever it takes?"

"Ok Lord, so now You have our attention."

Sometimes the more I longed to see purpose in his layoff the more oblivious it seemed, but when I sought for understanding, I found it in God's word. The more I sought His word, the more I heard Him say, "Be still and know that I am God." You know, sometimes the hardest thing we can do is WAIT! Yet, even when we can't hear His voice, we must keep listening and we must keep running the race.

God always finishes what He starts. He had begun a work in me and He would finish it. *Philippians 2:13 says, "For it is God which worketh in you both to will and to do of his good pleasure."* The Lord had begun a work in me and I knew He would not stop until His work was completed.

My Journal entry December 2, 1999:
"Lord, I am trusting that Your silence means that You are making plans to bring into my life a greater revelation of Yourself, one greater than I have ever known. Empty me of anything that would keep me from You and fill me with Your love. Humble me, for I am Your faithful servant."

I don't think I really understood humility or the ramifications of asking God for it at this time, but I later realized that an appropriate definition of humility is exactly what Christ patterned for us: *Humility does not mean that we think less of ourselves. It means that we think of ourselves less.*

Continuing to Purge by Fire

January 1, 2000
Two months after the layoff, my mother-in-law went to be with the Lord. This was another loss and another empty space in our hearts. Ollie McGowan, better known as "Grandma," was a spunky little woman who still did her own gardening in her early eighties. She had always liked being independent, having her own place, and making her own decisions.

She was a tough little lady. She only went to the hospital to have the last one of her six children and that was only because of complications. For over forty years after that she didn't see a doctor. She loved me and though she may not have said it many times, I understood her love by the way she treated me.

My husband grew up very poor. His parents were hard-working share croppers who raised not only their six children, but also two other children as their own. They had very little materialistically, but one thing they did have was love for each other and for others. They still do.

Grandma loved to make quilts the old fashioned way with a pedal sewing machine and quilting racks that hung from the ceiling of her home during the winter months. There wasn't any need for her to start a quilt in the summer because she stayed busy canning and freezing vegetables from her garden. I will never forget her apron and her freezer key that she always kept in her pocket.

She and her husband Omer taught their children to work hard and make an honest living. They treated others as they themselves wanted to be treated and that was with respect. I had wonderful in-laws, the best I could have asked for.

Waiting on God

As time passed by, I felt like I was in limbo. I was hanging in a balance wondering what was going to happen next. I guess a good way to describe it would be just "out there somewhere." We were going through the motions of day-to-day living, yet lacking direction and focus. It was a ritual of uncertainty as Charles and I kept wondering what more could we lose. I knew God was watching over us and it was evident in His provision, but whenever I would ask Him for purpose He said again, "Be still and know that I am God. Wait on the Lord."

Trouble on the Home-front

There is no home like your church home and when things aren't right on the home-front an emptiness exists in the hearts of those who reside. That spring Satan saw an opportunity to create some problems within our church family and

56

differences of opinions became an abscess that festered into a boil.

Being in a leadership position as pianist, I found myself kind of in the middle of a mess. I am not one to take sides because I believe there is only one side and that is God's side. If we all stayed on His side, we wouldn't have the difficulties that we do have in our churches today. Satan had his hay-day and it became increasingly more difficult to inspire the congregation to worship. The people who had taught me how to love were on opposing sides over biblical issues and opinions. Many of their happy faces were now grim.

This was another loss. I finally took a leave of absence from my position as pianist just to get away from the discord. I had enough uncertainty in my life. I offered my services as pianist to churches who were in need and for a year Charles and I traveled all over the local area. It was a time of healing for us. Everywhere we went we heard messages that were uplifting and encouraging. It was another way that God showed His love towards us. Even though I had my own needs, I believe He still used me to bless others during that year, as I was also blessed.

Sometimes removing ourselves from a situation allows us to get a different perspective and this is just what happened to me. God began to reveal things to me. I started to see that He really had not turned away from us, like it sometimes seemed, but that He was working His will and way in our lives one step at a time. I started to see how far we had come in the healing process. I started to enjoy His presence, but in a peaceful, patient kind of way. It was as if I didn't need to know the plans He had for me anymore. I just needed to trust Him to show me when He felt I was ready. I continued to wait on the Lord.

In June of that year, our youngest son, Nathan and his bride Sharon, were married. Though I gained a daughter, I still lost "the presence" of my son. To a mom, this is a bittersweet time of learning to let go. Happy as I was for the both of them, there again was an open, empty space in my heart. It was a different kind of loss.

Those of you who are pet lovers will relate to the next part of this story. If you are not, just bear with those of us who are. By the way, I believe God gave us animals to illustrate His unconditional love.

For twelve years, a little black and tan Miniature Pinscher named, Turbojet, was a part of our family. He had lived through some pretty horrendous situations in his life and because I was the one who usually nursed him back to health, he was very attached to me. In his old age he had become blind, weak, and frail. I knew on the day of the wedding that a decision was going to have to be made, but I prayed that God would allow him to live until after the wedding so that another loss would not spoil the joy of the celebration. After all, he was a member of our family.

On Monday morning, two days after the wedding, I was the one who had to take him to the vet. While holding him in my arms he took his last breath. It was another kind of loss.

His death was devastating to all of us. After burying Turbo that evening, my husband and I sat in our backyard swing and thought about all our losses. It seemed the wounds of our hearts were deepening instead of healing. We spent hours comforting each other, crying, and pondering God's ways. I don't think either of us realized that even in our despondency, we were seeking God's presence. We were asking Him to make Himself known to us and to teach us His ways. Yet, all we could hear was, "Be still and know that I am God. Wait on the Lord."

Our oldest son, Paul, was to be wed in October of 2000, to his bride Suzanne. This was four months after Nathan's wedding. But when he found a house to rent that he didn't want to pass up, he moved out at the same time as Nathan. We were empty-nesters now for sure!

No job! No mother! No children! No dog! No church! It seemed that "no" just meant "what's next?"

Three weeks later, a quarter-pound, bright light entered our lives. Though I had vowed to never allow my heart to be broken over a pet again, I gave in and Abbigale, another Miniature Pinscher, entered our lives. She became and remains a reminder of a little spark of joy in the midst of our storm. She wrapped herself around both our hearts and became our "little girl." Okay. For those of you who are tired of the dog story, I will continue.

Paul and Suzanne married in October and again we were so excited about having another daughter in our family. As pleased and thankful as we were that our sons had both found their perfect mates, there still was a void. Again, it was a different kind of loss.

We had been through a year of dark valleys, but somehow we could always see a ray of "Son-shine" leading us. I would have to say, even in the darkness of our days we knew God's love was protecting our hearts and drawing us closer to Him.

You see, when the Holy Spirit lives within our hearts, there is always hope. When we believe God's word and His promises, there can be joy, even in the valley of despair. The "Son" was our ray of hope. Though the storms of life were battering us, we fought hard to keep our feet firmly planted on the solid rock. I denied the temptation to ask, "What are "we" going to do?" Instead, in prayer I said, "God, I trust You and I know "You" know what you're doing."

I am not going to tell you that I wasn't constantly looking for the mountaintop, but I can tell you that I started to enjoy the stream that flowed through the valley. I started to savor the fragrance of flowers in the fields and enjoy the cool breeze, as the mountains sheltered me from the hot sun. Yes, there can be peace in the valley. God provided a place of refuge while he prepared to complete His work in me.

In James 1:2-4, God had taught me to "...count it all joy, Knowing this, that the trying of your faith worketh patience.

But let patience have her perfect work, that ye may be perfect and entire, wanting nothing." I knew that God would make all these trials a blessing because they were bringing me to my knees and closer to Him. He had me where He wanted me and I have never stood taller than at this time, when I was on my knees. God showed me that indecisiveness is the postponing of obedience. I definitely wanted to be "decisive" not "disobedient." My decision was to follow, but did my willingness to be obedient mean "whatever it takes?"

In August of 2000, I was introduced to a business opportunity that was a definite divine appointment from God. He used this new territory to show me things about myself I had never known and some I had never admitted. He placed me in the presence of people who believed in me and encouraged me to do things that stretched my belief and abilities. Things like: traveling to places I had only dreamed of going, speaking to large groups of women, and leading others. I found myself having fun again. I spread my wings and began to travel across the United States to business meetings and conferences. Before long, I was enjoying myself so much that I was taking people with me on my journey. I soon found myself in a leadership role in the company and a mentor to women in all walks of life. Since God had divinely directed this path, I considered my business a mission field and used opportunities to mentor women as an avenue to strengthen their relationship with God.

Thirteen months after I started my business, I resigned my position as a registered nurse, except for working when needed. Things were going great! I had joy in my life again. I had a reason to smile and laughter felt so good. My business had a purpose in my life and it was to build my confidence and self-esteem. Since it was a company that made God its number one priority, I also grew in my faith because I depended on God to provide and I was surrounded by women of faith who challenged me and kept me accountable. I was proving myself as a leader and I was finding that I had skills I never knew I had. Since my business was in sales, every month was dependent upon my willingness to work and wait on God's blessing.

I loved spending my time teaching and training women to become successful in all areas of their life: emotionally, financially, socially, and most of all spiritually.

Charles continued to work for the local cable company while I built my business. But in August of 2003, he was laid off again. The department he had been hired to work in closed, leaving him again without a job. By now he was fifty-eight years old. So I asked him, "What would you do if you could do something that you enjoyed?" After all he had been through, he deserved that much. He thought for a moment and then he said, "I guess I just enjoy cutting grass." I said, "Then why don't you buy yourself a mower and start cutting?" He did just that! Today, Charles has built a successful lawn care business and he no longer has to worry about layoff. As long as God sends rain and grass grows, he will have a job! God turned a gas-man into a grass-man.

When I was discouraged and overworked, God blessed me with an alternative. When Charles was distressed about a second layoff, God blessed him with an alternative. The Apostle Paul said that he was able to find contentment. I thank God that even though we were both in positions that kept us walking in faith and depending on Him, He gave us something that we both enjoyed and by doing so, He allowed us to be content while we "waited on God." He is an awesome God.

God's preparation sometimes takes a long time and He will not allow us to move forward until we are ready for the next step. I want to share with you an entry in my journal. This entry was written two years and nine months before my "Close Encounter" with God and three and a half years after the Women of Faith Conference. This will give you an idea of my heart's desire to serve God and where I was in building my relationship with Him.

March 24, 2003

"Lord, I give it all to you: past regrets, present problems, future ambitions, my fears, my dreams, weaknesses, habits, hurts, and hang ups. I put You, Jesus Christ, in the driver's seat of my life and I take my hands off the steering wheel. I will not be afraid; for nothing under Your control is out of control. I am a masterpiece by design and clay in the Potter's hand. I can handle anything because I know that You will give me what I need to accomplish Your will for my life. I want to know you as my Father, my Savior, and my Guide. I want to rest confidently in your abiding, unconditional love for me. Take my life and use it for Your glory. From this day forward I am Your servant. Take me and use me according to Your will. Amen."

On May 9, 2004, I endured another loss. My dear, sweet Dad went to be with His Lord. He was 85, outliving all expectations since having his first heart attack in his early fifties. Knowing this fact didn't ease the loss, but knowing with assurance that he was in Heaven with God did ease the pain. After many years, he was now at peace.

The thing I am most grateful to my Dad for is his example of unconditional love. He knew what it was like to endure pain, suffering and rejection, yet he still loved.

If Christ had called down the angels to remove Him from the cross, if He had interrupted God's plan for the sake of revenge on those who had mocked and scorned him without reason, then the meaning of unconditional love would not be the same. He loved and He forgave. He even asked God to forgive them "...for they know not what they do". How incredible, how marvelous is Christ's love.

Knowing my Dad, I rest assured that he now sits in Heaven looking upon my life and sees that: I have learned my lessons well. I now know, from his example, how to let God love me and I know how I should love others, even those who reject me and persecute me.

In order for us to show love we have to know love. Harboring grudges, bitterness, and even hatred can suffocate love. The Bible says, "love is kind." A heart full of love has no room for anger or resentment. A heart full of love understands forgiveness. A heart that doesn't know God cannot fathom this kind of love.

But for the soul that accepts His love and forgiveness there is peace and joy everlasting. I am so thankful for what my Heavenly Father did for me on Calvary and what my earthly father taught me through the way he lived his life.

Satan wanted to fill my heart with guilt for not being the daughter I always should have been. He had done so for most of my life. But my faith was steadfast and sure and I was able to overrule his deception with God's acceptance and unconditional love. I had allowed Satan to rob me of blessings in my past, but he was not going to steal from me anymore.

God loved me enough to send His Son to die on a cross for my sins. My sins…before I had committed them. He loved me enough to prepare a way for me to find forgiveness. I didn't have to beg His forgiveness the day I accepted Christ as my Savior. He offered it freely. So did my Dad.

When God Says Move

The place where we lived was a constant reminder of old things that were passed away. I wondered if they were meant to be a thorn in my flesh, as the Apostle Paul said. One day a man came to our door and said that his mother wanted to buy our home, if we would consider selling it. We had made several attempts to sell since Charles' layoff, thinking one day we would surely have to downsize, but for over a year we had not advertised. Long story short, three weeks later God had sold our home, we had purchased another one, my brother David had helped us update it, and we were moving in. God was so in control of the whole situation. We closed on three loans in one week, one of which was a construction loan that we only needed for six days. I whole-heartedly believe that God is not the author of confusion. When He is in the midst of our circumstances, everything is sweet peace. I stood in awe and amazement at how every little detail worked in sync as the transition unfolded. If we had stood to the side, I believe that God would have moved us in somehow because it was part of His plan.

I had returned to the position of full-time pianist, after my year's leave of absence, and I was enjoying seeing God work in the lives of his children. He had blessed His people. The church had gone through a time of healing, just as I had. He was restoring fellowship, joy, and love. It felt like home again.

I never doubted God moving us across town, but there was uneasiness and a question in my heart and mind about leaving our home church. Our new home was approximately thirty miles away. For seven months we traveled back and forth. A typical Sunday was spent on the road with only an hour or so to rest between services. Every Sunday we would pass so many churches, some of them within a mile or two of our home. A voice would always say, "I have another plan." I felt God was telling me to leave my position at the piano, but I loved our church family so much that it was hard to think of resigning. I kept telling myself, "Since I don't have a clue where we would go and surely God wants me playing the piano, it must be okay to stay here and serve until God gives me 'definite instructions' on where to go." But God doesn't always work this way. In fact, rarely. He wants to know if we are willing to follow, like Abraham, even when we don't know where we're going. If I was to be obedient, I had to follow His leading. The hardest thing to do is leave where we are comfortable, but when God says "Go," we must go. I was about to enter the unknown, but I was willing to trust God. So, I resigned.

I had grown more spiritually in the eight years we had been at this church than during my entire Christian life. I had so many great memories. These were the people who had taught me how to love others. I had watched as their love had allowed them to overcome bitterness and differences of opinion. This is where I had been able to give back in ministry by leading them in worship with my music. Like all churches, this one had also endured trials, but I loved it there. It was home. But I loved God more and He said, "Follow Me."

I resigned with tears over yet another loss, but I had peace in my heart and I looked forward to what God had in store for us, knowing that He never takes anything away without giving us something better in return. If He closes a door, He opens another one. If He moves us, it's to a higher level. With God there is no demotion, only promotion. I would walk by faith.

God had proven Himself time and time again. For five years we had realized that there really is life after layoff, if you just continue to trust God and walk in His will. He had blessed our faithfulness. He had given us a beautiful new home when we had thought it would be hard to keep a roof over our heads. He had met all our needs. We were even abundantly blessed.

You know, even when we can't see Him working we can rest assured that He is. Even when He says, "Be still, wait on the Lord," we can know without a doubt that He is working all things for our good. I was excited to see what God had in store for us. I knew His hand was upon us. I envisioned a new church, a new opportunity, new friends, and a new mission field. What and where would it be? Only God knew that. I was just anxious to get about my Father's business.

God's Ways Are Not Our Ways

The pathway I was on became treacherous, steep, dark, and uncertain. Little did I know of the dangers that lurked around the next hurdle of my race. Little did I know that my journey was about to take a detour that wasn't going to include a new church, but instead a long period of silence. It wasn't going to include a new friend, but instead a reacquaintance with an old one, my Heavenly Father. It wasn't going to include a new mission field, but instead a new ministry.

The story you are about to read is precious and personal to me. Were it not that God gave me specific instructions to share it with you, I would keep it to myself as a precious jewel. It is true and as factual as I can remember it to be. Its purpose is to encourage you to embark on a journey of discovery for yourself. I can only tell you that what I experienced is worth all the pain, suffering, and tears. It is worth the anguish, uncertainty, and the solitude.

Every fiber of my being wants you to hear me. There is a God in Heaven who longs to have a relationship with you. He wants to fellowship with you on a one-to-one basis. He wants to be "the One and only One" in your life. He longs for you to walk with Him. As the old hymn says, "He walks with me, He talks with me, and He tells me I am His own. The joy we share as we tarry there, none other has ever known."

If I had all the ink the oceans to fill, I could never write enough words to express to you the feeling of knowing God's presence. How could I explain feeling the touch of His hand on mine? How could I relate to you the brush of an angel's wing across my hospital bed? How could I get you to realize that this story is not fiction, it is as real as I am?

I am humbled and grateful for how God revealed Himself to me in His three persons. He answered my prayers to know Him more and in doing so, He took an ordinary woman and made her an extraordinary witness to His glory.

I want God to place me behind the cross so that you can see Him, not me. When you remember this book, don't let it be about me, let it be all about Him. God didn't say, "Write this book, it will make you millions." He said, "Write this book that it may bring Me glory."

I would suggest that you place yourself in a quiet corner if you are not already there because I believe God's power will be made manifest through the remaining pages of this book. What you have read thus far has only set the stage for the next and best act. I believe that by the time you are finished reading the next chapter, you too will have cast your eyes towards Heaven to see a vision of what God has in store for your life. That life will include an up close and personal relationship with Jesus Christ who connects you with God the Father and God the Holy Spirit.

I am nobody special, but one thing I am is "blessed." I am blessed to be a chosen servant of God, called to bear witness of what He has done in my life. Though I am unworthy of His love, I am here to tell you that His power can change even a broken vessel like me and make it useful.

This story is not about some spooky tale of spirits, but it does include an interaction with God the Father, God the Son, and God the Holy Spirit. I call it by the name God instructed me to share with you, "A Close Encounter of Three Kinds."

Chapter 2

A Close Encounter of Three Kinds

Almighty God – My Healer

What on earth is happening that Heaven knows about?

In December of 2005, I found myself in the midst of the greatest challenge of my entire life. Yes, another test of faith, but one that would be life-changing and one that would give me the story that I had said I did not have. It was a culminating event that took all the circumstances of my life and placed them into a melting pot to be tried and tested by fire. It was a time for my faith to be stretched, yet refined. This experience was going to be my proving ground.

In order for God to be able to use me He had to make sure of my intentions. He had to make sure that my heart was willing to suffer loss and sacrifice. Jesus said, "Take up thy cross and follow me." What was I willing to let go of in order to gain all? Would it be "whatever it takes?"

The refiner's fire will purge and cleanse us and if we can stand the heat, it will purify us and bring us forth as gold. God had been pruning me and preparing me for more than seven years and now it was time for me to be refined. In order to prepare me for the heat, God was about to engage me in a battle of faith versus fear.

The Bible says that only after a grain of wheat falls to the ground and dies does it bring forth fruit. I had been praying that God would use my life to bring forth abundant fruit for years. I had to die to self before His will was to be accomplished. I had to empty myself of foolish pride, un-forgiveness, greed, and control. In His refiner's fire, He was going to remove the impurities from my life so that He could work through me to bring honor to His name. In the process,

He would create in me a clean heart, totally surrendered and submissive to His will.

December 17, 2005

It was a typical holiday weekend and also our first Christmas in our new home. Charles and I wanted to share our blessings with our family and therefore we had celebrated by having about forty of them over for dinner. There was lots of good food, great fellowship with loved ones, and entertainment on the guitar by my Uncle James. I played the piano, everyone sang carols, and we also enjoyed solos by my Aunt Jean. There were lots of hugs and wishes for a wonderful holiday season.

I went to bed around 11:30 p.m. after everyone had gone, except for our son Nathan and his wife Sharon. They were living in Atlanta, Georgia at the time and had come to Augusta not only for the family get together, but because Nathan's birthday was the next day. On that day we would also be traveling to Charles' hometown for Christmas with his family.

I was a bit tired when I went to bed, but otherwise I was fine. I was excited about getting to see everyone in Metter. Christmas in my husband's family always means a house full of people with lots and lots of good country cooking. I loved my extended family. They had always been so good to me and included me from the very first time I had met them. They are wonderful people with a heart of gold.

I had always been a healthy person with no chronic health problems, other than allergies. In fact, other than the flu or an occasional sinus infection, I was never sick. I ate healthy and always tried to take good care of myself. My schedule was always hectic. I kept myself busy doing lots of things and I liked my life that way. I traveled a lot with my business and prepared and held weekly training meetings for consultants. I was the church pianist until the previous Sunday, I sang in the

69

choir and solo. I was a seamstress for over thirty years and anything else I could squeeze into my schedule.

Prior to December 17, I had not been sick. I did not have a cough or congestion and before going to bed that night I had no indication of an onset of sickness. Somewhere around 4:00 a.m., I woke up with a severe headache and chills. My mind was clouded as if I was heavily sedated.

I guess it was my quivering that awakened Charles. As he proceeded to cover me with additional blankets, he made a remark about how he could feel heat radiating from my body.

I was a person who was rarely sick and it was very unusual for me to have a fever. I thought maybe we'd better check my temperature. My first thought was, I bet I have the flu. My next thought was; I won't get to go to Metter today for Christmas!

Charles awakened Sharon because she had once been a nurse and knew much more about caring for the sick than he did. This was something that was totally out of his league. I had always been the caregiver since I was a nurse. He was at a total loss when it came to nurturing the sick.

Sharon took my temperature and much to my surprise, it was 105.2. Since my normal temperature runs usually around 97 degrees, I knew something was wrong. This was not normal, even if I did have the flu. My neck was stiff and my head was pounding. It didn't take much to convince me that I needed to go to the emergency room. Even though I knew I was sick, I never would have guessed the severity of what was happening inside my body.

I had worked only part-time as a nurse for several years since starting my business, but I remembered that I had worked a four hour shift the week before. I started trying to diagnose my condition based on contact that I had had with patients. I worked in Rehab so none of my patients were supposed to be sick (at least that we were aware of). Most of them were recovering from things like hip or knee surgeries.

The more I tried to think, the worse the headache became. I could hardly open my eyes to the light. I thought maybe I just had a migraine, though I had never had one before. But if that was the case, why did I have the temperature?

After about five hours in the emergency room, some intraveneous fluids, and Motrin, I was sent home with a diagnosis of "Viral Syndrome." Nathan, Sharon, and Charles had asked repeatedly for something else to be done, like more labs or a chest x-ray, but their requests were denied. They knew that I was acting any way but normal, yet they were unable to convince the doctor that anything else was wrong with me. He kept insisting that all I had was a virus. I was discharged with the usual protocol: Motrin and Phenergan.

I have no recollection of the next four days. In fact, once we left home that Sunday morning I was pretty much incoherent from then until the following Thursday morning which was December 22nd.

During those four days I am told that I carried on conversations and seemed to be alert, but I remember nothing. A very dear friend and business associate of mine, who is also a nurse, told me that she called repeatedly and was very concerned because she could tell that I was growing weaker every day. My husband said I slept a lot, but like most untrained persons, he thought it must be the Motrin and fever. To him, as long as I was sleeping, I must be comfortable and free from pain so he just let me sleep. He never realized that I was drifting in and out of consciousness.

I know it had to have been the Holy Spirit who uttered these words on Thursday morning because I do not recall making the statement. My husband says that when he awakened he asked me how I felt. It was then that I said to him to "Take me back to the hospital." I don't remember going and I remember only bits and pieces about being in the emergency room. I have no idea how Charles got me dressed, what he put on me, and how he got me in the car by himself.

Little did either of us know, the disease process that had been attacking my body for four days also affects its victims neurologically. It is after hearing the story from my family and the doctors that I realize how serious my condition was by

71

the time I returned to the hospital. I know that it was a divine intervention on God's part that took me back.

By the time I returned, I was severely dehydrated from the fever and I was extremely weak. I still had a temperature and a tremendous headache. My respirations were shallow and labored. This time the doctor listened to my lungs and then checked my oxygen saturation. I did not have a cough or any indication of congestion. In fact, I was unable to produce a sputum specimen. Because there was little air exchange when the doctor listened to my chest and because my oxygen saturation was extremely low, a chest x-ray was ordered. We waited for the results and when they came, it was so astonishing that the doctor brought the x-ray to my bedside for me to see. I don't think he could believe it himself. I can barely remember our conversation and the x-ray was just a blur.

Since I did not have a cough, initially, there was not much concern about respiratory complications. But when the x-ray was viewed it showed that my lungs were opaque. This means that both the right and left sides were obliterated by infiltrates. There was only a small amount of lung tissue in the upper right quadrant that was oxygenating. This meant that the oxygen requirement to support my vital organs, including my brain, was insufficient. I was deprived of life-sustaining oxygen. No wonder I was drifting in and out of consciousness!

My doctor's first impression was that I had a severe case of bilateral pneumonia. In fact, he said I had one of the worst cases he had ever seen. I was told that after several days in the hospital for IV antibiotic treatment, I would need to rest and recover for eight to ten weeks at home. I can remember this part of his conversation with me. I think it was because I was so shocked to hear that I could be so sick, so fast, and with so little warning. I said to myself, as if speaking to him, "But you don't understand. I am a very busy person. I don't have time to take eight to ten weeks off. I have a business to run. And besides, it's Christmas! You can admit me, but I just know, I will be out of here by Christmas!"

Even in my weakened state, I was sure that I could beat his eight week bed-rest prescription. I had things to do and places to go. Surely I would be up and going in no time. After all, it's just pneumonia, right?

I couldn't deny the facts. My blood oxygen saturations were extremely and dangerously low. I was in respiratory distress. I was placed on IV antibiotics and admitted to a step-down unit for monitoring. I was, of course, on oxygen, but it didn't seem to help my shortness of breath. I can remember gasping for air.

My oxygen levels continued to drop and neurologically I continued to drift in and out of consciousness. I would awaken long enough to respond to the voices of my loved ones, but drift immediately into unconsciousness.

The next morning my condition was worse than the day before. My blood work was skewed, I still had a severe headache, and my respiratory status was worsening. Despite the antibiotics, the chest x-ray showed no improvement. My respirations were labored and shallow. An acute care physician was called in to consult on my case. This was his first impression:

This fifty-three year old female was admitted with significant bilateral pneumonia and shortness of breath. Her admitting diagnosis is community acquired pneumonia which is very severe. The chest x-ray reveals four quadrant pneumonia that is mimicking adult respiratory distress syndrome, at this point. I am extremely concerned about the fact that the patient is currently on 50% oxygen and is unable to bring up sputum. The patient does have an elevated liver function test with generalized malaise and some amount of musculoskeletal symptomatology which would be consistent with an atypical pneumonia such as Mycoplasma Legionella. I would recommend treating her aggressively as follows:

73

1. Administration of oxygen and an arterial blood gas to rule out acidosis. If this is present she will need to be transferred to the intensive care unit for possible ventilation and life support measures.
2. Broad spectrum antibiotics. I doubt the presence of Methicillin-resistant Staphylococcus Aureus, however, that would be something that needs to be looked at since the patient works in the hospital and that is more prevalent at this time.
3. Monitor renal function closely.
4. Echocardiogram to rule out any possibility of cardiac dysfunction
5. If the patient does not improve within the next twenty-four hours a bronchoscopy will be done to diagnose the pathogen causing the pneumonia.

This consult may mean nothing to you unless you have a medical background, but if you understand any of it, you can easily see that my condition was guarded and serious.

By Saturday morning, Christmas Eve 2005, my condition was so grave that a decision had to be made concerning my prognosis and care. I was in acute respiratory failure.

My sister-in-law, Melba, had spent the night with me and she was present along with other family members. I had sent my husband home to rest the night before since he had been at the hospital all day with me that day. He had not yet arrived that Saturday morning.

Though I was in acute distress, I can recall being asked by the physician for my permission to be placed on "life-support." A signature had to be obtained for ventilation. I was intermittently coherent, so it was going to have to be mine. I asked him what my options were and he said, "You most likely will not survive without it." Though I was having almost no periods of awareness, this was one time when God stirred me into reality. I asked myself, "Not make it! Does he mean I might die?"

Being a registered nurse, I knew the ramifications of being on a ventilator. I knew the chances of complications. I knew that a great percentage of those who are placed on life support don't survive and if they do, many times they suffer from brain damage due to insufficient oxygenation or other complications such as: a stroke from a blood clot, bed sores, renal failure, congestive heart failure, loss of muscle tone, and the list goes on. Many times death is due to complications, if not from the disease process itself.

I also was aware of the fact that if there was no justifiable reason to keep me on life support, no hope for a recovery, or that I would live the remainder of my life connected to machines or in a vegetative state, my dear husband was going to have to make a decision to unplug the machines. I knew that this would be the most difficult decision he would ever have to make. It would be devastating to him. How could I put him in that position, yet how could I not give myself the option? This was not a decision that I could contemplate. Even the length of my state of awareness wasn't guaranteed. The doctor had to have an answer right then, not later. I could tell from his voice that he was anxious to get my answer so that he could proceed with treatment.

Let me stop right here and ask you: What would you do if you found yourself in this situation? I could hear the voices of my family around me encouraging me to say yes and that I would be okay, but I knew that it was only their fear speaking. They were hoping that the idea of a few days to rest my lungs would be sufficient and that soon I would be back to normal again, but I was the one who had to say "yes." I was the one who had to sign my life away. I was the one whose life would be at the mercy of machines to keep me alive and support my vital organs. I was the one who would have to trust God to heal me.

My heart sank inside of me as I thought of never getting to say goodbye to my husband or never getting to enjoy another Christmas with family. This was Christmas Eve. What a way to celebrate! I dreaded the unknown, though I had no fear of death because I knew I would spend eternity in Heaven. I knew that I would be sedated and placed in a drug induced coma and I admit, the thought of being unaware of what was happening to me created anxiety.

I thought to myself, but what if this is my time to die? If I said yes, would I be interfering with God's plan to bring me home to Heaven? I wondered if I was about to meet my Savior? What if my opportunity to really know Him was going to be when I walked with Him in Heaven, not here on earth?

God had always been so good to me. He had blessed me with a loving husband and two wonderful sons. He had given them precious wives who loved them the way we had always prayed they would. God had taken care of us financially and blessed us for our faithfulness to Him. We had always given Him praise for these things. We never lived an extravagant life, but God had blessed us with health and happiness. He had brought us through trials and tribulations and we gave Him the glory for that too. We never lacked because He had always supplied all our needs. We had kept God at the center of our home and our relationship. We had not always been the example that maybe we should have been, but we tried to teach our children to trust God, to obey Him, and to serve. We tried to lead them by example. I tried not to think of good-byes. I was confident in a Sovereign Lord who has promised me that I will live eternally with my loved ones because they also belong to God. It wasn't the fear of death that I dreaded because I knew that God would walk me through the gates of Heaven. I didn't regret not getting to travel to exotic places or to see the world. It wasn't that I might never find success or achieve some great reward or lay claim to a great accomplishment.

So, what would be my greatest regret? My greatest regret was a guilt, a dread, and a fear that I had not done all I needed to do for Christ while on earth and that now my chance might be over.

I regretted that I might have sung my last song of praise to God or that I might have played my last melody on the piano. I regretted that I might have had my last chance to witness for my Savior or that I might have missed my last opportunity to encourage a believer in their struggle with temptation or grief. I regretted that I had not loved more, laughed more, and let go of more.

I tried to picture myself standing before my family and the familiar faces of the people in my church that I loved so dearly. Had I experienced my last opportunity to minister to them in song and selfishly receive a blessing from doing so? Beyond their faces I could see, in a blur, the faces of those I had not had an opportunity to meet. Did their faces represent opportunities that I had missed to share the gospel?

I thought about my desire to write a book that would encourage and inspire others in their walk with Christ. This was something I had never tackled because I thought I needed a story. Other than my poems and journals, what legacy would I leave behind that would make a difference that I had lived at all? Who would remember me fifty or one hundred years from now, if the Lord tarried? Would my friends and family members remember me for the way I led them spiritually or would they remember my music, sewing, or laughter? Would they feel that they really knew me or that there was still so much about me that they wished they had known?

I thought as well about the women who were my business associates. Who would lead them and guide them in building a business God's way, as I had always tried to do?

My thoughts were on things eternal. What had I done with my life that gave it value, or better yet, what had I allowed God to do with my life that gave value to the lives of others?

I knew I could have done so much more. I could have been a better witness. I could have been more loving, sharing, and giving to those less fortunate than myself. I had not sung enough songs or played enough melodies. If only I could just do these things once more! Could it be that God would give me another chance? Could it be that He was not finished with me yet? Could it be that He was preparing me for the greatest part of my race or could it be that my prayer to know God more intimately was about to be answered as He ushered me into His presence?

So little time had passed since the doctor had asked for my permission to be placed on a ventilator, yet so many thoughts had raced through my mind. In my heart, I cried out to God to help me for He is my Great Physician and then I said, "Okay. I will do it." As I spoke the words I also prayed, "Lord, Thy will be done." I knew that these may be the last words I would ever utter here on earth.

Fast Is Still Too Slow

There was a sudden race for time. As soon as I made my mark on the consent form, the doctor told my family to say their good-byes and then he ushered them out the door.

He then proceeded to shout orders to the nurses. They were to get me prepared and downstairs for a bronchoscopy in order to extract a sample of sputum from my lungs for culture. They were going to attempt to clear some of the mucus from my lungs (which my doctor later described as glue) and finally they would insert the endotracheal tube down my throat and into my lungs. I would then be connected to a ventilator.

It seemed like there were a hundred or more medical staff around my bed all at once. Each one was poking a tube or needle in some part of my body. Everyone seemed to be in such a hurry and you could feel the adrenaline rush in the atmosphere. There was a nurse sitting at my bedside pulling with all her might to get my wedding ring off and it felt as if she was going to dislocate every joint in my finger. It was such as relief when she was finally able to remove it and I couldn't help but wonder what she would do with it.

This may seem insignificant to you in the scheme of things, but it was just another part of me that someone else now had control of. I was losing control moment by moment and soon I wouldn't even have control of my mind or body. I had no idea, at this point of my journey, that this was just the beginning of a long list of things that would lose their importance to me because God was making plans to change my priorities.

There were lots of voices coming in and out of the room, doors were slamming, and paper was rattling from the sterile packages being opened for procedures they were about to perform. I could hear the urgency in their voices as they shouted commands across the room. I didn't open my eyes, I just listened. I knew that my life lay in a balance between Heaven and earth and that God was the only One who could tip the scale.

Being a patient could almost be considered a violation of your rights. Once you sign the consent for treatment, it's as if you give permission for them to take over your body. I knew that everything they were doing was to help me, but it seemed all they were doing was hurting me.

Their movements were mechanical and methodical as they prepared to take away my control of respirations and place them on a machine.

It was such a strange feeling. I felt as if I was listening to what was going on, but it was all part of a bad dream. I tried to wake myself up from the dream, only to find that I was in the midst of reality. It was me. It was my life. I was helpless and defenseless. I was in God's hands.

I have had surgery several times before and I know what it feels like to be put to sleep, but this feeling was different. This time it was not for a time-limited surgery. It was going to be an indefinite period of time on life support until my body was either able to heal or unable to fight.

I'm not going to tell you that I didn't feel any anxiety or apprehension. After all, I am human. But truthfully, it was hard to feel anything at all. Everything was happening so quickly. I was drifting in and out of consciousness, but when I would be in a state of awareness my thought was, this just can't be happening to me!

I am a nurse. I should be the one performing these treatments on someone else. It felt uncomfortable and odd to be the patient and not the nurse.

I kept thinking that surely they would soon sedate me. I wanted to open my eyes, but that would confirm that this scenario was not a dream, but indeed reality. I was so extremely weak that my body felt like it was sinking into the bed. It was as if I were being lowered into a grave, but still able to hear voices above ground.

There was movement and I knew from tilting to and fro and the sound of clamoring wheels that I was on a gurney and in transport to the operating room. The overhead lights flashed quickly through my closed eye lids as we passed them one by one. In my mind I had the sensation of what it must feel like to "walk the green mile" as one is about to face the death sentence.

To everyone around me this was just a procedure. To them it was a routine that they had performed probably hundreds of times. The difference being, they had not performed it on me.

I could hear the gurney banging into the revolving doors as they wheeled me into the operating room. I wanted to hear my husband's voice just one more time. I wondered how long it would be before I would hear it again, or if I ever would.

Charles and I had always been inseparable, but now we were going to be separated by the doors of an intensive care unit...doors that divided two people who had lived as one for thirty-five years. I felt so isolated. I felt alone, even though I was surrounded by a room full of strangers who only knew me as "the patient." Nobody called me by name, they just talked among themselves. I was a body with a number and a life-threatening disease that was requiring immediate treatment. They were just intent on doing their job!

They didn't know me as a person. To them I was nobody special. There was no particular accomplishment in my life that was important to them or that determined their level of treatment. They didn't know my past, my family, or where I lived. They weren't treating me because of my title or degree or accomplishment. They didn't know my walk with God or that I sang or played the piano. They weren't working to save my life because they saw me as necessarily valuable. They were doing what they were trained to do; treat the symptoms and save a life and for that I am so grateful!

They did know that I was a nurse who worked in the same hospital. I remember hearing someone say, "She is one of us."

There were no familiar voices and even if there had been, no one was talking to me anyway. I had this urge to say something, anything, because I knew once I was on the ventilator I would not be able to communicate. I just wanted someone to notice me and appreciate the fact that I was a real person who was still alive and listening to every word they were saying.

I wondered if I would ever speak again. I thought to myself, maybe I could sing them a song while they prepare to connect me. That was a dumb idea. I tried, but I was so weak and so short of breath that I could not even speak above a faint whisper. It was so faint that nobody even heard me try. Since I couldn't sing to them, I decided to sing praises to God, only in my head.

Soon my fear and anxiety was replaced with peace. I started to think of the pleasantries in my life like a quiet walk in the neighborhood or sitting on the porch swing with my husband. I thought about many of the people in my life who had blessed me in one way or another.

There was a chill to the room and a smell of alcohol. Bodies brushed against my face as they leaned over my bed to move my near lifeless body side to side in order to position me for intubation. I kept thinking, surely they will sedate me soon.

There were a few of the nurses or technicians who would briefly explain what they were about to do to me, but it was done in such a mechanical way. It was almost as if their script was memorized and rehearsed. They didn't pay attention to whether I heard what they said or not. It was just something they had been taught to do in school. I wondered, what happened to "nurturing the patient?"

I guess I should be grateful that at least a few of them did maintain my dignity by telling me what they were about to do to me. Others just worked around me as if I wasn't even there. Some were at least gentle and I could feel the kindness in their touch.

I have always been a touchy, feely kind of nurse. I believe there is healing in a warm pat of a hand or a gentle back rub. It's a way to connect with a person without saying a word.

I now realize the importance of a gentle brush on the cheek, a stroke of the hair, a reassuring word, a pat on the arm; all those things I was used to doing for my patients.

I longed for this kind of touch. I wanted to feel human and connected in some way, not just a body. I was a real person with real emotions and real feelings. As long as I could feel their touch, it meant that I was still alive.

I knew by now that the only person I was going be able to have a conversation with was God. I had been praying almost constantly, but now it was time for God and I to find our special, quiet corner in my heart and mind so that He could talk to me and I could listen. I concentrated on listening for His voice and this helped to drown out the noises around me.

For days I had struggled to breathe. I was tired and so fatigued that I could hardly make my chest rise with inspiration. For two days I had been asking God to let me get better so I could go home. He obviously had different plans for me. My condition wasn't getting better and I certainly wasn't about to go home. At least not my earthly home!

I guess it must be human nature to think that sudden illness will never happen to us. We tend to think that anything this life-threatening comes with some kind of warning or with time to make preparations. This is not true. I had no time to prepare for this, at least not physically or mentally. Looking back, I can see that God had been preparing me spiritually for this journey for a long time. He had actually planned for this occasion all my life. For years I had sought for Him, prayed to Him, leaned on Him, trusted Him, and yearned to know Him. Now I desperately needed Him.

For ten years I had been praying and seeking a deeper relationship with Him; one that would take me to a higher level of understanding and wisdom, one that would take me to a new level of obedience, and one that would allow my life to produce abundant fruit.

God had prepared me by testing and growing my faith and belief in Him through layoff, death, and loss. Now I was ready to exercise my faith to the highest degree as I trusted Him to work a miracle in my life and heal me.

I asked God to allow His peace to permeate my being and calm my spirit. I asked Him to take control of the hands of those who were caring for me and to guide their every move. I asked for grace to bear my burden. I asked Him to care for my family when I could not. I asked for strength to accept His will as He drew me closer to His heart. Lastly, I asked Him to allow the testimony of my life to bring honor to His name. I asked Him to work His will in and through me. In my mind, I think I just assumed that He would restore my health, that this would be just another valley, and that my life would go on as it always had.

Suddenly, I realized that there was a presence in the room that was greater than all the staff put together. It was the presence of God. I couldn't see Him or touch Him, but I knew He was there. It was a presence that replaced my loneliness and gave me assurance that He was a power much stronger than the doctors and nurses. He was much more powerful than the disease that was claiming my body minute by minute. No one else seemed to be aware of Him, but He was real to me. He came to me when I needed Him most and He revealed Himself to me as My Healer and the Great Physician. I was surrounded by Almighty God and He was in control.

His Spirit hovered over the entire room as if He were giving instructions to the hands of those who were caring for me. The chill I had felt before was gone. It had been replaced by a warm blanket of God's love. He had laid it over me to protect me, shield me, and separate me from the pain.

I am sure that God brought with Him a host of angels who camped around the operating table. I tried to picture in my mind how the scene must look from God's vantage point. Here was one of His children laid out as if on an alter ready to be sacrificed. His eyes were on me, yet He was everywhere.

I am sure the angels were following orders as they made sure everything was carried out according to His plan.

I tried to imagine how I would feel if I were watching this scene take place with one of my own children, as my Heavenly Father was watching me. I knew it must break His heart to see His child in pain, yet He knew that this valley was necessary in order to prepare me, test my faith, refine me, and make me a useable vessel. Little did I know, but this was also His opportunity to introduce me to Himself in His three persons. He said, "I am your Healer, I am the Great Physician, I am Almighty God," but there was more of Him to come. He was answering my prayer to know the Triune God.

He is a Sovereign God who is always in control and knows all things. He knew what was going to take place in the coming days and He knew the faith it would take to pass this test. I am so grateful that He saw me worthy of testing.

He had always known that this day would come for me. He had prepared me for this day throughout the fifty-three years of my life. Through all the circumstances, the struggles, the rejections, the trials, and the heartaches as well as the many, many blessings and ways He had always taken care of me, He had fashioned a willing heart. But to what extent would He test my willingness to be obedient to Him? How much testing would I have to endure in order to prove my love for Him?

I had a choice. Either I could give in to fear and end up doubting His ability to take carry me through this trial or I could stand on His promises to work all things for my good because I loved Him and longed to be used for His purposes.

I chose to stand, despite my fear. I trusted in His healing power, knowing that He could heal me if that was His will. He would use me to bring honor and glory to Himself if He left me here on earth or He would give me a glorified body in Heaven. Either way I would be healed.

To calm myself even more I began to recite scriptures to myself like *Psalm 23 and the Lord's Prayer*. Others were:

"I will lay me down in peace and sleep; for thou, Lord, only makest me dwell in safety" (Psalm 4:8).
"show me thy ways, O Lord; teach me thy paths" (Psalm 25:4).
"for thou, Lord hast not forsaken them that seek thee" (Psalm 9:10).
"I sought the Lord, and he heard me, and delivered me from all my fears" (Psalm 34:4).

On and on the Holy Spirit brought to my mind verses that confirmed my resting place. Gone was my fear, panic, and anxiety. I felt peace.

I remember a drape being placed over my face in preparation to insert a triple lumen catheter into the right subclavian vein in my neck. I was thinking, I hope they know I am not asleep yet!

I overheard a female voice (probably either a nurse or anesthesiologist) on my left ask the doctor who was on my right if he was ready to sedate me. He said, "Yes, she has already been given the paralytic." She said, "Did you say that it had already been given?" He said, "Yes." (This is very important) She said, "Then we are not going to be able to fully sedate her." I thought, oh boy. Here I am paralyzed stiff as a board, without the ability to respond and I am going to be awake through all of this! Lord, I need You!

You can thank God that this little mishap was even in His plan because without the ability to converse and commune with Him over the next eleven days, this book would not have a plot, I would not have a story, and God would not have had my complete attention.

The doctors might have been performing surgery on my lungs, but God was performing surgery on my heart. He was filling it with a fresh anointing of faith to carry me through. It was a faith I would need to finish my race. My need was for healing, but it was more than just physically. I needed God to restore my soul. I needed to know He was there with me and He made His presence known to me more than ever before. He is God Almighty who is and is to come. He is Jehovah God who reigns. He is my Refuge and He is my Strength.

I was drifting into unconsciousness. This was God's way of protecting me through the most painful procedures. The last thing I remember telling God went something like this:

"Lord, I thank you for saving me. I thank You for the many blessings you have given me in my life. I thank You for assuring me of Your presence by surrounding me with Your protection and the warmth of Your loving arms. I pray that You will use this experience to bring glory to Your name. Keep my mind and thoughts on You, and only You. Guide me, protect me, and teach me to trust You more. Whatever it takes, reveal Yourself to me as never before that I may know You not only as my Savior, but my Father and Your Holy Spirit.

Like the calm before the storm, help me to know that the seriousness of my situation means that something of eternal significance and magnitude is about to happen in my life. Let me express my love to You with complete assurance that whatever my lot Thou hast taught me to say, "It Is Well With My Soul."

As I drifted into unconsciousness, I was being sheltered in the arms of God, protected by His grace and mercy and I was safe and secure in His love. I had no idea what God was doing, but somehow it didn't matter anymore. I trusted Him.

ICU (I see you) Though My Eyes Are Closed

The next thing I was aware of was being in ICU. There were people standing around my bed. Though they were talking softly, I recognized their voices and I knew it was my family and friends who were earnestly praying for me.

Of course, I was paralyzed to keep me from fighting the machines so I couldn't open my eyes to see them, but I could hear them. I might have been in a drug-induced coma, but I was not sedated. For the sake of a better word I will hereafter call my state of mind "awareness." I drifted in and out of sleep, but when I was awake I was aware of everything going on around me. Even though I was aware, I was unable to give the world any inkling that I was anything but unconscious.

I could hear the conversations of the doctors and nurses around my bed. Most of them by the way, weren't very encouraging. In the beginning there was a nurse who sat continuously at my bedside monitoring the machines for changes in my vital signs, my kidney function, and respiratory status. One nurse or another was continuously hanging another mini-bag of antibiotics, drawing blood or passing fluids into my stomach through a tube in my nose. There was intensity in the noises of the room and a distinct smell of ICU. I vividly remember the crackling noise of a thermometer being placed in my ear on a continuous basis.

I remember remarks about not being able to sedate me and orders from a physician to keep giving me more medication. I lay there thinking, if they ever get me completely sedated I will probably never wake up with all these drugs in my body!

My sense of awareness was highlighted by hearing the voices of my loved ones and friends. They would tenderly whisper in my ear, but the heightened sensitivity of my hearing caused their voices to ring loud and clear. I could hear the prayers from pastors, friends, and family. There were groups of familiar voices at the foot of my bed. They spoke in a hurdle like a coach anticipating the next game plan. I strained to hear what they were saying because I didn't want to be left out of the conversation. Couldn't they tell somehow that I could hear them? I wanted to be in on their prayers and I wanted to feel like they were talking to me, not about me.

I could hear a quiver in their voices as they tried to hold back the tears. Off and on they would talk to me because the nurses had told them that I would be able to hear at the time, just unable to remember anything when I woke up. I am sure they never imagined that not only would I remember, I would also live to tell about it!

As my family tried to convince me that I was getting better, I could tell they were trying to convince themselves of the same fact. After all, I was the one who was hearing the comments behind closed doors. The things I was hearing did not sound very encouraging as far as my hope of recovery. I heard the reports and I heard the comments from those who were taking care of me. But I also knew that God was able to heal me if He chose to do so.

Everyone was worried and distressed over my worsening condition. All I did was lay there still and silent, unable to respond in any way. I wanted so badly to be able to reassure them that God was in control and that I was resting in His care, but I could do nothing except trust that the same God who was with me and who was comforting me with words of assurance was also comforting them.

God allowed me glimpses of my surroundings, though my eyes never opened. It was the familiarity of a voice that allowed me to picture a face; like the face of my dear husband Charles. I could sense him leaning over me to kiss my cheek.

This was hard for him to do because at five feet seven inches it was a struggle for him to reach over the side rail and around all the tubes that were connected to my body. I could hear the despair in his voice and I knew how badly he was hurting, yet he was still trying to encourage me by telling me "Hang in there babe. You're going to get better."

At the end of each visiting hour, he would be the last one to say good-bye. It was our few minutes together. During this time he would tell me about all the people who had come to be with them that day. He talked about beautiful flowers that had been brought, but had to be taken home because they weren't allowed in ICU. He told me about fruit baskets and meals that people prepared and brought to the waiting room. He and my children kept cards, journals, and notes because they knew I liked those kinds of things. He talked to me as if we were having a normal conversation and that was exactly what I needed him to do. It was a one sided conversation because all I could do was listen, but it connected me with the world outside of ICU.

I felt so much better knowing that people were taking care of my loved ones when I couldn't. This brought me great joy and made me appreciate the many compassionate friends and family members that God had blessed me with.

I wanted to know what was going on outside of the four walls of my ICU room. I wanted to hear about family and friends and how God was working in their lives through my situation. I wanted to hear that people were giving God the glory for the life He had allowed me to live, not about how I was dying.

I was always anxious to hear the announcement of visiting hours. It seemed like such a long time between them. Those who visited were only allowed in my room for thirty minutes and it passed so quickly. They came in continuous shifts to cast their eyes on my near lifeless body.

At night Charles would have to leave the hospital because there was no where for him to rest in the waiting room and no one was allowed in to see me during the night anyway. But oh how I hated to hear him say good-bye. I knew this meant that I had a long night ahead of me. He would always assure me that he would be back first thing in the morning, and he was.

I knew he didn't want to leave me. I could tell by his voice that he feared what might happen to me before he could return. Leaving me was like leaving a piece of him behind. I know because I felt the same way. Even though he knew nothing about medicine or how to take care of me, I felt protected and safe when he was in the room. I always have and always will.

When Charles would leave for the evening, I thought often about how Jesus must have felt as He hung on the cross. There was a moment in time that He was separated from His Heavenly Father. I believe what saddened Him the most was not the price He had to pay for our sins because He came willingly, but rather His separation from God. In my humanity, I could relate. But Jesus came to fulfill the Father's will out of love. God was using my situation to give me a glimpse of how hard it is to feel separated from those you love so that I could understand "His" love.

Not only was it hard for Charles to leave me, but he had to go home to an empty house. A house that only a few days before had been filled with expectations and Christmas joy. Now Christmas had come and gone and there was no joy, only worry and uncertainty. The house that rang with music and singing a little more than a week before now was cold and silent.

You would have to understand our relationship to know how much he meant this and why, but several weeks after I came home from the hospital Charles shared with me how difficult it was for him to come home on Christmas Eve.

When we had moved into our neighborhood eight months earlier, we had been told stories about the "luminaries" on Christmas Eve; how the entire neighborhood places them around their property at dusk on Christmas Eve and how everyone lights them at the same time to reveal a glowing, winding pathway through the streets. I had really looked forward to seeing this sight. Since he was at the hospital with me all day and until visiting hours were over, Charles knew that our yard would probably be the only dark one in the neighborhood. He was so much more concerned about me than luminaries that I am sure the darkness would only have matched what he felt in his heart.

He knew how much I had looked forward to this event and therefore, it broke his heart to know that I was going to miss it. Worse than that was the haunting fact that I may never get to see it.

He told me that as he entered our neighborhood late that evening, it truly was a beautiful sight to see, especially when he rounded the corner and entered our street. It was then that he could see that someone had placed luminaries all around our yard for us and he said the entire yard glittered like his "candle of hope."

Broken-hearted, he entered the house and fell to his knees in despair. He said he cried out in pain from a broken heart and that as he prayed he asked God to take him too, if His will was to take me because he couldn't imagine living life without me.

Now you know why he is my hero! Jesus said that there is no greater love than to lay down our lives for another. I am so blessed that my husband loves me this much.

I always knew when Paul was in my room. I looked forward to the soothing, cool cloths that he would place on my forehead. It was something he knew to do that might make me feel better, and it did. That is except for the night he left the wash cloth on my forehead. After everyone had gone it flipped down from my forehead and fell across my nose and mouth. I had to wait until another nurse came in to move it. That was one time I was appreciative of the ventilator breathing for me.

Paul has always been a person of few words, but I could always tell when he was there because a mother knows these things. It was his presence that I needed most and he had his ways of making that known without saying a word. His wife Suzanne, is also a quiet person, but always had something to say to encourage me before she left the room. Her parents were faithful to stay at the hospital with my family and I don't think they missed a single day. Suzanne's mom is an experienced nurse so she was perfect to interpret the medical lingo for my family.

Nathan and Sharon were not hard to miss. They talked to me, rubbed my face and arms, and tried their best to solicit a response from me. I tried, but I could do nothing. Sharon kept the nurses on their toes by asking questions about my lab reports and x-ray's. She would ask me, "Are they taking good care of you Ms. Karen? Are you in pain?" She and Nathan paid close attention to changes in my vital signs on the monitors. I remember the coolness of Sharon's tiny hands on my arm. I couldn't reach out to her, but her touch meant so much to me.

Our sons are different as night and day, but each has his own very special qualities. I wanted so badly to be able to respond so that they would find a glimmer of hope. But my eyes were frozen shut and nothing moved because I was paralyzed. The drugs were given to keep me from fighting the ventilator, but they were also preventing me from communicating with those I loved. I wanted to tell them that I could hear them talking, but all I could do was lay there motionless. I wanted to be able to console them and tell them that I was uncomfortable, but not in extreme pain. I wanted to say anything that would make it a better day for them. I wanted to take their hurt away, but I couldn't. I was helpless.

Most of all, I wanted so badly to tell them about the encounter I had had with God in the operating room and how He had continued to fill my room with His presence. I wanted to let them know that when they were not able to be in the room with me, I was not alone. How would I ever explain the feeling of God's presence in a way that they would understand? I hoped maybe they could feel it too. If only they could know the peace that I felt in His presence!

When it was not visiting hours, life went on as usual for the ICU. It was such a noisy place and so full of activity. There was often a code blue and when I would hear it called I just hoped that it wasn't me they were running to. Even though I couldn't take a breath, I couldn't help but imagine a sigh of relief when they passed my room instead of entering it.

When I would be in my state of awareness, I would spend my time praying and thinking about the things I was hearing. Since I was a nurse, I understood most of the reports that I heard being passed back and forth from nurse to physician. I heard the nurses talking to themselves as they recorded my vital signs on a frequent basis. I also heard them expressing their own opinions about my deteriorating condition.

I also thought a lot about what God was doing in my life. He had my total attention and we fellowshipped continuously. He used our conversations together to drown out the bells, buzzers and alarms that surrounded me. It was a precious time as He drew me closer and closer to Himself.

I listened to the conversations around the nurse's desk as they discussed their lives and things that seemed so important to them. Funny how insignificant their distresses seemed to me. Not because they didn't belong to me, but because when compared to facing eternity, nothing seemed to hold much significance. Here I was lying on a bed with my life in the balance and they were complaining about what their husbands did or didn't give them for Christmas, a sweater that didn't fit or the drudgery of having to return it. I thought, what a problem!

Nothing mattered more to me at that moment in my life than spending precious hours talking and listening to God. I could have filled my mind with other thoughts, but I chose to focus on Him. Sometimes I almost felt guilty that I was enjoying such a journey. I was in constant communication with God, I was blessed, and I was enjoying every moment of our time together. I had no needs that were greater than leaning on Him. He was all I needed.

I wondered about the relationship God had with each of my nurses. I prayed for them to know Him. I could hear them talking about the "herd" of people who gathered in the waiting room on my behalf. It was a true expression of God's love and they seemed to be in awe that one person could draw such a crowd. That person was not me. The people who were gathered in that waiting room were there to watch God work a miracle. I often got a kick out of hearing the phone ring at the nurse's desk and then someone yelling, "get Karen's nurse, this has to be one of her family members calling!"

Sickness has a way of giving us a different perspective on life. I felt I was on a roller coaster. One minute I would be contemplating death and eternity and the next minute I was thinking about how I was going to handle life. It didn't seem to bother me so much either way. I would handle the situation with optimism, hope, a lack of fear, and incredible strength with God's help.

I trusted God to issue me a measure of grace every moment and to help me cope with my mind's inconsistent death or life issue. I knew that He rarely gave more than I needed at one time so I kept asking Him over and over. I also knew that He would pour out His grace on me just when I needed it, not before and not after. I found God's first measure of grace in my ability to see my circumstance in light of His "glory," and His "perfect will," not my own.

This enabled me to see beyond the present to a vision of a future that God might be planning for me. It was a glimpse of what God could do with my life, if He chose to leave me on earth. Serving Him has always been so important to me that the thought of Him choosing me for a special task excited me. Thinking on things above kept my thoughts positive and my spirits uplifted. His word says that without a vision, the people perish. God was using my visions to rescue my perishing heart.

My arms were tied to the bedrails, which was to keep me from pulling out the breathing tube. My life was sustained by machines that continuously beeped and rang with alarms and the ventilator that controlled my every breath swished and hummed to a constant rhythm.

There were IV lines and medication drips attached to machines that constantly signaled time for the next dose. Nurses were checking vital signs or drawing labs constantly, x-ray techs were taking chest x-rays, and respiratory therapists were doing treatments on my lungs.

Unless they were performing a treatment on me, it seemed they were oblivious to the fact that I was even there. It was a routine shift for most of them. It was a way to get through the difficult stress of death; a scene often witnessed by a nurse in ICU.

When I was in a state of awareness and I would hear a not-so-good report, I would ask God, "Well, what do You think about that?" I asked Him because I knew that He knew the outcome. But, like He does sometimes, He kept what He thought to Himself. He just said, as I had heard Him say so many times over the last few years, "Be still and know that I am God. Wait on the Lord."

The circumstances seemed so surreal. It was as if I were standing on the outside of a mirrored glass looking in at what appeared to be my body, but in lifeless form. God was there with me showing me things about my life that I needed to change, accept, let go of, or forgive.

He began to open doors to my memory that had been closed shut by intent. It was my means of protecting myself. Only God knew that it was time for the wounds to be healed. This time He gave me a new perspective on the situation. One by one He emptied me of the things that kept me in bondage. These were the things that would be necessary for Him to remove in order to purify my heart.

There was a *rejection* that had caused feelings of *resentment* that I needed forgiveness for. There was also a need for my *acceptance of God's unconditional love*. There was an issue of *pride* and *self-confidence* that needed to be replaced by a God-confidence. There was an issue of *control*

95

and *self-sufficiency* that had to be removed so I would let go of the steering wheel of my life and let God show me that His grace was sufficient for me.

There was an issue of *greed* as God showed me that all the blessings of my life had come from Him. I had done nothing to earn them or deserve them. They were His to give and His to take away. He didn't need them for He had His own, but He showed me that He gave them to me that I might share with others. There were undeserved feelings of shame and guilt that I had allowed to be placed on me and I needed to let go of them.

I was learning who I was in Christ. The things I thought had made me who I was were not me at all; they were just what I did. The only thing that could make me whole was God. Everything else became insignificant as I lay each thing at the foot of the cross.

My mind began to shift from earthly things to eternal things as God allowed me to view my life through His eyes. He started to replace my old thoughts of guilt and shame with new thoughts of love and acceptance.

I had always had visions of what I wanted to accomplish for Him, but they always seemed unreachable goals because I was looking at them through my eyes.

As I became more acquainted with Him, I began to see that nothing is too big for God. I realized that I had spent my whole life trying to figure things out when all I had to do was turn them over to Him. Freedom erupted from a volcano of pent up emotions. God was using this time in my life to draw me closer to Him. I had nothing else to distract me. I was totally focused on listening to His voice.

I knew God had a plan and that He would bring it to fruition. I had faith enough to know that He had allowed this unexplainable incident in my life for my good. In this valley of the shadow of death I would find Him, My Healer, waiting and ready to restore my soul, but not until He was finished with me.

I had always managed to keep one hand clinging to my way, my control. There had been times in my life when I had drifted out of fellowship with God, but that was because I wasn't pursuing the relationship. He never walked away from me, I walked away from Him. That was many years ago. I thanked God for never giving up on me.

I praise God that He has kept me from harm many times in my life. As my shepherd, He has always drawn me back into His fold when I would start to wander. Not only did He seek me until He found me, but then He guarded the gate to prevent anyone or anything from harming me. I had a healthy fear of not having God's presence in my life. I knew I needed Him. I knew that I could not make it through any of life's challenges without Him, especially this one!

Never Too Late!

God planted the desire in my heart to please Him and to know Him personally and intimately on the day I accepted Him as my Savior. Throughout my life I had always wanted to be in the center of His will. I wanted this so badly that I spent so much time asking Him to show me His will that many times I was too blind to see that I was right in the middle of it. This was one of those times.

My prayer life was not always what it should have been, which would account for the reason that I often failed to hear God's answer. I read my Bible, but not as diligently as I needed to. I lacked wisdom because I didn't ask for it and therefore I found some portions of the Bible difficult to understand. I knew a lot of scriptures, but I couldn't always tell you where they were located. I wanted to understand God's word and I desperately wanted to hear Him speak to me. I knew that in order to get different results, something had to change. I began to earnestly seek God through His word, through prayer, through Christian books, and through people I admired and respected.

I am a people watcher. I knew many people who had what they called "religion," but their life didn't reflect what they claimed to have in their hearts. Then there were some who were one person on Sunday and another on Monday. I wondered, if God is Lord of their life, then what do they do with Him from Monday till Saturday?

What I wanted was not a pretentious, pious attitude of worship. I wanted fellowship with God. I wanted to know Him so well, that He became my closest and dearest friend. You know, the kind you talk to "all" the time and not just on Sunday morning.

Let me share with you a little tid-bit. If you have peace, joy, and contentment in your life, more than likely you are walking in the will of God. If you are miserable, confused, unhappy, or have an empty feeling and lack peace in your life, it's very likely that God is using your uneasiness to draw you into a deeper fellowship with Him. There is something that He is trying to show you or teach you. It may be that He has a different direction for you to go. This is where I was.

He will use your uneasiness to move you to a new place. God is not the author of confusion. Satan is the one who wants to keep us wondering and guessing. We will always know that we are walking in the power and presence of God by the peace in our hearts that only He can give and by the fruit our lives are producing.

Another thing that will keep us from experiencing God's peace is when we have an unforgiving heart. A lack of yielding to the will of God will also create uneasiness and a lack of peace and direction. When these things are missing in our lives, we will lack the pleasures of joy and contentment. The uneasiness we feel is one of the ways the Holy Spirit speaks to us and a way that the Holy Spirit is working in our lives to bring about change. It is therefore a good thing.

While I was in ICU, I thought about how much I needed God and how helpless and dependent I was on Him to deliver me from this illness. I so needed the constant reminder of His presence and the feeling of security it brings.

When I was a little girl the safest place I could find was always in my daddy's lap. I tried to picture myself there. I tried to imagine the smell of his hair, the roughness of his hard working hands, and his crooked little finger that was from a break that never healed properly. I thought of the many nights I would practice my hairdressing skills on his head. He never minded because he was my daddy. All I had left were my memories of him. The reality was that my father was already in Heaven and I wasn't a little girl anymore.

So, in my mind, I crawled up on the lap of my Heavenly Father because He is the "father to the fatherless." As He held me in His arms, I felt content, safe, and secure. He reassured me that He was going to take care of me through this valley. Together we peered through the mirrored glass to witness more of my life.

He showed me my need for His love. It was an everlasting, unconditional love. He said, "Karen, I am all you need. My grace is sufficient for you. It is I that you need to please, no one else. I will show you the way, but you must be willing to follow." Despite my faults, my failures, and my needs, He loved me just for being me. He loved me without conditions.

I saw faces of loved ones that I had not seen for a while. Some of them I needed to forgive. Some of the faces needed to forgive me.

There were also faces of those I needed to love more. There were many faces of loved ones that I had neglected to tell how much they added to my life. Some needed to hear why they were so special to me because I had never taken the time to really share my admiration for them.

Coupled with this, were the scenes of what was to come; such as opportunities to share the story of my incredible journey and my "Close Encounter" with God, my Father.

As we watched the scenes unfold, we discussed the significance of each character and how they played such an

99

important role in helping Him to make me the person He wanted me to be.

When I was distressed about all the things that I wished I had done, He comforted me. In my weariness, He carried me. When I couldn't go on in my own strength, He shared His strength with me. He showed me what it meant to know Him as my Heavenly Father.

Soon the relationship with my father that I had missed for so long was being replaced by God's amazing love. He was teaching me of His unconditional love and in His presence, I found comfort, peace, and understanding.

A Turn for the Worse

I was awakened on this particular morning by the conversation of two nurses who were discussing my condition. They were saying things like "this one is not going to make it." While making routine rounds, my doctor had asked for my lab report and when he saw it, he said that it was "that of a dead person."

There had been days and days of unchanged chest x-rays. There were days of fluid overload and threatening congestive heart failure. There was also a constant threat of kidney failure. But one thing that wasn't happening to me was "improvement."

Walking Beside Still Waters

I could almost feel the warm sea breeze blowing in my hair and it reminded me of being on a cruise ship. As I gazed at the beauty of the azure seas, I marveled that God took such care in giving us things of beauty to enjoy. The water was so still that it looked like it was made of glass. It sparkled as if it were "liquid diamonds."

There were yachts and sailboats gliding through the water. There was even a huge, pristine yacht that housed a baby grand piano. How fantastic is that! This personal yacht was so white against the blue water that it looked like fresh fallen snow against a clear blue sky. As it made its way through ports of call, its beauty demanded all the attention due to its majestic splendor. I thought to myself, how awesome it would be to travel all over the world with nothing else to do but enjoy God's magnificent creation. Sounds like a dream doesn't it? No, it sounds like Heaven.

I recall very vividly watching this program on the television that was in my room. It was on the Travel Channel. I guess my nurse had noticed that my vital signs would stabilize and I would relax when this particular program was on, so she would always turn to this channel during her shift to keep me calm.

Charles and I had visited the Caribbean Islands several times and the scenes on the program reminded me of the beauty and wondrous works of the hands of God portrayed by the deep blue waters in this part of our world.

I had never seen this particular program before on our cable network at home, but I sure was enjoying it. It brought me such peace during such a time of great discomfort.

The show wasn't all about yachts and water. Sometimes the theme of the show would change to RV'ing. There were miles and miles of green rolling hills. On one program the RV stopped in a campground. There were no human beings around, but through the window of the RV, I could see lions and bears harmlessly meandering around a picnic table.

I pictured myself hiking a winding path that extended up a mountainside where sheep were grazing. I could see it in a distance. It never crossed my mind to be afraid of the wild animals because they all seemed so peaceful and harmless. It was so calming to watch these programs. I was so uncomfortable from the breathing tube and the inability to change positions. Watching the programs gave me a sense of serenity and therefore, they calmed my soul.

In case you haven't caught on yet, let me tell you what I realized about three months after I came home from the hospital. There was "no" Travel Channel or program about RV'ing, though it was as real to me as life itself. It was a vision of Heaven.

This realization came about one night while Charles and I were watching television. It was about three months after I went home from the hospital. I asked him if he had ever watched this particular program on the Travel Channel. He continued to flip channels, as men so often do (sorry to stereotype), while not paying much attention to what I was saying. I wanted him to find this channel. I knew he would enjoy seeing the beautiful water because he was also fond of the Caribbean. I kept telling him how much I enjoyed watching the program while I was in ICU, how it brought me peace and comfort to see the beautiful, crystal blue water, and how it eased my pain and discomfort. I told him about the yacht and the baby grand piano too.

By this time he was actually listening to what I was saying. With a disturbed look on his face he said, "Babe (his playful name for me), you didn't watch television! You couldn't have seen these programs because you never opened your eyes. You laid there still and silent. I'm not even sure there was a television in your room, but even if there was, you couldn't have seen these things because you were never awake.

I had been concerned about my memory and my inability to analyze or concentrate since hospitalization. I often teased him about having the excuse of being brain damaged when his only excuse was senior moments, but I knew the vivid scenes in my memory were real.

Quite shocked over this bit of new information I said, "Well, how about the times when I would blink my eyes to answer you or when I would squeeze your hand?" His mouth flew open in amazement as he said, "Babe, I know you think you saw those things, but you couldn't have because you never opened your eyes. Oh how I hoped and prayed to see your blue eyes. I would have given anything to feel you squeeze my hand and know that you heard me, but you did nothing for days and days. You gave no response at all. It was as if you were dead."

In glory, honor, and praise I share with you that God allowed me to visualize the splendor of a walk through the valley of the shadow of death. It was a picture in my mind that God gave to bring me peace and calm in the midst of my storm. He allowed me to experience Psalm 23.

His peace filled my soul as He led me beside still waters and allowed me to glimpse the crystal sea. He led me through green pastures and I had no fear because I knew His presence was with me.

My body was struggling to live, but my soul was rejoicing and basking in the glory of God. He took my attention away from my present distresses and gave me a glimpse of what Heaven will be like. If for no other reason than the beauty, it was evident that God was there. His presence filled the sky and the earth. It was the most peaceful and serene experience of my life.

Okay, so it wasn't the Travel Channel, it was a walk with God. Which would you choose? In Psalm 23, David gives us a picture of what it means to walk in peace with God. For me it was also a vision of tranquility that soothed my weary soul. It was a reassurance that I was not walking this journey alone. The 23rd Psalm took on a new meaning for me that day. The scriptures came to life as I experienced what David must have felt. Oh, I am so blessed.

I also realized that God in His loving kindness had protected my heart by allowing me to think that, at times, I was responding to my family to encourage them, while in all actuality, I was not.

Knowing that I was doing nothing to help them through the pain would have been discouraging and overwhelming to me. It would have made it easier for me to have felt defeated. God let me believe that I was somewhat communicating with my family in order to protect my heart. It was His way of raising me up for the scriptures say that He is "the lifter up of mine head." He taught me to walk with Him even in the valley.

This was just another way that God used to reveal Himself to me. I quoted the verses of the 23rd Psalm so many times while I was in a coma. God used them to build my faith and trust in Him by showing me that His word is still alive. He kept my mind fixed on Him and on eternity, not my situation. Thank you Lord, for your living word. *"...my heart said unto thee, Thy face, Lord, will I seek"* (Psalm 27:8).

A Close Encounter with Jesus Christ, God's Son

Days passed and my physical condition grew worse. I could tell from the conversations I overheard that hope of my surviving was fading. I was more aware of the pain and discomfort as my body grew stiff and immobile. My neck ached so badly from being in one position for what seemed hours at a time. My back ached from the turning and twisting of the ICU bed. Its purpose was to prevent the formation of bed sores from immobility, but every time it would tilt me it felt as though it was going to dump me out of the bed and onto the floor. It was a frightening feeling since I knew I would not be able to catch myself. I was paralyzed.

I hated it when they would suction my lungs. To explain: At frequent intervals a respiratory therapist would come in to give me a medication treatment which consisted of several puffs of medication (kind of like an inhaler) through the endotracheal tube which led down my throat and into my lungs. The medication was to loosen the secretions in my

104

lungs so that it could be suctioned and removed. One of the most horrible things I had to endure was suctioning!

Whenever I would hear the puff of the inhaler it would awaken me. It was a sound I learned to dread because I knew what was coming next. There is no way to prepare yourself for having someone suck the life right out of you. For years I had performed this same treatment on my patients, but I never realized how frightening it was until it was happening to me.

I will do my best to paint this picture for you by using an illustration. Imagine yourself being placed in a vacuum food storage container, being connected to the vacuum, and then the switch turned on. Oh, the best part...once all your air has been removed, the container is sealed leaving your lungs deflated and leaving you gasping for air. Not only are you gasping for air, but the treatment makes you need to cough so then you are losing more air. It's a horrifying feeling... like you are being suffocated. I can't think of a better way to describe how it feels. I just know that if I ever find myself having to perform this procedure on another person, I will have a lot more pity on them for having to endure it.

The tube down my throat connected me to the ventilator and it was so very uncomfortable. Whenever the nurses would turn me, I could feel it like a metal rod refusing to give in by maintaining its position in my chest. My mouth was gaped open because of the big tube down my throat and my lips felt parched from the fever and my inability to moisten them. I couldn't swallow so if any saliva happened to accumulate it had to drool out of the corner of my mouth.

I couldn't move my tongue and it felt like a chunk of lava rock in my mouth. It felt like my face was covered with the tape that was securing the endotracheal tube. Since I am sensitive to tape, my face was constantly itching from the irritation, but of course, I couldn't even scratch an itch! The tape often got hung in the hair on my neck and created a painful tug. It just had to tug until the bed shifted or someone tilted my head because I couldn't turn my own head to relieve it. The tube was taped so securely against my lip that it created an ulcer that took three months to heal. I was helpless and totally dependent on someone else to notice and care for my every need, even to wipe a tear from my eye.

I could feel the projection of the tubing as it waddled across my chest towards the ventilator which sat at my bedside. I felt like an astronaut who was tethered to their source of oxygen on the space ship. Off and on, water would accumulate from condensation in the tubing. This caused a loud gurgling noise. It was just one of the many noises I became familiar with in ICU.

As all patients do, even when they are immobile, I could feel myself slide to the foot of the bed because my feet would end up resting against the footboard. This wasn't too hard for me to do since my body was almost the length of the bed anyway.

Eventually the nurses or assistants would come in to hoist me back up to the head of the bed with such a fury that I thought they would toss me through the wall and into the adjacent room. This taught me to appreciate bed positioning. It felt so good for my body to change positions.

And the pillows!!! They would pack so many around me to support my extremities and keep them aligned that I felt as though I was being packed for shipping. There were foam boots on my feet to prevent foot-drop and stockings on my legs to aid in circulation to my immobile limbs. The beautiful thick, white, elastic stockings made my legs feel so hot, I thought they were on fire.

My arms were tied to the bedrails in extension and oh how I wished that someone would come and just bend them a few times for me. Only one time do I remember a precious therapist removing all the paraphernalia so that she could contract and extend my motionless limbs. Her touch was soft and gentle as she slowly went through each joint on my arms and legs, even my fingers. I will never forget the relief I felt from her touch.

The room was always smothering hot. Even though I couldn't move to touch myself, I could tell that my body was clammy because I stuck to the sheets when they would turn me.

Then there was the nausea. Because I was continuously being fed by a tube which ran from my nose down into my stomach, it was not unusual to have my stomach fill up so much that it would reach a point of overflowing; especially when nurses would add water after meds. This was very frightening. I just knew that whatever this disease was, if it didn't take me, I was going to end up aspirating and that would surely do the trick. Can you imagine being that nauseated, not being able to swallow, and not being able to say a word to anyone or be able to ask for help? Don't forget, I was in a coma, but I was aware.

It seemed I was fighting an unending battle with the discomfort. I tried praying my way through it, but sometimes it seemed God didn't hear my prayers. It seemed like hours between repositioning which was the only relief for my discomfort. No one was aware of my pain. To them I was "in a coma."

I hated to complain to God because I knew He was spending so much time with me already. When I didn't get an answer right away, I tried to accept the fact that I must be exactly where God wanted me. So instead of asking Him to remove the discomfort, I asked Him for grace and mercy to endure it. I knew that He had a purpose for my suffering and I knew that He would help me overcome it or bear it. I stayed attentive to His voice because I didn't want to miss anything that He was trying to teach me.

It was during this most difficult, discouraging, and challenging time that God revealed Himself to me in my "Close Encounter of the 2nd Kind." This time it was with Jesus Christ, my Savior, My Redeemer, and My Friend. He is the One who promised to never leave or forsake me and I needed Him close beside me to help me get through this trial of discomfort more than ever. I needed His friendship, the Friend that would help me bear my burden. I needed to hold His hand and hear Him tell me everything was going to be alright.

At times when it would seem that I just couldn't bear the discomfort any longer, I would think about what He did for me on Calvary. When I thought about how much He suffered for me, it made me feel unworthy to complain of my pain. I praised Him for loving me so much. This was the way I was able to handle my discomfort. I felt ashamed to complain about my pain when He had suffered agony for me. I asked Him to make my trial a blessing and to draw me closer to Him through my need for Him. I asked Him for mercy and strength to endure.

How could I have asked Him for any more than that, after all He had done for me on Calvary? I had no right to ask "Why me?" He was my Savior. He knew what was best for me and He knew what I was able to bear. I didn't want to emerge from this difficulty pitiful. Instead, my desire was to emerge powerful by the strength and power of the One who lives within me..

I couldn't see Him, of course, but I could envision His face and the tenderness in His eyes. I have had so many people ask me if I saw a bright light or a long tunnel. They also ask if I saw Jesus as a figure or face.

No, I did not. No one can look into the face of God and Jesus is God. But I could feel His presence and it was real even though I couldn't see Him. I didn't need to see Him for I knew He was there. I could feel the touch of His hand on mine. I could sense His compassion. It was almost as if I could hear Him say, "My child, I would take this pain from you, but my Father finds it necessary. Therefore, I will help you bear it." Thank you Jesus, my "burden-bearer."

In humility I said to Him, "Lord, all that I am, I place on the alter so that You can alter all that I am." He used my encounter with Him to humble me in His presence. I wasn't good to anybody at that time, but in the eyes of God I was "a moldable vessel." I was going to have such a story to tell when I woke up!

You may ask, "How were you aware of His presence?" Have you ever been asleep at night and have your mate gently reach over to hold your hand? It's something my husband does often. It's his way of saying, "I am here." In the dark I can't see him, but I am sure of his presence because I feel his touch. It was the same sensation when I felt the hand of Jesus Christ. There was such security and compassion in His touch. I knew that it was not only Christ's hand that was touching me, it was the hand of God. I have always known that He was with me since the day I accepted Him as my Savior, but this time His touch was different. It made me feel clean, pure, loved, and accepted.

To have had the opportunity to commune with God the Father was awesome, but to be doubly blessed by being in the presence of His Son, Jesus Christ was almost more than my heart could stand. I was so blessed. At times I felt almost unworthy of the fact that He loved me enough to want to spend this precious, personal, one-on-one time with me. He didn't say much, He didn't have to. He just held my hand and walked me through more of my valley.

I would ask myself, "Why not me?" He is my Savior. He died for me to show me His love. He promised to always be with me. God, in His Holy Spirit, had introduced me to Christ as my Savior when I was five years old and now He was introducing me to Him as my Redeemer and Friend. Only a God who "is" love could express His love to me in this way.

I had prayed for fellowship with Him and now He was answering my prayer in a much bigger way than I had ever imagined. I had always imagined a sense of His presence in my life, but this was more than sensing it, I knew He was there. Our fellowship was up close and personal as Jesus Christ sat on my bed holding my hand and feeling my pain.

In my encounter, He showed me that He was more than just my Savior. He was loving me into submission by allowing me to get to know Him more. My encounter with Christ was similar to that of my Heavenly Father, only His characteristics and purpose in my life were different. Jesus left Heaven to come to earth out of His love for me. He was teaching me about His unconditional love. He came to save me from my sins. He came to fulfill His Father's will and that was to provide redemption for my sins. He died and rose again to sit at the right hand of His Father's throne in order to intercede and plea with Him on my behalf. He is preparing a place for me in Heaven and one day I will live eternally with Him. That's who Jesus is.

Jesus was there with me in ICU as a friend who stays closer than a brother. He sat quietly by my side, never forsaking me as He has promised. As a mother who knows how it feels to sit by the bed of a severely ill child, I could understand the empathy Christ had for me. He knew that my suffering was necessary in order to bring about change. He was interceding on my behalf with His Heavenly Father and I am sure that He felt my pain. I prayed:

"Jesus, my Lord and my Savior, You suffered so much more than this for me. You loved me enough to give Your life in order to redeem me. How can I do less than praise You and give you glory in my suffering? Whatever it takes to bring me closer to You, I am willing to bear it. Help me to endure for Your name's sake. I ask You to work Your will and way in my circumstances for I trust You with my life."

I came to know Christ as my Companion and Friend, one who longed to spend time with me. He understood my suffering because He too had suffered. He came to earth in human form that He might know the feelings of man. He sacrificed His life for me when He took my sins and made them His own and He bore my guilt and the guilt of the whole world upon His shoulders on Calvary.

Jesus was the One who could turn my tears into laughter and all my rain into sunshine. That's what my Savior did for me. He knew God had a reason for allowing me to travel this path, but since He couldn't take it away, He helped me to get through it. He knew that my pain was for my own good and that it was necessary. He knew that after refining, pruning, and chipping away all the debris of my life, He would have a vessel that was worthy of being used for His purpose. I would be a branch ready to bear fruit. I thank you Jesus for loving me this much!

I have had a few people ask me if I ever felt that I was under an attack of Satan. I can tell you that I was under a divine attack because God in His loving kindness was using my situation to draw me more and more into His presence. He was making me more and more dependent on Him and yet I felt such peace.

If I was under an attack from Satan, I was ignoring his blows because my mind was fixed on Heaven. If there was a battle going on over who was going to win me, Satan had lost before he ever got started because greater is He that is in me than he that is in the world.

Then you also have those people who have the nerve to suggest that there must have been some hidden sin in my life to cause God to bring such "judgment." I think it is so sad that Christians see God as always wanting to punish us. I love Him and I am called according to His purpose. That means all things are allowed by Him for my good. I praise Him for the refiner's fire. Even what man might mean for evil, God means for my good.

God does not work this way. He does not sit on His throne looking for some reason to pour out His judgment upon us. Don't misunderstand me, for nothing upsets Him more than when we sin against Him. But He loves us into submission and sometimes that means through the furnace. It is not His will to separate us from Himself because of His judgment, but rather to draw us nearer to Himself in love.

111

Oh child of God, if you are going through difficult times and if you have confessed any known sin in your life; it may be that God is just trying to deepen His relationship with you. He is trying to fellowship with you and maybe He knows that the only way He can get you to talk to Him is if you find yourself in need of His help. He loves you so much!

It's a sad thing, but sometimes God has to use some pretty drastic measures to get our attention. Some of us can be more stubborn than others. Many times we choose to include Him in our lives only when we need Him to intervene on our behalf. Instead of waiting until you have a need, look to Him as the friend He longs to be. We should be turning to Him in our want of a relationship with Him, not because of our needs or desires. Don't make Him a casual acquaintance. Make Him your closest friend. It has been said that we become like the five people we hang around most. What a better example to follow than to follow Christ.

I have been told many stories about how my family and friends ministered to other families who were in the ICU waiting room. Some of them were elderly and had no one to encourage them and pray with them.

That's the kind of friends and family God has so blessed me with. They shared food, time, and love with those who were less fortunate. In this respect, God was letting His glory be shown through the lives of His servants. If He chose to use my sickness as a means of strategically placing His servants in the right place at the right time, then I am so blessed to have been chosen as the reason to bring them to a place of serving. By their acts of kindness and love God was glorified and they will be blessed.

God worked in the waiting room just as He did in my ICU room. God's people joined together in one accord to pray and ask God for my healing, according to His will.

I believe many lives were changed because of the witness of what love between a man and a wife is all about. One of my dear friends has told me since my hospitalization that the relationship between her and her husband was strengthened as they witnessed the bond of love between my husband and me.

I was in a coma, but God was using my sickness to bring healing and restoration to relationships. He was using my illness to build hope and faith in those who visited. He was using His people to minister to others. He was building their faith and He was using me. I am so blessed to know that at the same time He was revealing Himself to me He was building relationships in the lives of the people I loved. He is such an awesome God and so worthy to be praised!

In the long time span between visiting hours, I prayed and communed with God. By this time I was so weak that I let Him do most of the talking, while I listened. I didn't want to miss anything He had to say or any instructions He might have to give me. This sure wasn't the time to miss hearing from Him. I needed to make sure I got every detail right. I was near death and that left little room for error.

The Human Car Wash

I have to take a moment to share with you a funny little story that occurred between one of the visiting hours.

There were two nursing assistants who came in to give me a bath. One of them recognized me and started telling the other one that she had met me at a local department store one day several years before and I had been especially nice to her (I like to make people feel special). She went on to say that since I had been so nice to her, she was going to give me her very best shampoo and bath.

Get the picture here: I am very, very ill and I am in a coma. I am on life support and I am unable to acknowledge that I remembered meeting her too. She started talking to me, but of course, it was a one way conversation. That didn't slow her down a bit. She went on talking as if she knew I could hear every word. She would ask me questions, knowing that I couldn't answer her. She assumed that I wasn't aware of her presence, but what she didn't know was that I could hear every word she said! I thank God that I had been nice to her because I would hate to know the kind of bath I would have gotten otherwise. Let this be a word of warning; be nice to everyone you meet. You never know when you might see them again!

Well, when she said her "best bath" I had no idea her best meant a Saturday evening head to toe scrub! I have never been so soaped, washed down, and lotioned in all my life. I thought for sure that she was going to skin me and then drown me with water before she hung me up to dry. I don't know where all the water came from or where it went, but she must have poured gallons on my head! All I could think was; this must be how a car feels as it goes through a car wash!

And just like a drive-through car wash, it didn't take her long to do her thing either. She was in and out of my room in no time and left me stacked up, packed up, smelling good, and she even changed my bed. My only complaint was that I wished she had tried to dry my hair rather than leaving it rolled up in a towel. I hate to think how it must have looked after it dried! But at least it was clean. I mean squeaky clean! I never got the chance to see her again, but if I ever run into her I will be sure to thank her for the trip through the "human car wash!"

I had to tell you that story because even though I was deathly (and I mean deathly) ill, and even though I was in a coma, her special treatment brought a smile to my heart.

Smiles are hard to come by in ICU. There are so many people dying around you and you hear the families mourning. I couldn't help but feel their loss. It reminded me of many times in my career as a nurse when I was witness to the passing of an individual. There is such a difference in the ones who transition into Heaven versus those who are facing eternal damnation because of rejecting the Savior. It is amazing how God can use the testimony of our faith, even in the way we handle our sickness or death. Precious is the passing of a saint of God, but frightening is the look of horror on the face of a professing nonbeliever.

God's glory filled every corner of my hospital room and there were those who knew something was different about being in my space. It had nothing to do with me. It was the presence of the One who was with me!

One day a nurse who was leaving shift was standing next to my bed giving report to the oncoming nurse. She made a remark about how glad she was to have been assigned to me. Why? Because she loved the "peaceful feeling that permeated my room."

I thought to myself, if only her eyes could see through my eyes. If only she could witness the presence of Christ as I had and that she could know that it was He who permeated my room. If only I could tell her that she was standing in the presence of God!

I believe God smiled when He heard her comment and I thought I could even hear the flutter of angel's wings as they lifted them in praise to God for how He, in His marvelous power, is able to be everywhere at all times. I was surrounded and protected by the arms of God, the hand of Christ, and the wings of angels. I am still amazed that God chose me to be an eye witness to this wonderful encounter.

My conversation with this nurse happened much later, but her remark placed such a burden on my heart that I made sure to ask her about her relationship with Christ as soon as I came out of the coma and was able to speak. I would have recognized her voice anywhere and if not her voice her habit of "popping gum."

She had no idea what I meant when I asked her about her relationship with Christ. Her response was, "I go to church with my grandmother." She had based her salvation on being a church member all her life. She lacked understanding and I could tell by the confused look on her face that she knew little of what I was talking about when I told her that being a church member was important, but it wasn't what was going to get her into Heaven. I told her that Christ wasn't concerned with how much "religion" we had. He was more concerned about the "relationship" we had with Him as our Savior and Lord.

I shared with her a brief synopsis of my encounter with God and encouraged her to seek a personal acceptance of Christ as her Savior and then to grow in her wisdom and knowledge of Him by seeking to know God intimately. I never saw her again, but I pray the seed I planted was nourished and that God will use that seed to bring a harvest. She was one of the first people I spoke to after I was taken off the ventilator. I could barely speak above a whisper, yet God gave me an opportunity to witness to this young lady, even from a bed in ICU. When God says "Go," He means that we are to be a witness for Him "wherever we are." I take His command seriously.

My sense of hearing was extremely intensified while I was in a coma. I think God wanted to make sure that I heard everything He said to me during those days in ICU, so He beefed up my hearing. Every slamming door, every voice, every lid opened, and every beep was extremely loud and unnerving. The nurses and doctors chatted at the desk just outside my room and seemed unaware of the fact that the patients (at least this one), could hear. They talked about what they did to celebrate Christmas and all the good food they ate while I lay connected to a feeding tube down my nose for my Christmas dinner!

I have talked a great deal about a personal relationship that was being built during this time with my Heavenly Father and His Son. The walk I had with them was a pleasant distraction from the news of my condition. My blood counts dropped which required the administration of blood. My renal function was guarded. My body was extremely swollen due to the fluid overload. The excess fluid was putting pressure on my heart. This created a threat to tap the sac around my heart in order to withdraw some of the fluids. As we say in medicine, I was headed "down the tube!"

By this time, the doctors knew they were up against something much bigger than a typical pneumonia. The powerful antibiotics I was receiving had proven ineffective. Instead of improving, my condition was failing and I was even nearer death. An infectious disease consult was ordered to see if one more doctor might have another idea for treatment. All the efforts, so far, had been to no avail. Nobody seemed to know much about this strange, unidentified "bug" that was destroying my lungs.

On the seventh day, December 28, 2005, another doctor was consulted. He was a thoracic surgeon who had an idea that what they were dealing with was not an infection, but rather an inflammation in my lungs. If his theory was correct, it was a miracle that I was still alive. In order to prove his theory he needed to do an open lung biopsy, immediately! There was danger in the procedure, especially in my condition.

He painted a grave picture for my family, but reassured them that he would do everything he could. He told me, many months later, about going to the waiting room to explain to my family my condition versus his treatment plan. He said there were so many people in the waiting room on my behalf, that he knew he had to do everything he could to save my life because it was obvious that I had so many people who loved me. I thank God that I do.

He obtained consent from Charles to do an open lung biopsy. If he was right, he knew he would have to work fast in order to halt the progression of the disease and save my life. Charles recalls this day as one of the most heart-wrenching, discouraging days of his life. He was having to face the fact that soon I might be gone. The clock was ticking faster and faster and every minute was a blessing.

Though I was still in a coma, I remember this doctor standing at my bedside. He told me his name and then he said, "Karen, you are a very sick lady. I promise you, I am going to

117

do everything in my power to save your life." As he turned to leave the room and prepare for my surgery he told my nurse, "In twelve hours she will be getting better or she will be gone."

He took me immediately to surgery where he extracted two tissue samples. He started me on steroids and placed two chest tubes in my lungs to drain the "glue-like" substance. His approach was to treat this disease process as an inflammation, not infection. Since the antibiotics had failed to produce improvement, he concluded that my body may be having an auto immune response to whatever it was that was attacking my lungs. If this was true, my body was actually attacking itself. One of my physicians told me later that my blood was stripped of all its protein (which is its power) because everything in me was fighting to combat the inflammation in my lungs.

In my research since hospitalization, I have found that the disease he suspected causes the lung tissue to become fibrous. This means permanent lung damage and decreased oxygenation. The purpose of treatment is to halt the process of fibrosis and prevent any further damage from occurring.

The symptoms of this disease are insidious and they mimic those of pneumonia. The problem is that in a great percentage of cases, patients succumb to the disease before the actual culprit has been identified or before an accurate diagnosis has been made.

Hopes were that my body would respond to the steroids and there would be a cessation in the development of fibrous tissue. If I survived, the possibilities were that I could end up a respiratory cripple, who was dependent on oxygen; a candidate for a lung transplant; or best choice, my lungs would have minimal scarring and I would lead a relatively normal life. As the minutes passed by, more and more of my lung tissue was being affected. If this new treatment didn't work, then I most probably would have only a few hours to live. If his suspicions were wrong and the disease was not what he thought it to be, we would have run out of options.

118

I knew that only God Almighty, the Great Physician, could spare my life and it was going to take a miracle.

I listened to everyone talk about my future and all I heard were if's, and's and but's. I trusted the doctors, but I trusted God more. So I asked Him:

"Lord, you hear what they are saying. You knew it was going to come to this point and You know the outcome. I believe that You can still heal me, even though they don't see much hope for recovery. So does this mean that these folks are about to tell me farewell or does it mean that they are about to witness a miracle? If it's a miracle, I thank You for allowing it to be me."

I think everyone who knew me, knew of me, or knew my family and friends were on their knees as word traveled about my prognosis. Churches all over the country were contacted and God's people were interceding on my behalf. I must share with you a story about one of those prayers because I know God will use it to strengthen your faith in prayer as He did mine.

We have a Christian television station in our area with a twenty-four hour prayer line. My good friend and co-minister in music called his mother to ask her to be in fervent prayer because the doctors weren't giving me much hope of surviving.

She felt led to call this television station to request prayer. The host of the program prayed for me on the air. She asked God to send a new physician to consult on my case (He had already done that). She asked Him to give this physician a new idea for treatment (He had already done that). She asked that this treatment would bring about a change in my condition within twelve hours, according to His perfect will. (He was working on that)!

Even as this prayer was being offered on my behalf, God had already worked out the details to accomplish the request.

How could it not amaze you and build your faith in the power of praying in His will, to know that God did answer and His answer was exactly as she requested? His will was already being accomplished before she ever uttered a word.

He blesses our faith with His faithfulness. Don't you just know that God was thrilled to hear so many of His children praying to Him? How sweet are the voices of praying saints of God. He longs for this kind of relationship with us. We cannot and should never expect to change God's will. Rather, the purpose of our prayers is to ask Him for the ability to accept His will.

Reality Check!

I began to rethink the possibilities. All this time I had been asking and expecting God to heal me. I just assumed that He would. After all, how could He not want to use such a willing heart as mine?

But as I stood on the brink of death, I began to wonder. Could it be that His intent was to heal me by giving me a new glorified body in Heaven? You see, the word "heal" holds different connotations.

Healing can mean restored to perfect health. It can mean restored to even better health than before illness. It can mean healed, but not whole, and it can mean restored in the soul.

Could it be that God was finished with me here on earth? Was He pleased with what I had done? Would He find me faithful to the finish? I wondered how many opportunities I had missed to serve Him. I felt there was so much more I could have done. There was so much more I wish I had done. Was it too late?

My body was so weak and tired of trying to hold on to life. There had been so many days of struggling, praying, searching, and listening. I had enjoyed my walk with God and I felt closer to Him than ever before. We had walked and talked and He had taught me so much about myself, His purpose, and His ways. He had allowed me time to reflect on my past. He had shown me the error of my ways and He had loved me for my efforts to please Him. He knew my heart's desire was to honor Him in life or in death. He had humbled me and put me in a place of total dependence on Him. For the first time in my life, I truly understood what it meant to say, "I can do nothing on my own."

Even with all the faith I could muster, I was reaching a point of despair. Not because I didn't trust God, but because I was so weak I couldn't see how I could hang on much longer. I guess I thought I needed to or that God needed my approval by saying, "Okay, it's time to go." I wanted so badly for Him to find me faithful to the finish. I searched for strength, but I was so weak I couldn't even think about praying anymore. After all, what more could I say to God that I had not already said?

The only thing I kept saying over and over again was, *"Lord, I just can't hold on without You. I don't have any more fight left in me. I only want Your will to be done. If You are continuing to work a miracle in my life then please give me the strength to endure this race and help me have the faith to finish it. Let my life honor You, whether it be in Heaven or on earth."*

Had God answered my prayers to know Him more just so I could get a glimpse of what real fellowship with Him will be like in Heaven? Had He allowed me a glimpse of a coming attraction called, "Your Eternal Home," by giving me visions of crystal seas and rolling meadows? Was His purpose for this valley a way of preparing me for the transition? Had He developed our relationship and increased our fellowship together for His benefit in Heaven or mine here on earth? Was I ever going to have the pleasure of sharing the story of my "Close Encounter" with my family, friends, or the world?

As I lay there trying to figure out if my life on earth was ending or my eternal life in Heaven was beginning, my doctor entered the room with the pathology report from my biopsy. He gave my nurse the results. It was just as he had suspected.

It was not an infection they had been treating for approximately eight days. It was an inflammation of my lungs triggered by the infection. His suspicions were correct. My body was fighting to destroy whatever it was that had attacked my lungs. In the process it was also destroying my lungs. The name I heard was "BOOP." I later found out this stood for "Bronchiolitis Obliterans Organizing Pneumonia."

I heard the doctor say, "This pathology report could very well be her death sentence." I said, "Okay Lord, get my mansion ready because I'm coming home!"

I felt a sense of urgency. I wanted to spend my last hours considering all the blessings God had given me in my life. I thought positive, happy thoughts. I couldn't speak and I was still in a coma which meant I would never be able to say good-bye to my family. The only person I could share my deepest, innermost thoughts with, was God. I would continue to talk to Him.

I was determined to walk into Heaven loving Him and praising Him. There would be no whining or complaining coming from this child of God. I would be powerful, not pitiful. Illness had taken over my body, but it had not taken over my spirit. I continued to believe in God's power to heal me and I knew He would if that was His will, but I also made known to Him my willingness to accept His perfect will.

I filled my mind with my favorite songs like, "It Is Well With My Soul" and "How Great Thou Art." I wanted to sing the words to "You Raise Me Up," but I thought I would save that one for on my way up to glory.

I thanked God for allowing me to share my life with my best friend, my husband Charles. I thanked Him for the joy of being a mother to our children because they had so blessed my life. I thanked Him for the joy of using the talents He had given me. I thanked Him for the family and friends who had loved me. I thanked Him for the privilege of being able to walk in His presence and know the feel of His touch. I thanked Him for peace in the midst of my storm-tossed sea. I thanked Him for being the Rock to stand on when all else was sinking sand. I thanked Him for being my Friend, one that stood by me when I was all alone. I thanked Him for the lessons I had learned and the things He had shown me about my life. I thanked Him for the hard times and the lessons that had been difficult to learn because they had only made me stronger. I thanked Him for teaching me that faith comes from hearing and hearing comes from the word of God. I thanked Him for sending His Son to die for me. I thanked Him for freedom.

On and on I praised God for allowing me to experience a relationship with Him. It took a lifetime for me to realize that to really know Him, which was my heart's desire, I needed to thank Him and praise Him for "all" things. I didn't allow Satan to tempt me with negative thoughts. I just kept praising God. I thought, soon I may be joining Heaven's chorus and forever I would praise Him, what a blissful thought! I had peace.

I thought about all the last things I had done because if this was the end of my life, everything was going to be my last. I thought about the last time I told Charles how much I loved him. I thought about my last kiss and hug from him and from my children. I thought about the last time I walked through our home, the last meal I had prepared, the last time we had fellowshipped with friends and family and the last sermon I had heard. I thought about the last time I had snuggled with our little dog, Abbey, or petted our big dog, Dottie. I thought about the last time I sang in church, the last time I played the piano and the last song I heard on the radio. I thought about the last time I had prepared a meal for a bereaved family or sent a note of encouragement to someone in need.

I thought about the last time I took a moment to smell the roses, gaze into the sky or enjoy a simple breeze. I imagined the taste of my last meal and the comfort of my favorite robe. I tried to remember the last compliment I had given, the last friend I had made, and the last good deed I had done. I thought about the last time I had witnessed to someone or shared God's love. I thought about all the people in my life who were so special to me and the last time I had told them so. I thought about the last time I saw my Dad and the wonderful legacy he had left behind. I thought about the last ride in my car and the last cup of coffee I shared with my husband on our porch swing. I thought about the last poem I had written, the last teaching I had done, and the last place God's will had taken me. I thought about my last day at work and the friends who had shared the last night shift with me. Since I had missed Christmas 2005, I tried to remember last year's special moments, for it was my last Christmas. If I was about to enter Heaven, everything I had done in my life here on earth had been done for the last time.

Had I been grateful enough for all God had given me in my lifetime? Had I really served Him with all my heart? Had I been willing to sacrifice all for Him?

I continued to praise God for the many "last" things I had done until I drifted back into unconsciousness.

I was stirred by a voice in my room. My first thought was, am I still in the hospital or already in Heaven? This was a very defining moment because God brought me back to awareness to complete His work.

A voice whispered to me, "Karen, do not be afraid for I am with you and I am your God." I am sorry to say that it was an unfamiliar voice, but one that I soon recognized. I had heard it many times throughout my life, though many times I had ignored it or dismissed it as unimportant. It came from deep within my heart. It was a voice soft and low, sweet and tender. It was non-threatening, gentle, and kind, but purposeful and direct. It was the voice of the Holy Spirit.

A Close Encounter
with the Holy Spirit

Obviously, I had gone through a long list of "lasts," but one thing I had not done was hear my last words from God. There is one more person of the trinity and God wanted me to get to know Him better. God's introduction to Himself was not yet complete. It was now time for me to have a "Close Encounter of the 3rd Kind" and it was going to be with the Holy Spirit.

The Holy Spirit had lived in my heart since the day of my salvation, which had been for forty-eight years. I had never given Him the opportunity to fill me, nor had I given Him complete control of my life. Because He is there to be our Guide, there had been many times in my life that I had heard His voice, yet ignored Him or decided my way was better. His voice had been unfamiliar because I had not sought Him enough, however, I could recognize it because I knew it existed and I had heard it many times. His nudging I had often dismissed as unimportant and continued to do things my way. I had spent my life expecting to hear from God in a bolt of lightening, not a still small voice. My lack of faith and willingness to follow Him were a result of my pride and need for control. All my life I had wanted to please God, yet my lack of relationship with the Holy Spirit resulted in my disobedience. God began to show me that the emptiness I had always felt inside and the need I had to know Him intimately stemmed from my lack of complete surrender to the voice of the Holy Spirit.

How could I have neglected the One who lived inside of me? How could I have missed being filled with this gentle One who lived within my heart in order to guide me, teach me, and show me the way?

The Holy Spirit was there to comfort me and walk with me through the remainder of my journey. I was ready to give up because I didn't have the strength to keep hanging on and I was trying to do it in my own strength. But that was until I heard God say, "Not yet, Karen. There is still someone you need to encounter. You were introduced many years ago, but now it is time for you get to know each other more intimately."

Then the Holy Spirit said, "Karen, you are going to need Me to carry you through the rest of your journey. Without Me, you will not make it. You will need Me in order to finish your race because I am the One who will show you the way. You will need Me because I will pick you up when you fall and I will carry you. I will provide a map for you to follow and I will make sure you have the necessary tools to finish your race. I will equip you with the skills to climb high mountains and I will equip you to forge the deep valleys. I will connect you with your Heavenly Father and through our connection you will find the faith to finish. I will comfort you when you are weary and I will teach you the path of righteousness. Are you willing to follow me, whatever it takes?" I had heard this question before!

His voice was sweet and kind and I knew He spoke to me in love. *"Of course I will follow you,"* I said. *"I will follow You wherever it is that You would have me to go. I realize now how much I have missed by not walking in complete obedience to Your will. I have put my selfish pride ahead of obeying You. I have let my ambitions and goals get in the way of my being able to hear from You. I have searched and longed for You and yet You were there all along, waiting patiently for me to obey. Holy Spirit, fill the empty places in my heart. Let me overflow and then fill me again. I no longer want to wander in aimless desperation. I want to walk in Your will. Remove from me anything that might hinder my hearing Your voice. I will follow You, even if it means in death."*

The closeness we shared was unspeakable and full of glory. Nothing else mattered to me anymore. I had found my resting place and I wanted to forever abide there with Him. I realized that all my days of trying to figure things out on my own were to no avail because they only deterred the blessing from following His leading. I realized that my life and the plans I had made never mattered in the scheme of God's plans for me. I had missed so much by not getting to know Him.

Not only had I encountered the Holy Spirit, I felt eternally connected to God. I had been in His presence. I had been in the presence of Jesus Christ; my Redeemer, Savior, and Friend. And now I was in the presence of the Holy Spirit. He was the One who would guide me to my next destination, whether that was to be in Heaven or in God's purpose for the remainder of my life here on earth. I knew that if I ever lost my way, He would be the One to love me back into submission and He would do so unconditionally.

My heart was surrendered, but there was still some unfinished business that God had to take care of. My conversation with the Him went like this:

He said, *"Karen, We've been walking and talking together for a while now. You say you want to serve Me with all your heart. You say you will do whatever it is that I ask of you. You see that I long to give you the desires of your heart and I know you mean what you say, but there are some things you need to let go of first."*

"Okay," I said. "You know that I have always wanted my life to bring forth abundant fruit. I want You to use me and work through me in order to make a difference in the lives of others. So what else do I need to do?"

He said, *"Karen, but you are not listening. What are you willing to give up in order to follow Me?"*

I said, "God, I give you everything, for nothing is more important to me now that doing Your will?"

He said, *"Name it; what do you mean by everything?"*

I said, "I give you my house, my car, all my earthly possessions. Everything I own is Yours."

He said, *"These are material things, Karen. They are blessings that I have bestowed upon you. They are Mine anyway. If I wanted them, I could take them back. If I wanted more, I have a storehouse of abundance. Karen, there is more that I want from you. What are you willing to give up in order to follow me?"*

I said, "Okay, Lord, I give you my job, my career, my finances, my title and any accomplishments. Anything I did that I thought made me who I was, I give to You because I now realize that who I am, is Yours."

He said, *"These are things that can be replaced. I want more."*

I said, "Lord, I give You my husband and my children. Use them for your service. Have your will in their lives. I want to be worthy of Your love."

He said, *"But they already belong to me because they have accepted Christ as their Savior. There is more."*

"What more could you want Lord? You have removed my pride and my need for control. In my helplessness, You have emptied me of myself and my ambitions and filled me with a desire to do Your will and Your will only. You have answered my prayer and revealed Yourself to me in an up close and personal way as my Heavenly Father, Jesus Christ, and now Your, Holy Spirit. I now know what it means to have an intimate relationship with You. I have enjoyed our fellowship and I want to be filled with Your power.

You have humbled me and now in complete surrender I am in submission to Your purpose. You have removed a heart of stone from past hurts and regrets and You have broken down walls of unforgiveness and shame that were preventing me from becoming the person you created me to be. You have replaced my greed with a heart of love. As I lay here in this bed, helpless and emptied of all the things I thought made me who I was, I am a new creation in You. What more do I have left to give you?"

He said, *"There is one more thing that you are holding on to and I need to know that it belongs to Me too. With it, I can take you and use you mightily for the kingdom of Heaven. Without it, there remains a wall that separates My will from your will."*

I spent what seemed to be hours contemplating what more God could want from me. I felt like my twelve hours were running out and that my future depended on my willingness to surrender whatever it was that God was asking for. What could He possibly want that I had not already given Him?

I was so physically and mentally exhausted I could hardly think anymore. I was losing my hope for recovery and felt I was fighting a losing battle with life. I needed the Holy Spirit to raise me up and enable me to keep pressing on. But I also needed to figure out what it was that God was asking me to give to Him because my decision was separating me from my obedience to Him. My body wanted to give up, but my mind wanted another chance to live again. I longed for another opportunity to show God how much I loved Him by serving Him with all my heart and all my will. I was broken, but not destroyed. If I went down in defeat it would be because I surrendered, not because I gave up.

Ah, surrender or give up. I could surrender my existence to Him or I could give up my right to be sanctified and set apart for His will. I could cling to "my life" or I could cling to "His purpose" for my life. I said to myself, "I have nothing else to give, but me; my life, my existence, my will."

Like a bolt of lightening out of the sky, it hit me. I realized that who I am "not" is a wife, a mother, a sister, a nurse, a business owner. Who I "am" is a child of God who was created to live out my life for God's purpose, not my own.

I have been justified and sanctified for His kingdom. I am a joint-heir with Christ. I am the daughter of a King. I have been bought and paid for by the blood of Jesus Christ. There is nothing else that I can I give Him except "me."

This had to be what God in His Holy Spirit was asking me for. He wanted to know if I was willing to exchange my will for His will so that He could use me to fulfill God's purpose. This surrender meant forsaking all else. It meant putting nothing else before Him. It even meant my willingness to die if my life would bring Him more glory in my death than in my living. I thought of the song, "I Surrender All," and I meant it!

When God said "all," He meant all of "me," including my life. Now I understood. God had been grooming me for His purpose for my life. He had been waiting for my willingness to surrender "all" and walk in faith and obedience to His will and His purpose. My whole life had been a series of events that had prepared me for my Heavenly Father's "eternal purpose." Surrendering to Him meant that my life would now have its purpose. I would obey Him.

In sweet abandon I said,

"It's Yours Lord. I give you my breath, my life. What you do with it is up to You. Whether You choose to leave me here on earth or whether You bring me on to Heaven to live forever in Your presence, I sacrifice my will for Your purpose.

You have shown me that my life has no purpose without You. Take me and use me to bring honor and glory to You and You only. I can now see beyond the things that I thought made me who I was. Who I am is Your devoted servant. You have taught me Your way. I will live the remainder of my days serving You, however long that may be. That is all that matters to me now. And if You choose to leave me here on earth for a while longer, I ask You to give me the faith to finish my race. I will honor Your name by giving You the glory for the experience of getting to know You in Your three persons and I will share the story You have given me until the day I transition to my eternal home. Thank you God for loving me."

The Holy Spirit said,

"I accept your life and I will use it to bring honor to God. You will be alright because I will be with you. No longer will the two of us be separated. I will fill you with my power and in my strength your weakness will be made strong. Together we will fulfill God's purpose

for your life. Follow me and I will show you great and mighty things that otherwise you would never have known. There will be days that you may doubt My leading, but trust in Me by faith. I will not lead you astray. I will connect you with your Heavenly Father who loves you so. Abide in me."

The curtain on God's stage of preparation had closed; at least for this act. I had given Him my life. What He would do for the final scene was up to Him. I was going to trust in Him and follow.

No longer did I feel a sense of loss? Oh, I had given up a lot. I had given Him "everything," but I felt I had gained more because the alternative to living here on earth for a Christian is eternal life in Heaven. I would be a winner either way. If He chose to leave me here for a while longer I promised Him that I would spend the rest of my life sharing my story and proclaiming His name, His mercy, and His miraculous healing. I only wanted His will for me.

If He took me to Heaven, I would spend eternity sitting at the feet of Jesus, forever praising Him. In Heaven I would get to see my Dad again and I would await the coming of my loved ones. In Heaven I would never have to suffer again. There would be no more ventilator or pain.

There is no greater sacrifice than what Christ did for me on Calvary. How could I have thought that anything less than my "life" would be enough to sacrifice for Him? Either the Holy Spirit was to give me directions for the final portion of my race here on earth and my transport to Heaven or He was to be my Helper as I embarked on a marathon of service that God had prepared for me to yet accomplish. Either way, I found total peace and comfort from knowing that He was abiding in my heart. His presence filled me and I felt His power raising me up. My heart overflowed with joy.

I thought I had surrendered my life to God so many times before, but I had always maintained a grip on the steering wheel. I was now a passenger who was willing to go wherever

131

He needed to take me, instead of being the one behind the wheel.

He had been there all along, waiting patiently for me to surrender my will in order to accept His will. As much as I had craved the direction of the Lord in my life, I had missed it because of my stubbornness to listen and my lack of willingness to give Him control. I am not boasting about this fact, I am merely stating that I am so glad that I am able to share this with you in hopes that you will not waste years of your own life fighting the same battle.

My mind began to think of the possibilities. There were visions of what I thought God might have in store for me. After all, who would not benefit from the truth in my story?

My mind drifted back to ten years earlier when I sat in a stadium in Atlanta, Georgia at a Women of Faith conference. I couldn't help but think about all that had happened in my life since that time and how God had orchestrated a series of events that prepared me for this very present moment. Only by the unmerited favor of God had Charles and I both endured trials, tribulations, and loss yet grown closer to Him in a relationship that had sustained us and would continue to sustain us until God called us home.

I thought about my needing a story to tell and how God had answered my prayer with an encounter with Him. In my thoughts I imagined myself standing on stage and singing with Sandi Patty. I figured if I was going to fill my mind with pleasant thoughts I might as well dream big! I admire her testimony and her walk with God. He has put a new song in her heart and her powerful voice now resonates more than ever before of His grace. All power and glory be to God. He could do that for me too.

I could see myself standing before large congregations encouraging them to accept God's gift of love, deepen their relationship with Him, and walk in His will and purpose. My encounter with Him was a story I would forever tell. I couldn't wait to share it and I would make it my goal to disciple others.

The Spirit of God was speaking to me and without losing any of its force and authority; it enlightened, persuaded, moved, and edified my soul. He began to show me ways that He wanted to use the story He had given me. Not only would I share in spoken word, but He laid on my heart the desire to write the details of my experience in a book. He even gave me a title, "Faith to Finish" and the verse of scripture from which it was taken, Hebrews 12:1-2.

I claimed His promise in Psalm 22:25 and my heart accepted a burden for lost souls and Christians who were, like I used to be, missing so much by not walking according to God's will. He gave me hope for a future (Jeremiah 29:11), and a reassurance that He would lead me in paths of righteousness, even though my pathway was going to change. He promised He would be there to direct and empower me to accomplish all that He asked of me. My soul was about to burst to tell somebody, anybody, everybody about my "Close Encounter" with My God, My Redeemer, and My Guide.

Just to refresh your memory, this was all taking place during the most difficult twelve hours of my eleven day journey through the valley of the shadow of death. How awesome it is that in my deepest, darkest valley I found Him waiting with open arms to lift me up and carry me through.

The Holy Spirit was my bridge of hope. It was in my darkest hour that I realized my dawn was just in sight. It was when I had exhausted all my energy trying to make a difference my way that I learned that the difference had to begin in my heart and then become God's way.

I could not give away what I did not have. I could not tell others about how awesome it is to walk with Him until I had experienced that ultimate walk myself. My race led me into a personal, intimate, passionate relationship with my God.

If I was to share God's peace, I first had to obtain it myself. In order for me to speak with validity, I had to endure. I needed the power of the Holy Spirit on my life in order to accomplish the kind of things that I knew He wanted me to achieve for His purpose. For me to have this power, God had to empty me of myself and fill me with His Spirit. I couldn't thank God enough for His patience with me. I looked through the glass dimly and saw so many times in my life when He could have just given up and said, "She is way too much work!"

But He didn't. He continued to guide me with His light until my world became so dark that He was the only beacon I could see. With His light, the Holy Spirit illuminated my path, my destiny, and His purpose.

My broken heart He mended and in its place, the Holy Spirit placed a burden for lost souls who are groping around in darkness trying to find their way. I wanted to be one who would help them find it.

I would say that God was completing my registration papers about this time for He was about to enter me into the last portion of my life's race. I had agreed to be trained and to run with endurance and patience. I had no idea where this race was going to take me. I didn't care because I was just going to keep running.

I had been like the Israelites who wandered for forty years in the wilderness because of their lack of faith and obedience. I was tired of wandering and trying to make things happen my way. I was tired of trying substitutes for God's love. I was tired of being stuck in a pit that had been dug by the devil himself. It was a pit of doubt, despair, unforgiveness, and unworthiness. I had broken free of the chains that had held me back from being the person God had waited so patiently on me to become.

The children of Israel took forty years to complete an eleven day journey. I had also been on an eleven day journey and it took me forty years to get there. Now I was ready to head for my Promised Land. Another thing about these people is that they never crossed over into the Promised Land until the next generation because of their fear, lack of faith, lack of obedience and unbelief.

Not me, I was ready to run the remainder of my race with God by my side, with my Savior encouraging me, and with the Holy Spirit guiding me. I was willing to conquer new territory and fight the giants. I was ready to feast on milk and honey. Never again would I waste my time worrying about what other people thought I should or should not do with my life. I no longer needed man's approval, only God's approval. No longer was I afraid of what people might think about the decisions I made. As long as the Holy Spirit was guiding me, I had no fear.

I would never again fear death because I had stood at its door and known only peace. No longer was my focus on my abilities. All God wanted was my availabilities. He would equip me with what I needed to finish my race. My life was now dedicated to what He could do through me. As long as I walked closely by His side and obeyed His commands, He would be in control of the consequences. I was to just obey.

God had protected me by guarding the gate of my heart. He arranged my medications to make sure I was aware of my surroundings and yet able to communicate with Him. He allowed me to know the severity of my situation, yet He kept me from succumbing to fear and faithlessness by keeping my focus on Him. He reassured me that I would be alright because He was there.

Though in man's eyes my life seemed to be nearly over, in God's eyes it was just beginning. The best part of my journey was about to take on a different meaning and a defined purpose.

At the end of twelve hours, the same doctor who had given little hope to my family concerning my recovery, stood at my bedside rejoicing over the "remarkable improvement" in my condition. Finally my body was responding to the treatment.

The pathology report that he had called my "death sentence" was becoming a miracle in the making.

God had a different plan. He had taken a rapidly progressing disease that many times claims its victims within the first three to four days and used it to prove to the world that He is truly the Great Physician.

He took something out of man's control and placed it in His control. To God be the glory for the things He has done in my life. Now there was hope because it looked as though I had a good chance of surviving. Even though I was not out of the woods yet, in my heart I knew that I would be. God had given me instructions and He was going to help me complete them.

The Change

What was it that brought about the change? Oh, it could have been God using the brilliant minds of physicians and the skill and knowledge He had given them to change my course of treatment. I will give them just a little bit of the credit. It could have been that this miraculous body God created decided to heal itself.

I will always believe that it was my willingness to die to self and take up my cross and follow Him. I believe it was my ultimate test of faith. It was God's revelation to me of who He is and how He had waited so long for me to crave a personal relationship with Him. It was about freedom and peace from chains of my past. It was also about emptying me of all the things in my life that kept me from mirroring Jesus Christ. It was about complete and total surrender to His will and His purpose and it was about repentance and forgiveness.

God placed me in a position of total helplessness to teach me that I needed His help. I found myself flat on my back with no where to look but up, tied to a bed, unconscious, paralyzed and with a tube down my throat to shut me up so that I would listen to Him. He connected me to life-sustaining machines to humble me and remove my control. Then He blessed me with eighteen days in His presence.

I may not know until I get to Heaven, but I believe that "this reckoning day" was my turning point. It was the day I said, "It is Yours, Lord. I give you my breath, my life." It wasn't necessarily a change in treatment, a new doctor, a new idea, but a change in "heart." Mine was now a heart that was totally surrendered and committed to His purpose.

The Holy Spirit: My Guide

"Lord, will you be my guide?"
"Yes, I will. As we travel together I want you to remember that I know where I am going. Every stop along the way is important and we will stay there until you learn what it is I am trying to teach you. We may travel across snow covered mountains, rocky cliffs, or lush green valleys. Are you willing to follow me anywhere? Will you keep your eyes on me, whether the path is easy or hard?"
"Yes, Lord."
"There are lessons you need to learn first."
"Tell me what they are Lord."
<u>Lesson #1:</u>
"I want you to step where I step."
"But Lord, Your footprints are far bigger than mine."
"No, I will make them just right for you."
"But Lord, I know You sometimes walk too fast."
"I will never walk faster than I know you can keep up with Me."
"But I will get tired easily."
"I am your Shepherd. I will lend you My arm when you need help. I will carry you when you are weary."
"Lord, what if I stumble?"
"I will pick you up and heal your wounds."

137

Lesson #2:
"You are to follow Me in faith, even if you can't see Me."
"Lord, how will I know where to walk?"
"You will have a guide book called the Bible. Refer to it often for direction and also for reassurance that I am with you. I will never leave you nor forsake you."
"Lord, what if I become confused and lose my way?"
"Remember My teachings, My truths, and My promises. Remember who I am and always will be, Your God. Call out to Me, and I will hear you and show you great and mighty things which thou knowest not."
"Yes, I will follow You Lord."

My condition continued to improve from that day forward. By the tenth day on life support I was being weaned from the meds that had been paralyzing me and therefore I was able to barely blink in response. I could move my fingers enough to let my family know I was responding. God had sheltered and protected me with His loving arms and now He was transitioning me from a state of dependence on Him and the life-supporting machines to a more familiar world. I felt like I had been caught up in a very long, but wonderful dream. Now I was trying to separate the real from the spiritual.

I never wanted to lose the closeness that God and I had shared over the previous two weeks. There had been a time when I had reconciled myself to leaving earth and I was anxiously awaiting my eternal resting place sitting at the feet of Jesus. But here He was working a miracle, and I was right in the middle of its making.

I could feel God loosening His grip. Little by little He was placing me back into the world of the living. I believe His heart longed to bring me on to Heaven because He loves me that much, but He knew that the fields are white to harvest and the laborers are few.

God had created in me a servant's heart that wanted to reap an abundant harvest. I was willing to work the fields in order to reach those who needed to hear the gospel. I didn't know how I was going to accomplish all that He wanted me to do, but I trusted that the Holy Spirit would show me the way. I have often heard it said that it is through our most difficult trials that God is preparing us for our greatest triumph. I was so anxious to see what He had planned for me.

By the way, the pathogen that caused the infection has never been identified. I had a disease of magnitude with an unidentifiable cause. Do you see how God works? He takes the unexplainable and uses it to prove His power and glory.

God's underlying purpose was to heal me inside by restoring my soul, to create in me a heart that was surrendered to His purpose, and to deepen my relationship with Him.

God kept me in a state of awareness so that I would be conscious of my tremendous need for Him and also that I would be able to call on Him "from whence cometh my help."

No one knew by looking at me that I was aware, but inside my still body was an awakening spirit. It was one that was filling me, changing me, and transforming me into the image of Christ. It was the Spirit of God.

I was beginning to show signs of life and even though I was still connected to the ventilator, I was more and more aware of my surroundings and my body. I wanted so badly to communicate with my family and they could tell.

I was constantly nauseated from the tube-feeding and several times my stomach had been so full that it overflowed. I thought if I could just get them to put a suction catheter in my hand, I would be able to suction my mouth if the need arose. By the way, this is a totally different kind of suctioning than the one previously mentioned. It would not have done any good for me to have a suction catheter in my hand because my hands were tied to the bedrails. Also, I was still immobile from the drugs! This tells you that my brain wasn't working properly.

My family was so excited that I was trying to communicate that they were anxious to play along with my game of charades. Someone suggested that maybe I could write a note. Being the determined person that I am, I was sure this was a great idea if someone would untie my hand and give me a pen!

Before this brilliant idea my husband had been leaning over the bed trying his best to figure out what I was trying to say. I could barely open my eyes, but I glimpsed a pen in his shirt pocket. I kept hoping that he would lean over just far enough that the pen would fall out. That way I could grab it and write them a note. I had no idea of my weakness. I couldn't have grabbed a cotton ball let alone a pen! I don't know what I would have written on anyway. I just knew I had to tell them about the nausea before I aspirated. When they finally did put a pen in my hand, it felt like it weighed ten pounds.

I felt like a one-year old with his first crayon or a kindergarten student trying to write the alphabet for the first time. I had no control, even though someone was holding the pen for me. My vision was so blurred and my eye-lids so heavy that I couldn't see the paper. As hard as I tried, I couldn't form a letter. I didn't have the strength to even make a mark. I wasn't even sure how to form the letters or even how to spell the word. What was wrong with me?

Eventually a patient little nurse tried to help me by holding up a letter board, but I couldn't raise my finger to point to the letters so she laid it on my chest. Of course, being the professional nurse that I am, I was not trying to spell "suction," that would have been too easy. Instead, I was trying to think of the proper name for suction catheter, which is "Yankauer." After what seemed like an hour, I finally managed to point to "Y-a-n." But after all this grueling activity, I was exhausted, frustrated, and angry at myself for not being able to communicate my need. Still nauseated, I fell asleep.

Nathan and Sharon were at my bedside that night. Sharon said she was bothered all night that they were unable to figure out what I wanted so badly to say. She knew that it must have been important because I had tried so hard to tell them. It was important alright. After all, I was afraid I was going to aspirate and choke to death! I thought, now isn't this a picture! Here God is working a miracle to save my life from this life-threatening disease and my inability to communicate is going to cause me to aspirate. I didn't want anything interfering with God's plan to heal me.

The next day she and Nathan couldn't wait to get back to my room for visiting hour. They were so excited because they thought they had finally figured out what I was trying to say. The first thing they asked was, "Were you trying to say you had to yawn?" I thought to myself, well not exactly, but that was a good try!

It's something we laugh at today, but it wasn't quite as funny that day. I just kept thinking that we could all save ourselves a lot of trouble if they would just get the tube out of my throat and turn off the ventilator. Then I would be able to tell them anything. Maybe soon! At least I was improving.

The more they withdrew the drugs, the more I felt disconnected from my body. It felt like it belonged to someone else. My brain felt like it had been scrambled. It was hard for me to concentrate or hold a thought for more than a few seconds and it was hard for me to analyze my situation or think beyond the moment. It was kind of like waking up from a deep sleep or in a strange place and feeling disoriented. I found it hard to focus on the physical aspects of my life because I had been so preoccupied with the spiritual.

It tickled me that my family spent a great deal of time during visiting hour trying to tell me about all the things that had happened to me over the last two weeks. They asked me things like, "Do you realize Christmas is past?" "Do you know it's a new year?" "Do you know where you are?" "Do you remember getting sick?" It was funny. I couldn't wait to tell them that I probably knew more about what had happened than they did. I knew at least as much because I had witnessed everything first hand. I was so anxious to get off of the ventilator so I could talk to them!

My thought processes might have been returning, but my attention span was very brief. It was like watching a slide show one picture at a time. Blink, blink, blink. Everything was always in slow motion, including my brain! I felt like I was halfway between coma and reality. I was so aware of things going on around me, but it was hard to grasp that it was real. I was still connected to life support, however, I was breathing more on my own with less assistance from the ventilator.

Finally, I heard the nurses saying that my doctor was to come in that next morning to remove the life support. Yeah! Just a few more hours and I would be free from the machine that had been breathing for me over the last ten days. I would soon be able to talk and boy was I excited to tell them what they had missed! I knew I could make it a few more hours with God's help. After all, it was because of Him that I had made it this far.

The way I passed the hours was by continuing to praise God for His goodness. I quoted scripture and sang songs to myself. Sometimes I listened to the daily commotion that surrounded the nurse's desk. There has never been a day in my life that I was more excited. Soon I was going to be able to tell everyone about my "Close Encounter" with God. How awesome that was going to be. Soon my life would be back to normal, only better. My praise ceremony was interrupted only by periods of rest.

January 3, 2006

It was a long night. Anxious as a child on Christmas Eve, I kept my mind busy all night with songs, verses, and visions of singing with Sandi Patt. (Again, what a thought)! It seemed the next morning would never arrive.

I still couldn't open my eyes long enough to see a clock so the only way I knew it was morning was to listen for the change of shifts. I was growing impatient enough waiting for morning, but what a let down when I heard my nurse tell the oncoming day-shift nurse that my doctor wouldn't be there to take me off the ventilator until around 4:00 that afternoon.

Could I handle this discomfort for eight more hours? I fought a constant urge to gag from the tube down my throat and my body ached from immobility. Still, all I could do was wait. It seemed like God was really trying to get this point across, don't you think?

I knew I was getting better because I began to think for the first time about how awful I must look. My hair had been shampooed once in eighteen days (remember the human carwash) and then it was let dry on its own. I had not had make-up on for three weeks (this is sad for someone who sold cosmetics for a living). My mouth was pulled to one side, gaped open, and taped. I was sure if I was wearing anything at all, it had to be one of the hospital's "designer gowns!"

I wanted to look around so that I could place the sounds of ICU that had become so familiar to me, but all I could manage was an intermittent flutter of my eyelids. They felt so heavy that I had to really concentrate just to move them the slightest bit. This was enough for me to see the tips of my toes and the huge moon boots on both my lower extremities.

I thought about the possibility of bed sores from my immobility and wondered if my skin was still intact. The reality of what was ahead of me, as far as rehab, was beginning to concern me. At least I was able to think a little about what was coming next.. Since I had been a rehab nurse, I knew the results of immobility and what it could do to your muscles and joints. Oh well, I thought, at least I still have legs!

I thought about silly things like my wedding ring, but then I remembered someone nearly dislocating my finger when they were trying to remove it. I knew it must be somewhere. I wondered what my husband had put on me to bring me to the hospital and where my things were.

I wanted to feel something, anything; like my face, my hair, or even the sheets. I guess I was trying to exercise my spatial and tactile skills to see if they were still intact. In other words, "pinch me to see if I am awake." Everything had been so abnormal for days. I just wanted something to "feel normal." It still seemed so impossible that all this had happened to me.

I tried not to think too far past the present because that reminded me of how long I still had to wait before coming off of the ventilator. All I could think about was being free from the machines!

I smelled breakfast trays coming so I knew for sure it was morning. I thought to myself, Okay, I know my olfactory nerve is intact because I smell food. Of course none was for me. My breakfast was a bag of Hyperal that hung from a pole over my right shoulder and infused through a tube inserted through my nose and down into my stomach.

Two nurse assistants came in to give me a bath. As most did, they carried on their conversation over me and about me as if I wasn't there. Every now and then they would ask me if I could hear them like they thought I could actually answer them with the rod down my throat. I couldn't move so I wondered why they would ask me a yes/no question knowing I couldn't even nod. They took my lack of response as an indication that I couldn't hear them. If they had known that I could hear every word they were saying, I am sure they would have been a little more selective about the things they talked about. Oh the stories I could tell!

I had my usual morning chest x-ray and labs, but I was still on a ventilator. I heard other doctors come and go, but they weren't my doctor. I grew more and more exhausted as I tried to muster up enough fight in me to keep a positive attitude. It was the longest day of my life!

Now that I had my orders from God, I was ready to get on with my life. I said to myself, "Oh, if someone would just come and take this tube out, I would get up from here and be just fine."

"Consider it all joy" was all I could think. I had to find a way to have joy, even in this most difficult time. I had to keep thinking positive thoughts while trusting God that I wasn't going to be connected to this machine for the rest of my life. I could sense the powers that wanted to bring me down, discourage me, and threaten my faith. Satan would have given anything to have destroyed the experience I had recently had with my Lord. I really had to fight the temptation. I was so weak that I could no longer control the saliva that formed a continuous drip from the corner of my mouth. This was so humbling. I laid there thinking about all the spinal cord patients I had taken care of in my nursing days, particularly the quads who were at the mercy of their caregiver for every detail of their life. I thought about the patients who had fallen victim to stroke or brain injury. I wondered how much of me was still going to be intact. I continued to check things out.

I knew that coming back from coma was certainly not like it is depicted on television, but how much of me would return? What would my capabilities be? Would I be able to work or maintain my business? Would I be able to travel? What would be the effects of this disease I had listened to them describe over the last few days? Would I get to go home or would I have to spend weeks on a rehabilitation floor getting my strength and function back. Would I possibly have to spend time in a nursing home or would my family be able to take me home and care for me?

I wondered if I would have the same personality. I knew I had been oxygen deprived for days and that could result in some deficits, but how much would I be affected? Was the fact that I could think at all a good sign or were my thoughts caged within a body that was damaged goods? Was it a body that no longer would be whole? Would I be able to speak, sing, or play the piano? Would I ever be able to sew again or drive a car? I had nothing to do but lay there and think.

So, as I had always done, I turned my thoughts toward Heaven. I began to pray and thank God for choosing me and seeing me worthy of His forgiveness. I was so appreciative to Him for answering my prayers. I was humbled, but grateful for His grace and mercy. I didn't deserve the tremendous blessing of a precious walk with Him, but He freely spent time with me. I didn't deserve His healing, but He felt I was a vessel worthy of mending and putting to further use. I didn't deserve His love, but He gave it anyway. The more I focused on God, the faster the time seemed to pass. The more I focused on Him, the less discomfort I felt. The more I praised Him, the closer He drew me to His heart.

It was a stormy day and Nathan and Sharon were putting off a trip back to Atlanta in hopes that they could see me after I was off the ventilator. Every visiting hour I would hear them say how much they hated to leave. They so wanted to see that their Mom was returning to life. They wanted to have the opportunity to talk to me before they left. They were as anxious for me to be extubated as I was.

God had His reasons for allowing me another walk with Him before He freed me from the ventilator. I think it was as hard for Him to let go of me as it was for me to step away from His presence and re-enter the world of the living. I pictured Him feeling like I felt on my children's first day of school. I knew it was a necessity that they learn and grow, but I just didn't want to let go of them. I believe God has these feelings for us as well. I think He just wanted to savor the precious time we had experienced together for just a little longer. As ready as I was to hop on the bus and head to school, I had to keep depending on Him and wait on His timing. So we enjoyed fellowship together as He walked with me, talked with me, and told me I was His own. The joy we shared as we tarried there in that place, none other will ever know.

I was determined that Satan would not win the battle for my attention. As hard as it was, I was going to keep looking to God, the author and finisher of my faith. I would keep my eyes fixed on God. He would fight my battle for me. He had prepared a table before me in the presence of my enemy and I was determined to feast on the bounty of God. With His help I would overcome. I prayed that my test of endurance and patience would be a testimony to those who were also waiting. I would be patient and I would wait upon the Lord

Isaiah 40:31 kept coming to my mind. I would wait upon the Lord and as I waited, He would renew my strength. In His strength I would mount up as eagles. I would walk and not be weary. I would run and not faint.

I decided that while I was waiting I would plan a victory celebration to be held at church as soon as possible. I would share my incredible adventure through the valley of the shadow of death. Of course, I would be singing and so would anyone else who wanted to. We would have other testimonies and I prayed that lost souls would come to know the Lord through the power of the Holy Spirit. It would be a night that was all about God and His goodness. It would not be about me, it would be focused on honoring God and giving Him the glory. I rehearsed it. Oh what a night of celebration it would be!

This is the same kind of service I would have wanted if God had decided my journey was upward. Death is not permanent for those who have accepted Christ. It separates us from loved ones, but it comes with a promise of being with them again one day in Heaven; and for all eternity.

Death is not to be dreaded. I know this first hand now. There was such peace in the valley. The only thing final about death is that we leave this body with its sickness and pain to receive a glorified body in Heaven. The only things we take with us are the souls of those we have led to Christ. We are all living with a terminal illness called death. The scriptures tell us, unless Christ returns before, we are all going to die.

You may ask, "How could you have been at peace during such a difficult time in your life?" Because I know that God only works things for my good because I love Him and because I know that I was called according to His purpose. It is for His purpose, and His alone, that I live.

I know that for every trial, there is a triumph. I also know that with every promotion, there comes a test. I had been tested, and now I awaited the grade which would bring about my promotion.

My prayer for years had been that God would find me worthy to be used by Him. By being obedient and sharing the story of my encounter, I knew that God would give His purpose to my suffering.

In order for me to be able to help others, I had to know the power of God in my life. Now that I knew Him intimately, I wanted others to know Him as I did. I wanted to help others build their relationship with the Lord. Now I could speak first hand of His greatness and how He loved me so much that He chose to spend eighteen days in fellowship with me. He drew me close to His heart, He loved me, and He breathed new life into my soul. He gave me a message to give to His people. He said, "Tell them how much I love them, tell them what it is like to be in My presence, and teach them how to have a personal, intimate relationship with Me." I praise God for His faithfulness and for considering me worthy of sharing His message.

It's never been very important if people necessarily remembered "me," though I think we all would like to be remembered for something. However, it has always been my prayer that their lives were different in a positive way because they had seen Christ in me. I hope people will see that if He can use me, He can use anybody. I want my life and my testimony to be the bridge for others; a bridge of hope, forgiveness, and restoration. I want to be able to say that I ran my race all the way to the finish line, not to be the winner, just a finisher who found the faith to keep running in her relationship with God. There is no greater legacy.

God doesn't ask us to be perfect. Christ was the only perfect One. But what He does ask for is our obedience, our submission to His will, and our willingness to be used for His purpose, not our own. God wanted all of me, not just a part of me. Now He has everything.

1:50pm on January 3, 2006

"Karen, are you ready to get that tube out?" I felt like Lazarus must have felt, only this time Jesus was saying, "Karen, Karen, come forth!" But it was the voice of my doctor; the one who had come to remove me from the ventilator. Praise God, it was finally time!

I couldn't believe what I was hearing. Loud and clear were her words as if she was shouting them in my ear. I said to myself, "Of course I am, wouldn't you be?" I couldn't help but think that if she knew the story I had to tell, she would be ready to "get the tube out" too.

Fifteen minutes later, the ventilator was unplugged, the tube had been pulled from my chest that had sustained my life for eleven days and I was praising God for allowing me the privilege to continue in my service for Him. I couldn't help it. I kept repeating over and over again, "Thank you Jesus, thank you Jesus!" I wanted the world to hear me praising Him. My voice was just a whisper, but I strained as hard as I could to make my sound of praise be heard.

I was so excited about a second chance. I was ready to hit the road and start running because God had given me a job to do. It had always been my responsibility, but this time I would be more focused and driven to reach souls for Christ. This time I wouldn't let my foolish pride get in my way. This time I wouldn't have need for control because God had it all. This time I would let go of my past failures and I would move forward in my race, walking behind the One who knew the way. This time I wouldn't feel the need to prove myself worthy of being loved because I knew how much God loved me.

After a deep breath and a cough, there was a rapid sensation of a foreign object being pulled up through my chest and out my mouth. Words could never express the immediate feeling of relief I had once the tube was out. A large oxygen mask was placed over my face, a nurse made sure that I was stable, and then I was left alone in my room. For so long there had been nothing but noise and activity around me. For the first time in eleven days my room was silent. Gone was the noisy ventilator. Gone was the pump for my feeding tube. Gone was the tube down my nose through which I had been fed. Gone were the restraints that had tied my hands to the bed rails. Everything was quiet except for me. I couldn't stop praising God and I couldn't stop asking to see my family. Only nobody was listening, except God. Over and over I kept saying, "Thank you Jesus, thank you Jesus." I thought about how Moses must have felt after God spoke to him at the "burning bush." I too had received orders and I had an eternal focus, which was to do what God had told me to do.

I was breathing on my own, though I still had oxygen. I could speak, though my voice sounded like a hoarse frog and was so faint it was barely above a whisper. I was anxious and asking, "Where's my family? Can I see my family?" Even though I was so desperate to talk to them and even though my family was waiting patiently in the waiting room, they made me wait until the next visiting hour to see them. It seemed like forever!

I was hungry. I don't particularly like ice cream, but for some reason I kept thinking how good it would feel going down my sore throat. Ben and Jerry's "Moose Tracks" was what I asked for, to be exact. I don't know why this particular flavor because I had never eaten it before. Later, when my family started trying to find it, we realized why...Ben and Jerry never made it!

I tried to sing to make sure another part of me was working, but nothing much would come out. I thought, oh well, I could expect that it would take a day or two for my voice to come back. After all, my vocal cords had been pushed aside by a rod down my throat for eleven days. I would try something else. I tried to just say the words, but because of my shortness of breath and weakness, I had to take a breath about every other word. My heart so wanted to rejoice, worship, and praise God for His goodness. I gave it my best effort, though I'm sure I sounded terrible. That's probably why they closed the door and left me alone! I didn't care. I was alive and God had given me a story and a purpose.

When the visiting hour finally arrived I was so excited! I heard the nurse announce over the intercom that families could come in. Mine was going to be so surprised to see me because I was awake, I was off the ventilator and I was going to be able to talk to them for the first time in almost two weeks. I was beside myself with anticipation. My heart was racing.

Since only two or three persons were allowed to visit in the ICU at one time, my loved ones and friends took shifts coming back to see me. The first one to enter was my sister-in-law Lorraine. I had heard her voice and that of her husband, my precious brother Mike, many times while in a coma. I wasn't surprised that she would be the first person I would see coming through the door. As she rounded the corner and looked through the glass window of my room, she almost squealed with excitement. I will never forget her surprise when she realized that I was disconnected from the ventilator. I had a huge oxygen mask over my face, but that didn't make me hard to recognize. It didn't keep me from trying to talk either.

Nathan and Sharon were right behind her. They were also overjoyed to see that Mom had returned to the world of the living. Before this day, my visitors tended to linger around my bedside as if to get their last glimpse of me alive. Now the shifts were changing rapidly as each one ran out to let another one in to see "the miracle." It was so exciting!

Nathan and Sharon were trying to orient me. They had been told that it was likely that I would have some deficits from the lack of oxygen and the disease process itself. They were prepared for blindness, loss of memory, inability to recognize familiar faces and even the possibility of a vegetative state. I don't blame them for checking me out. I couldn't believe it myself. Joy and laughter had replaced a room filled with gloom. This Lazarus was alive!

I politely answered their questions and then I started to fill them in on some details - things about my experience in ICU that even they were not aware of. At first they probably thought I had been dreaming, but when I was able to recite conversations and give account to the things that had occurred, my story took on an air of validity. They were shocked, but oh, so happy! I shared details with them about what went on behind closed doors - like the "human car wash" and my nurse, the "gum popper!" I told them about prayer meetings at the foot of my bed and the cool cloths that Paul placed on my forehead. I couldn't stop talking! It was so wonderful to be able to communicate with my family again. I couldn't keep from praising God.

Of course, Lorraine ran to get my husband, Charles, who was so overjoyed he was in tears. My brother, David, was there with his wife, Melba. It was good to see him looking normal. When I was first coming around and barely able to open my eyes, I remember catching a glimpse of him leaning over me to kiss my cheek. His face seemed to be covered in a bushy beard and at that time, he had two noses, two mouths and four eyes. Now that I was awake, I guess I must have been really hungry. For some reason, I kept telling David that he owed me a steak for making it through this experience. It might have been because he is so good at grilling.

When Paul and Suzanne entered, they were so excited about the good news. Paul had been hiding some news of his own. Because of all that had been going on with me, he had not found a good time to share "good" news, but now he had more than one reason to be excited. Paul had produced his first film and it had been selected to be shown at a preview event in Augusta that following weekend. Actually, it was going to be on his birthday. I tried my best to reach up and hug him to let him know how proud I was of him, but instead, he leaned over to hug me.

I could name them one by one as they came in to see me, but for the fear of leaving someone out I will just say; there has never been, nor will there ever be, any faces that looked better to me than those of my family and close friends. They had walked through the valley with me and they had struggled from day to day to keep their faith. They had prayed for me and waited on God to answer. Now, praise God, their prayers had been answered. It was a miracle. I was exhausted by the time the visiting hour was over. I went to sleep, peacefully.

I rested soundly until I heard a familiar voice at my bedside. It was the voice of my dear childhood friend, Kay. She and her husband had driven to Augusta from Greenville, South Carolina, thinking they were probably going to be paying their last respects. You can imagine how surprised they were when they arrived in the waiting room to hear that I was not only alive, but off the ventilator, able to speak, alert, and coherent. I was so glad that she didn't have to see me as I had been, even though I am sure I still looked quite frightening. But she was glad to find me improving and it was good for me to know that she was there.

Word traveled quickly and many others were there during the next visiting hour to witness a miracle, a Lazarus brought back to life by the hand of God. I will forever give Him thanks for allowing me the privilege of continuing to serve Him! God had "…chosen thee (me) in the furnace of affliction (Jeremiah 1:6-9).

It's Not Over Yet

That evening I came to understand the meaning of a diagnosis I had seen many times on patients charts and that was…"Deconditioning" and "Generalized Weakness."

I had been trying to talk non-stop since being extubated, but I had been so busy talking that I had not realized that nothing else was moving except my mouth. I could not even turn my head.

I had my first meal that evening which was cream of chicken soup and ice cream. It wasn't a steak and it wasn't Moose Tracks ice cream, but it tasted good since I had not eaten in three weeks.

A nurse fed me. I thought she was just being kind and helpful. I had not tried to use my extremities, therefore, I had no idea of the muscle weakness that my immobility had created. Because I had not tried to move, I didn't realize that I couldn't move. She told me that a therapist would soon be in to work with me. I then began to realize that I was alive, I was awake, but I was not back to normal.

My husband had just arrived for visiting hour and he was allowed to come to my room while the therapist was working with me. He was still so excited about my being awake and breathing on my own that he had not anticipated what he was about to witness. Like most people who watch television, he thought once I woke up the worst would be over and soon everything would be back to normal. I knew from experience with head injury patients that this was not true. Still, in denial I thought, but I will be different.

My first session with a therapist was a rude awakening. Charles and I both realized that I wasn't out of the woods yet. I had survived the illness and I was getting better by the hour, but now I had to be rehabilitated.

I expected to have some weakness from being immobilized for eighteen days, but weakness is not a very appropriate word when you can't raise your hand off the bed, turn or lift your head, raise your foot, or even slide it across the sheets. There are no words to describe the profound, intense, incapacitating weakness that accompanied my return from a coma.

My first therapist was a tall, thin guy who looked to be about eighteen years old. He very politely introduced himself and told me he was going to check the strength in my upper extremities. After gathering some basic information we were ready to begin. He first asked me to reach up and touch my nose with my index finger. His request was somewhat of an insult to my intelligence since I had known where my nose was three times as long as he was old, but I thought I would humor him and obey his command. After all, this was his job.

Despite my sincere efforts to raise my arm, nothing happened. He reassured me that weakness is to be expected and then he proceeded to help me raise my arm across my chest, only when he let it go, it fell like a brick nearly knocking the breath out of me.

Then he tried to lift my arm towards my face. He was determined to show me where my nose was! This time when he let go, I slapped myself right in the face. I am sure this was not quite what he had in mind when he said to "…touch your nose." Not only was I frustrated, I was also embarrassed, humiliated, and exhausted. This was enough activity to require a nap.

A short while later, another therapist, much older, but shorter in stature, entered my room. He introduced himself and said he was there to help me "…sit up."

I thought to myself, you guys need to communicate. If I couldn't raise my arm to touch my nose for the other guy, how in the world do you think I am going to sit up?

But wanting to be a compliant patient I said to myself, "Oh well, I will humor him too." So I said, "Sure, let's do it!" After all, I am a very motivated person.

Needless to say, he did get me to a sitting position, but not without a lot of grunting, pushing, and pulling. That was on his part because "he" had to do all the work. I had no strength to help him. It was frightening to be upright. I had been flat on my back for so long that once I was in a sitting position, it felt like all the blood in my body rushed to my feet. I was dizzy, clammy, and faint. I had no balance and leaned to one side or the other unless the therapist had his hands on my shoulders to steady me. My head tilted downward and no matter how hard I tried, I couldn't lift it. Because I had no balance and no strength to steady myself, it felt like I would surely fall face first on the floor. I couldn't control my own saliva, therefore,

155

it drooled from my mouth and puddled in my lap. It was so humbling!

My back ached as it curved due to the weakness in my spine. It felt like my backbone had turned to jelly. I wobbled like an infant trying to learn to sit alone. He wanted to test my ability to hold my balance, but when he let go of me, I fell backwards across the bed. My whole sitting experience only lasted a few seconds, but it was long enough to exhaust me.

To add insult to injury, he also wanted me to fold a washcloth. Okay, by this time I had had just about all the humiliation I could handle for one day. I was exhausted from my attempt to sit alone and I wanted to go to sleep and forget that this experience had taken place. I had been doing fine, basking in the thrill of being alive, until these guys came along to burst my bubble. All they had done was shown me how infantile I was.

I thought, oh, who cares. I will show him how to fold a washcloth. Maybe his mother didn't teach him how or something. I felt so insulted that anyone would think that I was incapable of doing such a simple task.

I was wrong again. Humbling as it was and even though he propped my arms up and held them across my chest, I didn't have the strength to lift one corner of the washcloth and carry it over to the opposite side. Again, this was so humbling!

I thanked God when the therapist said that this was my last therapy session for the day. What a finish to my first day back to life! Feeling very helpless, tired, and struggling with the emotional side of my incapacities, I drifted off to sleep that night trusting God for a better day the next day. I knew that things could only get better. Tomorrow was another day.

It was a peaceful night, even though I was unsure of the future. I knew God would renew my strength because He had given me a job to do. After what He had brought me through I could handle anything, but only with His help.

The next morning I awakened to a breakfast tray being placed on my over-bed table. A very cheery, pleasant nurse named Kathy introduced herself and told me how wonderful it was to see me improving. It was so good to be able to talk to the people who had been caring for me while I was in a coma, instead of having to just listen to their conversations. Kathy was a Christian, so she appreciated the parts of my story that I was able to share with her. I knew immediately when I told her about my encounter with God that we shared a common bond and it was the Lord.

She was the one who had fed me dinner the night before so I guess she anticipated having to feed me breakfast as well. I was determined to feed myself, even if it took me all day. There was a tiny bowl of grits on my tray and that became my target. It seemed a million miles away, but when I told Kathy my goal, she agreed to let me try. I don't think she thought it was possible.

Reluctantly, she set up my tray and positioned me. I didn't even have the strength to open the packet of sugar. I couldn't lift my four ounce cup of juice either so we raised the over-bed tray and positioned the straw where all I had to do was tilt my head the slightest bit to reach it. I knew that if I tilted too far, I would not have the strength to lift my head and therefore would fall face-first into my tray. She lifted my arms, placed them across my lap, and elevated them on pillows to minimize the distance between my mouth and my grits. She placed my bowl of grits in my left hand and a spoon in my right. She propped extra pillows behind my head to tilt it forward and elevated my feet to keep me from sliding down in the bed. I probably looked liked I was in some kind of kung-fu position, but I didn't care. I was determined to regain my dignity. I would not give up until I had finished my grits!

Well, it took me two hours to feed myself that bowl of grits, but I did it and I didn't spill a drop! I was so pleased with myself and my accomplishment that everyone who entered my room that whole day got to hear about my successful attempt to be "normal," even the housekeeper!

I took another nap to recover from my energy expenditure. It seemed such a brief time before I was awakened by another therapist. It was mid-morning by this time and I was still exhausted from my "feeding frenzy," but I knew I had to work hard in order to get better. Working as a Rehab nurse had taught me that. Generalized weakness wasn't going to hold me back. I had orders from God and I needed to get to work!

This little guy did a few exercises with my lower extremities and as long as he was doing the movement we were getting along just fine. My legs were so heavy they felt like telephone poles that were attached at my hips. But then he said, "Karen, now we are going to stand you up." I thought to myself, "we" are going to stand up? Get real!"

It had been bad enough to try and cooperate with the arm raising and sitting up, but standing? What did they expect out of me? Not only was standing going to interfere with my safety, but this little guy was about a foot shorter than me. Even if he was able to get me to a standing position, if I were to collapse I would fold right over on top of him.

But I knew I had to start somewhere. With a lot of effort, we did it. I guess you could say we cheated because we also used a machine that elevates you and then supports you while you are standing. This might not sound like much progress to you, but to me it was a monumental step towards being able to walk again. I stood for a whole "thirty seconds!"

My body felt like it weighed a thousand pounds. Nothing wanted to move. I couldn't reposition myself in bed, I couldn't roll over, sit up, raise my legs, or raise my head without assistance! Every movement required all the effort I could muster, but I kept trying. The therapist showed me exercises that I could do between his visits – things like sliding my legs across the sheets (1 could move them only an inch or so) or trying to tilt my feet forward and backward. These sound like simple tasks, but they were grueling energy zappers for me.

Whenever I would awaken during the night I would try to move a different part of my body. Even if I couldn't move it, I figured I was at least exercising the connection between my brain and my muscles. I asked God, "How long will it take for me to get my strength back?" He was silent.

I am not sure of the time, but somewhere in the middle of the night I was awakened by the most intense, excruciating pain in my right side I had ever felt. It was so bad that it took my breath away. My eyes flew open and all I could see was bright light. Then I heard a familiar voice. It belonged to the doctor who had taken me to surgery to do a biopsy and place chest tubes. He now was ripping the tube out of the right side of my chest, and needless to say, without my permission!

Before I could complain or strike him, like I wanted to do (Forgive me Lord), he was finished, the incision was tied in a purse string suture, and he was gone. He had flown in like a tornado, done his damage, and then he was out the door. With my head still spinning from the pain, I managed to get my composure enough to ask the nurse for something to relieve it. Eventually, I went back to sleep.

January 4, 2006

Free at last, free at last. Praise God, I'm free at last!

It was a long day as I awaited transfer to a regular room. I kept thinking, if I can just get out of ICU and into a regular room, I will feel like I am making progress and my family and friends will be free to visit me at any time. I wanted anything and everything back in my life that represented normalcy. A room on another hospital floor wasn't home, but it was a step closer to home.

There were arterial lines to pull, bandages to be changed, machines to disconnect, etc. Little by little, the tubes that had connected me to IV poles and arterial lines for all those days were being removed.

My body felt anything but normal. I had incisions everywhere and I still had a chest tube on my left side. When I located it I couldn't help but recall the experience I had had the night before. I said to myself, "Oh no, that means I've got to go through that pain again!"

159

I had more tubes than I had realized. They were connected to arterial lines in my groin and to both my arms. There were bandages everywhere for reasons I wasn't aware of.

I felt bloated and swollen and I knew it was mostly from the steroids. I wasn't any help with repositioning, for all I could do was lay there like a big blob. But I could whisper, so it was hard to shut me up. Despite my need for oxygen, I kept a pretty constant chatter with whoever was in the room. Of course, I was still bragging about feeding myself grits as well. If no one was in my room, I chattered anyway, just because I finally could.

Just as they were about to transfer me to another bed that would take me to the regular floor, in came my doctor to announce that I wasn't going anywhere until he removed my last chest tube. I really had hoped that he had forgotten about it and that maybe it would become a extra appendage that I would carry around with me for the rest of my life. It would have been fine with me rather than endure the pain of removing it, but oh no, he had to have the pleasure of pulling it out!

At least this time he gave me some warning and didn't wake me up out of a deep sleep. He also gave me instructions on how to breathe as well as a signal when to start my panting. The second one was much easier, though still extremely painful. It was the kind of pain that one can endure only for a few seconds because if it lasted more than that you would just die.

I respected this man, though I did tease him about the night of pain. I told him not to be surprised if one night while he was sleeping someone slipped into his bedroom, turned on a bright light, and started pulling the hair off of his chest. I can't believe I really said that, but I did! He laughed a hardy laugh.

After I had thanked him for being influential in saving my life, he shared with me how close he had come to losing me. What means more to me than anything about him is that he didn't take the credit. He said that it was so good to see me leaving ICU and how beautiful I was compared to the first time he had seen me.

I made some silly remark about beauty because here lay a sales director for a cosmetic company who had not had skin care or make-up on for eighteen days. On top of that, I had a new "do" to my hair from the "human car wash." I could tell there was still tape stuck all over my face, though I couldn't reach up to feel it and I was wearing the beautiful designer gown known by all those who have spent a night in the hospital.

He snickered as he said, "But you are a miracle and God knows that doctors still need to see miracles every now and then." I agreed with him and put him on my list of "doctors I like."

The ride upstairs was like being let out of prison. The stuffy room in ICU was a thing of the past. The air in the hallway was cool and refreshing. I was headed to a private room where I could be with my loved ones twenty-four hours a day. My sister-in-law, Dale, was there to go upstairs with me. When we arrived at my room, Paul was there as well as a friend from church. Once I was settled in my room, I took a nap to rest from the activity of the morning.

It was so much more peaceful in a private room and out of the noisy ICU. Now I would finally be able to rest and with rest would come strength. Someone had to stay with me at all times, as you would figure based on the previous information, but at least I now had some privacy and my family could come and go any time of the day or night, not just during visiting hours.

Due to the nature of my illness I was taking large doses of steroids in hopes to minimize the pulmonary fibrosis. The medication alone can cause side effects such as diabetes. For this reason, they were carefully monitoring my blood sugar levels throughout my stay. Another side effect is mood swings. I am normally a very stable, quiet, even keel kind of person. In another chapter, I will talk more about the emotional effects this drug had on my recovery.

I continued on respiratory treatments, but my oxygen saturations remained stable. With therapy and support of my wonderful husband and family, everyday I became a little stronger. On January 7th, I took my first steps with a walker. It was only a few and I had a therapist on each side, but it was wonderful to be back on my feet again.

On January 8, 2006, my pulmonologist sat for about an hour explaining how different my life was going to be. In some respects, it was like receiving a diagnosis all over again. Though the inflammation was residing, I would be left with permanent lung damage. The extent would not be known for several months and possibly up to a year.

Her hopes were that I would not be what she called a "respiratory cripple," but that I would have to learn to listen to my body and pay attention to signs and symptoms of decreased oxygenation which would be evidenced by fatigue and shortness of breath.

I was to stay away from sickness due to my compromised resistance and I was going to have to reconcile myself to being homebound for several months as they monitored my progress. An infection of any kind would be dangerous and possibly life-threatening.

I was told it would take six months to a year to recover my strength and that I should be careful not to push myself beyond my limits. My resistance was zero so I would have to be careful about those who came to visit me. She encouraged me to limit visitors (she knew how many people had been at the hospital with me) and to spend most of my time resting in order to give my body time to heal. She also talked to me about eating a healthy, high-protein diet to stabilize my liver and blood values and regain my strength.

My primary physician, who is also a Christian, came in to pray with me and my husband and to give me some additional instructions. Together we praised God for his miracle-working power in my life. He shared with me how close I had come to leaving this world, but he rejoiced in seeing that I was improving. He said he was "…anxious to see what God was going to do with my life." I was too!

I had no idea how we were going to handle my disabilities once we got home, but we would figure it out. My doctors were anxious to get me out of the hospital and away from illness and the possibility of re-infection. They were going to send me home. This was some long awaited news!

I was trying to absorb all this information and make it my own. I still found it so hard to believe that this was "my" life we were talking about. I had stood so many times before a family explaining the same sort of things to them about their loved one. Now, the patient was me.

We were going to handle this with God's help. After all, look how far He had brought me already. Four days earlier I was still on a ventilator. Now I was getting ready to go home. We had to wait on some equipment to be delivered, but as soon as it arrived, I was free to go home. Yeah!

With great anticipation I was ready to face the future. That evening we would be at home; together as a family and celebrating our "late" Christmas together. We would be including the New Year because we were already over a week into 2006.

In my mind, I thought I could beat the odds. I was already making plans to attend a business seminar in March, which was to be held in Atlanta. I just knew that I would be able to make this event since it was three months away. To me, that seemed like plenty of time to recover. I knew my doctor said to give my recovery six months to one year, but I was young and determined. I was going to be just fine. I had faith in God and I was going to finish the race He had set before me, even though I was getting over a detour.

Yes, I had faith, but little did I know that God had not completed His test of my faith… or my patience.

January 8, 2006
Going home at last

Though I wondered how we would manage at home with my limited mobility, I was ready to get back to my familiar surroundings so I jumped at the chance to leave the hospital.

It was a warm January morning and a Sunday to be remembered. As I was rolled in a wheelchair to the entrance of the hospital where our son Paul was to pick me up, I took the time to look around me at the faces of people who were sitting in the lobby. Many, I'm sure, were awaiting admission to the hospital. Probably some were there for tests, some were ill, and some were preparing for surgery. I couldn't help but think that eighteen days before I had been where they were. So much had happened. God had been in that place with me. I said a prayer for them that He would gird them with the same loving care that He had given me. Most likely, some of them would not make it out of the hospital. I asked Him to give them the courage to accept His will.

I couldn't help but be grateful for being able to return home, but most of all I was so grateful for what God had done in my life during my stay. How miraculously He had worked to bring me through the valley of the shadow of death and place me on a mountaintop of restoration. I prayed for the souls behind the faces I passed and asked God to reveal Himself to these people as He had done to me. I asked Him to give them peace in their circumstances.

The sun felt warm and the air was crisp and cool as we crossed the threshold to the outdoors. My mind was clouded by uncertainties, but my heart was rejoicing in knowing that God was in control of my circumstances. I no longer would sweat the small stuff. Though my mind was fixed on finishing my course, I knew that I also had to focus on my continued recovery. I was no good to anyone like I was, not even myself. I had to get better and I was going to do it with God's help.

The ride home was peaceful as I took the time to thank God for His creation and for allowing me the privilege of seeing it again. Even in the midst of a southern winter, the barren trees looked beautiful to me. The sky was clear and bright blue.

As we drove home I prayed for the people in the cars that we passed. I couldn't help but think that they probably thought that their life would go on that day as it always had. I knew personally how suddenly it can change and how quickly it can be over.

We are all living with a terminal illness called death. We just don't know when God will choose to make it our time to finish our race. That's why we should live each day to its fullest. We should work for the Lord while it is day, for night is coming. Like never before, God had given me a sense of urgency to accomplish what He had left me on earth to do. My prayer became, "Show me thy will Lord." His answer was, "For now, be still and know that I am God. Wait on the Lord."

I was looking for "normalcy" in my life again. There just wasn't anything normal about having to use a walker and only being able to take a few steps at a time. It wasn't normal to take three people to get me out of a car and into the house. It wasn't normal to have to ask people to bring me things because I couldn't get up out of a chair. It wasn't normal to not be able to speak because my voice was still a whisper. It wasn't normal to have my husband shower me and comb my hair before we left the hospital because I didn't have the strength to raise my arms. It wasn't normal to use two hands to hold a toothbrush and have someone else squeeze the tube of toothpaste because I didn't have the strength to do it myself. It wasn't normal to not be able to stand at the sink to do these things. It wasn't normal to need assistance with toileting It wasn't normal to have my husband on the phone scheduling friends and family to come sit with me because I couldn't be left alone.

Having to be so humble also wasn't normal for me, but God was just beginning to teach me to walk as Christ walked. He showed me that being humble is not a sign of weakness, but instead a sign of strength. I learned the value of letting others receive a blessing from helping me when I couldn't help myself.

It wasn't normal for me to have my Christmas tree still up on the 8th of January. The first thing I wanted to do was order pizza and open our Christmas presents. I wanted to clear away the reminder of a Christmas that had passed while I lay in ICU with my family struggling to find hope. It was time to focus on a new year, a new life.

As our family gathered in our living room that night, we were all so thankful for the blessings of life and togetherness. We exchanged gifts, but none were necessary. Our greatest gift was in knowing that God had answered prayer and I was home. I had to let someone else open my gifts for me, but as appreciative as I was, nothing compared to the gift God had given me. It was the gift of knowing Him intimately.

I had no idea what the next weeks, months, or maybe years would hold. I refused to focus on the uncertainties. There was something I did know. I had experienced a "Close Encounter" with my God, His Son, and His Holy Spirit and I had received my marching orders to tell others what He had done in my life. I didn't know when He would bring it to pass, but knowing that He would fulfill His promise to me gave me something to look forward to in the coming months. My desire to do His will gave me a different perspective on my physical condition. I knew He would accomplish His will through me because I was a willing vessel, regardless of my weakness.

I couldn't hold a pen, but as soon as I was able to do so, I had a book to write. It would be my first and maybe my last, but it was an assignment given to me by the Holy Spirit Himself. I didn't know where to start, but I did know that I now had a story to tell.

I wasn't aware of it at the time, but there was still so much to be learned from this experience. Over the coming months bits and pieces of my memory would unfold and my mind would clear. Family and friends would fill in the gaps in my memory with details that many times, they didn't want to remember themselves. I wanted so badly to start writing it all down for fear that I would forget, but that day would come soon enough. For now, my mind was too scrambled and my hands too weak. I could barely keep a train of thought so it wouldn't do any good to be able to write anyway. This would have to wait another day or two (It ended up being more like five months)!

It was a quiet evening at home with my husband, our sons and their wives. There were a few phone calls from family members making sure I had actually returned home (no one could believe it), but I chose to let others answer the phone and give my thanks. Trying to talk above a whisper caused strain on my voice and I was already so exhausted from the days events.

As I sat and watched them all caught up in the details of caring for me, I couldn't help but be grateful that I could once again look into their eyes. What a joy to be in familiar surroundings! What a blessing to be at home!

Everyone was rather quiet. I think they probably didn't want to remind me of my recent experience and maybe they just didn't want to remember it themselves. Since they had been told that I may have some deficits, I think they might have been afraid to check me out too much for fear of finding some discrepancies. Maybe they were just as happy as I was that we were together again, and that was enough.

I realized very quickly that the time I had spent alone with God was personal and known only to me. I would be careful to share my story with them at just the right time because I wanted them to know how real it was and that it was not just something I had dreamed. The day would come for me to tell them of my encounter, but for now, the memory was mine to enjoy. Every voice, every remark, every prayer around my bed were all remembrances of a walk with God. It would take me a while to organize all my thoughts, but I had nothing but time on my hands. Tomorrow would be another day.

I could have spent hours lying awake trying to figure out how we were going to make it without my income or how long it would be before I would be able to work again, but instead, I left those things up to God.

I had other things to worry about - like how was I going to get out of the bed without rails or walk to the bathroom, shampoo my hair, or put on my make-up? How was I going to dress myself when I couldn't raise my arms or lift my feet? How would I fix a sandwich, let alone prepare a meal? How would I balance our checkbook or pay our bills and how would I clean my house or buy groceries?

Somehow, God would work it all out. After all we had been through; the rest had to be a piece of cake. I would take one day at a time and not worry about tomorrow. That's what God wanted me to do anyway.

I went to sleep cradled in my husband's arms. I was secure, safe, and at home, but anything but normal!

Chapter 3

A Dry, Barren Land

January 9, 2006

I awakened long before sunrise. My sleep had been frequently interrupted during the night by the many thoughts that kept racing through my mind. I couldn't help but recall the things God had shown me about myself and about my life. I wondered how He was going to help me accomplish all that He had instructed me to do for Him when I was so unable to do anything for myself. It was difficult for me to concentrate and my memory was also impaired. I was so afraid that I would forget the details of my experience that I kept playing the tape over and over in my head in hopes of imbedding the memories deep within my mind for safe keeping.

In the shadows of morning I gazed into the face of my wonderful husband. He had been through so much. I wondered how or if all this was going to affect our relationship. Was he going to get tired of caring for me? How long would I be unable to care for myself? How was he going to take care of me, work, and do the necessary chores around the house? Instead of a help-meet, I had become a burden. In my heart, I knew that he would do anything for me, but Satan used my mind as a stronghold.

I began to feel a sting of guilt. There was nothing I could have done to prevent this sickness. My doctors had reassured me of that. But because I loved Charles so much, I hated what I could see this ordeal had done to him. He had been so worried and now he was so overwhelmed over his new responsibilities. It was just about as hard for him to focus and complete a task as it was for me.

My hospital stay had separated us longer than ever before in our thirty-five years of marriage. The walls of an Intensive Care Unit and a sickness that came very close to taking me

169

heavenward had created a veil, but not one that overshadowed our love for each other. We were connected at the heart. From the time I was transferred to a private room till now, he had been so conscientious and attentive to my every need. Whenever I would apologize for being such a bother he would say, "You would do the same thing for me if you had to" and I would, definitely!

The transition from ICU to home happened so quickly that I'm sure he was as apprehensive as I was. He was so afraid that something would happen or that he might miss seeing the signs of a reoccurrence. Several times during the night I had felt his hand softly brushing over my face to see if he felt my warm expirations. I had felt his hand on my chest checking to see if it was rising and falling. At times I was aware of him rising up to look over at me, as if to confirm that I was still there. After many nights of sleeping alone and longing for my return home, I know he was trying to make sure he was not just dreaming. Sometimes He would awaken me to ask me if I needed anything and sometimes I just felt him holding my hand.

All these things brought back memories of our first night at home with our babies, only then he slept through it all. This time he was playing the role of mother and I was the baby!

I had awakened Charles several times during the night to help me with things like repositioning, toileting, medications, or for refreshment. You can see that neither of us got much sleep. It was very hard for me to get comfortable in bed and even harder to breathe lying flat so we played a game of musical bed and chair every hour or so. When I couldn't stand the bed any longer, he would help me to the family room so I could sit upright in the lounge chair. Once up on my feet, with the walker and his assistance, I could take the ten steps or so to the bathroom and to the chair, but it was a slow process. My balance was so poor and I was so weak that he feared my falling so he took every step with me, patiently. He was so tolerant. It was me who got frustrated.

Sitting upright made it easier to expand my lungs and less painful on the incision on my side where the biopsy was taken. Once Charles would get me settled in the chair, he would fall asleep on the sofa, afraid to leave me sitting up alone. Sitting in the dark, quiet room gave me a perfect time to talk to God and listen for Him to speak. I couldn't read because the drugs had affected my vision. I couldn't concentrate or keep my focus for very long anyway so I just sat, reminisced, prayed, and thought about the challenges a new day would bring.

It was as if I was on a new adventure. I had been on a journey through the valley of the shadow of death, but now the path that lay before me was of a different kind. It was a journey through the unknown – from sickness to recovery. It was a task of learning how to live in a body that felt like it wasn't mine. But it did belong to me and I felt trapped inside.

I was no longer sick in the sense of bearing infection, but my body was racked by the effects of the disease that had claimed my independence and left me totally dependent on others for "every" detail of my life.

I was already feeling the effects of the medication that was treating the inflammation in my lungs. I knew that the current dose was high and that the side effects would get worse before they got better. Over and over I sensed the tenseness and short temper and I had to be ever so careful not to give into those feelings. The last thing I would ever want to do was allow my tongue to offend those I loved. They had been so good to me. I needed them more now than ever before and they were working so hard to meet my every need.

I asked God to help me control my emotions. I am sure that there were times when the anxiety within me was evident, but I did my best to conceal the anguish and uncertainty of my physical and mental state. It was going to require a lot of patience to get through this part of my journey. I could tell that already.

It was 5:00 a.m. and I would start the day soon, but for this moment in time, I lay quietly next to Charles and watched him sleep. I felt safe and protected. Nineteen days before I was lying in this very same spot when he said I asked him to take me back to the hospital. So much had transpired. Charles had found himself having to make so many important decisions concerning my care while I was in the hospital; things such as signing his permission for my surgeries and biopsy, the administration of blood, or extensive blood tests. The one dreaded decision I still praise God that he did not have to make was to unplug the machines. His decisions were now going to be somewhat less complicated, but still important; like how to get my day started.

By the time Charles awakened, I had made plans for how we were going to handle my bath and how he was going to maneuver getting me in and out of the shower. I knew it was going to take a lot of effort and that it would require him to get in the shower with me. Not only would he have to hold me upright, but he would have to bathe me.

He carefully made sure that all my necessary clothing items were accessible as well as plenty of towels. He had a little different approach as to how we would handle the logistics of getting me in and out of the shower than I did, but when you are helpless you don't argue and I knew that his way would work just as well.

After padding the shower bench and the surrounding floor so neither of us would slip, we made our way inch by inch over the threshold of the shower door and finally I found a resting place on the shower-chair. I was exhausted by this time and out of breath so I was no further help to him. It was all I could do just to hold on to the chair and try to maintain my balance. My back ached from trying to hold my body and my head upright.

I will never forget the tenderness of his touch as he maneuvered around a five inch incision from the biopsy and two incisions where chest tubes had been. I had residual tape and bandages from IV lines on my neck, arms, and groin.

Seeing all this for the first time was a reality check for how grateful I was to be alive and home. Charles carefully monitored my every tilt or lean in fear that I would lose my balance and fall. He stood like a five-feet, seven-inch tower that guarded me from danger. At one point, he tenderly kissed the top of my wet head and told me how wonderful it was to have me home and how happy he was to be able to help me. He never complained. Instead, together we praised God that I was getting better. Even though I continuously apologized for causing him so much trouble, I know he wouldn't have had it any other way.

He encouraged me over and over again by saying, "One day it's going to get better babe and we are going to make it." I wanted to believe him, but something inside of me said, "How long?" I felt so extremely weak, frail, and dependent on him. I needed strength to walk through this barren land, let alone to climb the next mountain. I knew it would have to come from God above because "everything" was out of my control.

After a rest break, I insisted on brushing my own teeth. I had to sit in a chair and lean over the sink. Charles helped me raise my arms and place them on the counter so I could use both hands to hold the toothbrush, but I brushed them by myself, in slow motion. Everything I tried to do was so physically demanding and required so much effort. I realized how much I had always taken for granted; like the ability to jump out of bed and start a new day. I realized how ungrateful I had been for the little things in life, like being able to care for my simple, basic needs. Even though I had been a rehab nurse for sixteen years, I had failed to appreciate my abilities until I had disabilities.

I couldn't raise my arms above my head so Charles learned another new skill. It was blow drying my hair. He even got a lesson on how to use a curling iron (Sorry girls, you can't have him)! Those of you who know him will appreciate this fact and you will know that "hair-styling" is not exactly his cup of tea! He can coiffure a lawn, but grass is not quite the

173

same as hair! It wasn't the best looking "do" I had ever had, but it was better than the one I was left with after my "human carwash" experience in ICU.

We eventually managed to get me dressed. I don't think Charles had ever paid attention to all the necessary things women have to wear. To him, sweat pants and a shirt would have been just fine; and I mean just those two items! Though he was tolerant with my slow pace, I wasn't in a position to argue too much about his choice of what to wear. I was actually too weak to care so we kept my outfit for that day fairly simple. However, we did add a few more necessary items. After two hours, I finally made it to the recliner that was soon to be known as "my chair."

Charles doesn't know much about how to prepare a meal, but one thing he has always done is prepare our morning coffee. It's one of the few things he does know how to cook! We had decided to wait on breakfast that morning until we tackled the shower. I guess this was a pretty good idea since the shower turned out to be a two-hour long ordeal. I was exhausted and really needed some nutrition by the time he got me to the lounge chair…and a long nap!

I had to eat to take my medication so the next challenge was breakfast. As I said, he has never been one to favor cooking so this was going to be a step-by-step adventure. In my whisper voice I gave him instructions on how to prepare oatmeal. By the way, it was instant. I wasn't normally a breakfast eater so I already knew that oatmeal at 7:30 a.m. was going to be hard for me to swallow, but I had no idea how hard until he delivered my steaming bowl of… well let's just continue to call it oatmeal!

He listened well and I must say that he gave it his best try. Regardless of how difficult it was to swallow, I ate it anyway and I praised him for doing such a good job on his first attempt. I couldn't help but ask, "Oh Father God, how long before I am able to cook?"

The "substance" held a close resemblance to wall paper paste so at least I knew it would coat my stomach enough to protect it from the steroid I was taking. I figured this was the most important thing. After all, we were both learning new skills...for him it was cooking, for me it was being able to eat it!

Our biggest dilemma was trying to figure out ways to cope with my inabilities. We had to figure out ways to prop me up, ways to place things so I could reach them, how to position my plate so that I could feed myself, etc. As he tried so hard to meet my every need, He also tried to pretend that life was somewhat normal, though we both knew that it wasn't. He tried to ignore that I dropped things on the floor because I was too weak to hold on to them. He tried to act like he didn't see when I would spill my drink or dribble my food down the front of my clothing because I would miss my mouth. In his silence, I know he was trying to keep my spirits up. Sometimes when these things happened our eyes would meet and we would find ourselves laughing just to keep from crying. I was trying so hard to be independent and "normal."

Since I was unable to get up or move about on my own, my children had devised a plan to build a fortress around me with my walker in front and a table to the side which held all my paraphernalia. I had books, CD's, inhalers, medications, lip balm, the phone, and anything else they thought I might need and it was all right where I could see it. Except there was one problem, I couldn't raise my arms to reach for any of it. It's so funny how many things you learn you can live without when you can't get to them and when you don't want to keep asking for help!

By the second day I was learning how to simplify my life. Only the necessities mattered at this point. As a professional, I was used to wearing a suit almost every day with coordinating jewelry, shoes, handbag, etc. Now I wore sweats, no jewelry, I didn't need a handbag (I didn't even know where mine was) and I had simple hair that was in a different style every day, depending on who was caring for me. But I was so grateful that it was at least clean and brushed. The only make-up I managed to get on was a little mascara. My hands were so weak and shaky that this was evidenced by the little black dots that surrounded my eyelids. Charles didn't really understand the importance of wasting energy on mascara, but it made me feel better so he waited patiently as I attempted to apply it. It was doing something "normal" for me because I never left the house without my mascara. Charles had never minded my primping. In fact, we have a long standing joke about it. One Sunday morning, several years before, we were getting ready for church and I was applying my make-up. Charles kept watching me in the mirror and smiling. When I asked him what was so funny, he said, "Just keep going, you will eventually get there." I guess you could say he believes in the old saying, "If a barn needs painting, paint it!"

Instead of a full schedule with a long list of things to do for the day, as I was accustomed to, I now had one focus…ME! It took all the strength I had just to make sure that all the things that I needed to do for myself got done. Things like medications, inhalers, and exercises for my weak limbs.. I couldn't depend on my memory. I had to depend on whoever happened to be near me. Anything with lots of steps, even giving directions, would try my patience and overwhelm me. I had to focus on one thing at a time. Just thinking about a list of things to do, drained my energy. It was as if a portion of my brain was non-functioning!

The more important things, such as: scheduling doctor's appointments, therapy, Cat scans, MRI's, blood tests, and chest x-rays, were left in the hands of those who were caring for me. I couldn't deal with the decisions. I could barely follow directions.

A normal day, prior to illness, consisted of emails, mailings, phone calls to my unit and customers, planning and preparing for meetings, and doing coaching calls. That was in the morning. Then in the afternoon I held appointments or made new contacts. In the evening, I might have been out of town for an event or maybe even an overnight stay to work with consultants. My life was non-stop, until now. When God applied the breaks, He really "squealed" them!

My first doctor's appointment was scheduled on the fourth day after I returned home from the hospital. I started planning for that day two days in advance because I couldn't handle rushing or last minute stress. I knew Charles was going to need help getting me to my appointment. We had a list of names to call. There were so many friends and family members who wanted to help. Making that arrangement was easy to take care of. I knew we would need at least two hours to get me showered and dressed so I planned the time we would start. I would also need time for breakfast in order to take my meds.

Since everything I did was in slow motion, I knew I had to allow myself plenty of time. Little did I know that this would become a way of life for me. It was a life that was totally new and unexpected. It was a life of uncertainties and obstacles. It seemed that all I was able to accomplish in a day was to bathe, eat, and sleep, just like an infant.

After a few weeks of all this, I began to feel like my life lacked the fulfillment, motivation and will power I once had known. I was beginning to feel wasted and discarded. I knew that the results of high doses of steroids were already taking their toll on my emotions. I sought for wisdom and understanding from God. I was trying so hard to "be still" and wait on my body to heal.

I couldn't help but wonder how I was going to fulfill my promise to Him? How was I going to obey His call on my life to speak, share, and write? I had no voice, I had no energy, I couldn't write or put my thoughts on paper, even if my brain unscrambled long enough to allow me a sequence of thoughts. God was still using my circumstances to test my faith in Him to walk through this dry, barren land. I had to accept that the pruning process was not over. I was going to continue to seek

God and trust Him in all things, even though I didn't understand. I knew He had a purpose and that all things would be accomplished according to His perfect will.

Charles had always left the details of running the house to me. Things like: making sure bills were paid, bank deposits were made, checkbooks were balanced, grocery shopping, laundry, and even meal planning were not on his list of greatest accomplishments. How were we going to handle all of this? How were we going to pay the mounting medical bills when I was unable to work? How was Charles going to maintain his business, when he had to spend so much time caring for me? It was all so overwhelming, yet I knew that God would provide and that He would take care of us. We were going to take life one day at a time, take care of issues as they arose, and not worry about those that didn't. At least we would try!

My brain was still so clouded by all the drugs that sedated me, paralyzed me, and sustained my body's organs that I couldn't concentrate on an idea for more than a few minutes. Even in conversation I would lose my train of thought. If it was something that required analysis, such as bank statements, making appointments, or following up on medical bills, I had to let someone else handle it. I didn't trust my judgment and I began to suspect the possibility that I had suffered from something called anoxia (lack of oxygen to the brain) or maybe a mild stroke. I had difficulty with short-term memory and it was hard for me to focus. I had trouble with word finding as well. Normally, a way to aid in improving a memory problem would be to make notes, but my hands were too weak to hold a pen so that wasn't an option. I often busied myself by scribbling my name over and over again just trying to gain control of a pen. Still, my handwriting remained illegible.

The Prednisone had affected my eyesight so it was impossible for me to read and nearly impossible for me to watch television. Besides the problem with my vision, I couldn't remember what was happening in a program from one commercial to the next.

I needed to write so many thank you notes, but couldn't do that either. If I had been able to write, I would have been spending my day journaling my thoughts. My greatest fear continued to be that I would forget the details of my "Close Encounter" with God and if that happened there would be no book and no opportunity for me to use my experience to help others. God was continuing to build my faith in Him to accomplish what He had told me He would do through me. I was still learning to trust.

My voice was just a whisper. To carry on a conversation over the phone that was loud enough for the other person to hear strained my voice and caused me to be even more short of breath. So making phone calls wasn't an option either. This separated me from friends and family, especially long-distance ones.

I longed to read my Bible. I knew God had a message for me within its pages, but I couldn't read because of my vision and concentration so I settled for listening for His voice. He continued to say, "Be still and wait." Many times He spoke to me through others means; such as through those who came to visit me, music I listened to, or ministries on television.

My daughters-in-law, Suzanne and Sharon, made sure there was healthy, easily prepared food in the refrigerator and that all the laundry was done. Suzanne paid our bills and balanced our checkbook. Many friends and family brought meals and assisted with housekeeping. I was so grateful for all their help, but I felt so helpless. How would I ever repay them?

Charles had a list of people who lovingly gave of their time to come and be with me every day for the first four weeks so that he could work somewhat of a normal schedule. It was difficult for him to leave me, but one of us had to work and he needed a break from my constant care. He kept a calendar and a list of volunteers and he would call every evening to confirm their appointment to come sit with me the next day.

He was cautious to make sure no one came who was sick because of my decreased resistance and compromised immune system. I would listen to him giving explicit instructions to each one every morning about how I liked my juice by the chair, how and when I needed my medications, what time I would need lunch, and what I liked to eat. He carefully managed his work obligations around my sitters. We were going through a role reversal. I was the one who had always nursed the sick, but now he was learning the part very well.

At my three week appointment, my pulmonologist decided that I was in need of Home Health for some physical therapy. It was about a week later that I had my first visit. I loved seeing a new face because this gave me an opportunity to share my story with one more person, thereby answering God's call to share.

Though I had very little voice, I used it to witness to the therapists who came to care for me and any visitors I thought would benefit from hearing about my miracle encounter. I had never been much of a conversationalist, but now that I had something of eternal importance to share; I couldn't keep quiet. I would use my last breath to make sure I gave testimony to God's goodness to me.

I tried to encourage the friends and family who came to visit me. Sometimes they brought their own list of troubles and I would ask God to help me encourage them so they would leave feeling better after having been with me than when they came. I had no other outlet but to use the one God had given me and that was to bring Him honor by sharing His love, grace, and mercy from "my chair."

By the fifth week at home, after much coaxing, I convinced Charles that I was capable of spending a few hours alone during the day while he worked. It was good to have some time to be quiet and think, though I was so grateful for all those who offered to help me. I tried to be attentive to God's voice so that I wouldn't miss any instructions. I spent many hours napping to regain my strength and many in prayer to find it.

It was rare that I was ever alone for very long at the time because someone was always coming and going, like my therapists. I had people who called to check on me frequently and some who dropped by to check on me, as well. With lots of effort I could pull myself up from the chair and walk with the walker to the kitchen to briefly grab a sandwich or plate that Charles had prepared for me and I could make it to the bathroom by myself; thanks to an elevated commode chair. Finally, I felt like I was regaining some independence and it felt so good.

Whatever my doctors and therapists said to do I did it, plus some. If the therapist said to do five reps, I tried to do ten. If they said walk ten feet, I tried to walk twenty. I knew that I was no good to anyone like I was so all my efforts were devoted to getting better and stronger. It was so hard for me to put so much attention on myself. In fact, being self-absorbed was probably one of the hardest things I had to adjust to.

I have always been focused on others. My life, my business, my ministry was always about others. I was so used to my freedom and my ability to work, travel, be creative, and just be active. Now I was having to find ways to occupy my time while sitting in a chair thinking of myself and what I needed to do to get better.

I was battling emotions that I had never felt before. The effects of all the drugs were playing with my mind. Satan was using this as a stronghold and he was fighting me like never before. Nothing would have pleased him more than to bring about doubt and discouragement in my mind as he attempted to threaten my faith. Some days the battle was not one of anger, sadness, or depression, but more a lack of "any" emotion. If I had to explain how I felt inside, I think I would just call it "numb."

I now understand what it means in medicine when we describe a "flat affect." Mine was flat alright. Sometimes I wondered if I had forgotten how to laugh. It seemed that no amount of effort could muster up a smile. My face felt like it was frozen into a frown and the effects of the steroids were already causing it to swell making my skin taunt and my eyes puffy. I could tell I was retaining fluids and gaining weight and this was equally as disturbing.

One day I cheated myself out of a good laugh by looking in the mirror. It would have been a funny sight to see, but the person who looked back at me was a stranger and I didn't want to laugh at her; I wanted to cry with her. My lack of emotion didn't allow me to muster up a good cry anyway. I just stood with my walker, gazing in the mirror at someone who resembled me, but didn't feel like me. As I looked at who I had become in outward appearance, I began to wonder how much more of "me" I was going to lose. I had given God everything during our walk together in ICU, or had I? Was I willing to endure the changes in who I thought I was in order to become the person He wanted me to be, even if this included my outward appearance?

Yes, I was. I won't say that it was easy, but again I asked God to forgive me of my pride, to continue to humble me if that was what it was going to take to keep me close to Him, to walk with me through this dry, barren land, and to give me the grace to bear the pruning process that He continued to perform in my life. I had to let go of my pride, accept that the changes in my body would not be permanent, and keeping moving forward. I had to learn to laugh in order to learn to live.

Few people knew of these raging emotions. My husband has always said that I have a lot of people fooled. I didn't want to give in to doubt, despair, or defeat. I knew these were not my true feelings, but instead a mixture of circumstances and medications. I wasn't proud of how I was feeling (here goes my pride again), but I couldn't seem to help the way I was feeling. I thought if anyone saw how I was struggling, they would see it as a lack or faith or a sign of weakness. I didn't want to appear weak. I wanted everyone to see me as strong in faith and thankful to the Lord because I was and I still am. I wanted them to know that I gave Him praise for sustaining me and for bringing me to this point in my race, even if it was through a desert! I never felt closer to God than in my weakness. Even in the deepest pits of self-pity, He comforted me with the presence of His Holy Spirit. Over and over again, God reassured me that for this time in my life, He was all I needed.

I thought that by expressing my emotions, I would be indicating a lack of faith and that surely wasn't true. Nothing had grown or continued to grow more in my life than my faith in God and my relationship with Him. God had given me a promise to speak in "...a great congregation." I didn't know where it would be, but I wanted to be ready for the opportunity when it arose.

One day a very special friend reminded me that God's promise to speak "in a great congregation," might be one person at a time. What a revelation! I could do this, even if it was a brief phone call, a testimony to a nurse or therapist, or a card of appreciation. God could still use me to touch lives with His love, even from "my chair."

Charles was witness to every sleepless night, every frustrating, futile attempt to care for myself and every struggle to overcome the blows of Satan. He knew better than anyone, the effort it took for me to just get up and start a day. I could tell that he grasped for every little morsel of hope that would indicate I was improving. His hope was that I would return to the person I used to be. But where was she? I wanted so badly to find her, but I couldn't find her either.

For months on end, I spent many night after sleepless night in "my chair," alone in the dark. It was a time of solitude with God. Awake, but with eyes closed, I would recall frequently my encounter experience and I prayed and begged God not to let me forget the details before I was able to record them on paper. I didn't realize at the time that He was still creating my story. It didn't end when I was in ICU; that was actually just the beginning. Now I had a dry, barren land ahead of me… a time to continue to wait on God as He prepared me.

There were many nights I couldn't seem to pray. It was as if the words wouldn't come. I didn't know what to pray. All I wanted was for God's will to be done in my life and to complete His call. I was trying my best to understand. He had given me instructions…write a book and share the message I have given you. I could do neither. I couldn't even stand up by myself. I couldn't control my thoughts in a sequence long enough to tell a story, let alone have the voice to speak. What on earth was God doing here on earth that Heaven knew about, but I didn't? When I didn't know how to pray, I asked the Holy Spirit to pray for me in utterances and groaning God could interpret. I know He did.

There were times that God's love left indelible marks on my cheeks from the tears that flowed from my lack of understanding. He became very significant and real to me. My situation was in God's hands and this barren land was only my path to the Promised Land. I must keep trusting Him!

Sometimes when I didn't know how to pray, I would listen to CD's. There was one very special CD that I ended up wearing completely out. It was recorded by a family in our church and they are so dear and precious to me. There are several songs on this recording that really ministered to me, but one in particular that I played and rewound over and over again is called, "God Still Answers Prayer."

Though all I could do was tell God that I believed and trusted Him to fulfill His promises to me, it seemed enough and all He wanted at that time. In His still small voice I would hear Him whisper, "Karen, be still and know that I am God. Just keep waiting."

I knew that the Holy Spirit was praying and Christ was interceding on my behalf. I knew that no one knew my heart's desire more than God Himself so I made the decision to abide in Him. I had to free my mind of the feelings of urgency and just sit back and enjoy fellowship with Him because our time together was precious.

It was during those first few weeks at home that I began to realize that even in my weakness, I was strong because I was depending on God to meet all my needs. By faith, I trusted Him to be all that I needed when I didn't even know what I needed. When I felt like I had hit rock bottom, He was always the Rock at the bottom. I would hear Him say, "Hold on my child, joy comes in the morning."

Little by little, I began to regain my strength, but remained easily fatigued. Little by little, I became able to attend to most of my self-care activities which was a big boost to my morale. The last thing I wanted anyone to do was to feel sorry for me. After all, I had been witness to the awesome presence of God.

I sometimes sensed that people had difficulty knowing how to approach the subject of my inabilities, even my loss of voice. They would try to convince me that it was sounding stronger, but I knew it wasn't. Not significantly so anyway. On their face I could see that some of them were not at all convinced of this fact either. I think some stayed away because it was hard for them to see the person they had known before reduced to a state of dependence. One friend told me many months later that he had to turn his head to keep me from seeing his distress when he witnessed me coming to the door with my walker. If he had only realized, this was a big improvement. I was so happy that I could finally get to my feet and maneuver around the house a little on my own.

I saw my pulmonologist frequently at first because it was necessary to monitor the fibrosis that was occurring in my lungs. I continued to take large doses of steroids to minimize the damage to my lungs, but at last she was beginning to taper the dose. Yeah (I could write another book on the side effects of this drug)! I fought a constant battle with emotions. One day I would be up and the next day I would be down. It was a roller coaster ride I hope to never have to take again. I had never had a problem with weight gain, except when I was a child, but I soon found myself to be thirty-five pounds heavier. This didn't help my emotions either. I had developed a moon face, hump back, and rounded shoulders as a result of the Prednisone. I retained fluids making my feet and hands swell to the point that I could hardly wear my shoes and my clothes were all uncomfortable. Nothing fit anymore and clothing that constricted my breathing was definitely not tolerable! Most of the time, I felt like I was wearing a straight-jacket anyway because of the constriction of my lungs.

I was another person, a stranger. I didn't look like me, I didn't walk like me, I didn't talk like me and I didn't act like me. I tried my best not to let other people see the pain that I carried inside me. I tried to keep a positive attitude, though some days the pain would penetrate the mask and the facial expression told the story of the turmoil inside of me. Charles could always tell and God used him to encourage me with the same words he had said so many times, "Babe, it's going to get better. We're going to make it." Somewhere deep inside of me I knew that the person I once recognized as myself must still exist, only God was making her better.

I was in a battle to maintain my faith and I was determined that the devil was not going to destroy the work God had already done and was continuing to do in my life. It took shear determination to get out of bed every morning to do "nothing." I thought many times that the walls in our home were going to swallow me up and one day Charles would come home and find me gone. To cope, I tried to picture myself healthy and "normal" again. I just wanted one day every now and then to say, "I feel good."

At times, I felt disoriented and I would lose track of time. I also felt disorganized and unable to pull things together. My weakness and shortness of breath continued to threaten my independence, my motivation, and my self-determination. If I pushed beyond my limits, I would fall prey to difficulty breathing and a physical fatigue that was debilitating.

I was amazed at how God removed things from my list of priorities. It was necessary because my priorities were based around my abilities. I had so little energy that only the things that had real value were pursued. I tried to set goals, but they were only a way to the means…getting better.

Most of the time, I felt as if I were in my own little secluded world, outside of which people were oblivious of my situation. I watched from my chair as my neighbors had their morning walk. I even envied the garbage man who was able to jump off of his truck and run from house to house. I knew I was lonely when I watched for the mailman so I could wave hello. The thought of being able to jump in my car and go for a ride seemed like bliss to me. Occasionally someone would call, but few came. Still I leaned on the Lord in my solitude.

One beautiful, sunny day in late March, my husband suggested that I go with him while he did a small yard. It was quite a chore to get me into his big truck, but it was exciting to be outdoors. I never left the truck that day, but to be a part of the outside world was wonderful. I noticed things about God's creation that I had never really taken the time to enjoy. Things like: the sunshine on my arm as it rested on the window, the spring flowers beginning to show their colors, the people taking their morning walks, and the yards that were beginning to show green. There were children at play at the daycare playground enjoying the warmth of the sun and the birds were chirping loudly as if saying to me, "Welcome to the outdoors."

Something else I realized that day was how swiftly the cars were racing by. It was as if the drivers were all in a hurry to reach an appointment. They all seemed to be so focused on getting to their destination that it was impossible to make eye contact with them as we passed by each other. Many were on their cell phones, some were sipping coffee, and even a few were applying make-up.

Suddenly, I realized the fast pace everyone seemed to be moving compared to how slow my life had been. I realized that I used to be just like those people; running from place to place with my mind fixed on what I needed to do next, instead of on what was going on around me. It was easy to see that these people were just like I used to be; always in a hurry and running on a treadmill going nowhere.

God began to impress on my heart to pray for each person in the cars we passed that day. I asked Him to give me a heart of love for mankind and a passion to reach those who were searching for fulfillment, purpose, and direction in their lives. I asked Him to give me opportunities to show them that our life's purpose can only be found in pursuing God's purpose and that success is not measured by financial gain. In God's eyes success is finishing our race by faith. We are to be looking for our reward in Heaven, not here on earth. Success is knowing and having a relationship with God. That day I started to appreciate how He had slowed me down, even though it was nearly to a stop. It was necessary for Him to slow me down in order to turn me around, redirect my path, and set my feet on His direction for my life.

I knew first hand how it felt to be on the receiving end of God's "personal development" program. I still had a front row seat in His classroom. He obviously wasn't ready to promote me to the next level because He was continuously teaching me things about Himself and about me. Though my heart's desire was to serve and love others, before I could help them, I still needed help myself.

The people I saw that day weren't aware of me or my situation, but I couldn't help but ask God to continue to humble me and make me more attentive to those who are suffering, estranged, or lonely because I now was one of those people and I could relate. Where would I have been without His presence in my life? I had so many needs, yet He was all I really needed. God's lesson on this particular day was on humility.

If I was going to serve others, I had to know how it felt to walk in their shoes. Humbled and grateful to Him for allowing me to learn of His attributes, I knew what it felt like to lose health, lose self-worth, and lose freedom. God, in His mercy, was still working on me. As He comforted me, He was teaching me how to comfort others (I Corinthians 1:3).

At my three month appointment, I was given some very disturbing news. As my doctor explained the results of a recent CT scan, I was excited to hear that it seemed the process of fibrosis was becoming more stable. That was a good sign. But my next question to her was, "When will I get my voice back?"

As she turned to look me in the eye, I could tell that her response was not going to be what I wanted to hear. She said, "Karen, I know how much you love to sing, but you also know that the ventilator that damaged your vocal cord also saved your life." "Okay," I said, "So what does this mean?" She said, "I am afraid that since it has been three months and your voice has not improved, the damage may be permanent." I thought to myself, how can you make such a remark so flippantly? This means my whole life's purpose will change.

My heart began to race, my face flushed, and tears welled up in my eyes as I said, "Well, Moses had a problem with his speech but God still used him, so I guess as long as I have a microphone, He can still use me." I said it and I wanted to believe it. I had to believe it! Again my faith was being put to the test.

On went my mask as I tried to hide the pain in my heart. Was I exercising my faith or just trying to convince myself? I knew God had spared my life and He had given me promises of being able to share the story of my encounter with Him. Most of all, He had given me such a burden to help others grow in their personal, intimate relationship with Him. I was so anxious to "get about my Heavenly Father's business." But realistically, how was He going to use me to share a story if He didn't give me back my voice? How was I going to sing, as David did in the Psalms, if all I could do was whisper?

I was confused, shocked, and disheartened. A better word would probably be devastated! I didn't have to say anything to Charles for he knew my heart was broken. Another piece of me had been taken away. Without my voice, I felt useless in the Potter's hand. Without my voice to speak or sing and my hands to play the piano, there wasn't much left of me. Oh how I needed a touch from God at that moment!

I had kept such faith that my voice would return. In fact, I had never allowed myself to think otherwise. Now I wondered if anything about me would ever be "normal" again.

I had dreamed of standing in church, singing my heart out in praise and ministry. Even while I was in a coma, I had passed the hours thinking about the day that I would be able to tell others what God had done for me. I had tolerated the whisper of a voice for almost four months. I thought it was going to be a fleeting thing, but now I had been told that this might be as good as it gets! I must admit, I was angry, not with God, but with the illness that had now claimed another part of me and a very important part for sure (Forgive me, Lord, for my intermittent lack of faith)!

It had been one thing to lose part of my lungs, but my voice! What good would I possibly be in God's service without a voice? Why would God work a miracle, allow me to live, give me specific instructions concerning what He wanted me to do with the rest of my life, and then not give me a voice? This just didn't make sense. I was numb and oblivious to my surroundings as my husband made my next appointment and we turned to exit the door. As we walked to the car I fell apart. I was broken and wounded, but thank God, not destroyed!

I will never forget what happened next. We sat in the car a moment holding hands, but both quiet. I knew Charles was praying for me and I was praying for myself that God would give me the reassurance that He was still in control. I needed His strength to accept this new information and to know, that even in my weakness, I am still strong in Him. I needed Him to build my faith in the process of building my strength because I knew that He would work all things for my good. I trusted in Him and wanted more than anything in the world to do His will. I wanted to believe that He could use me, no matter what disabilities I might have.

No one knew me better than my husband. Though he would never consider speaking in front of a large group of people, he admired my willingness to do so and he was so proud of my personal and spiritual growth that gave me the confidence to do such things. He shared my passion and supported my belief in God's commandment to serve Him as I had been instructed. We were connected in spirit and he shared my pain. He knew my desire, he knew how much I loved to sing, and he enjoyed hearing me. He tried to console me, but this pain was almost unbearable. All I could say was, "Hubby, pray for me."

When he switched on the ignition, God spoke. Guess what was playing? Soothing my broken heart were the words to the song I had listened to so many times in the last three months. You can choose to believe it or not, but I know it was all in God's plan and it was His immediate answer to my prayer. He might as well have been sitting in the backseat singing the song Himself because the words came to me as though straight from His lips. He gave me His promise, "God Still Answers Prayer."

No, I would not give up and I would not give in. I served a God who had proven the doctors wrong one time and He could do it again. I didn't know His timing and I didn't understand His purpose, but I trusted Him to work even this for my good and His glory. He gave me peace.

I was sent to a specialist who found with videography that I had damage to one side of my vocal cord. It was sluggish and "dinged" due to the endotracheal tube that had been inserted down my throat while I was on life support. It wasn't anybody's fault that it had happened. I was just fortunate to be one of the few people who suffer damage to their vocal cords from intubation.

A speech therapist confirmed that the damage may very well be permanent, but she did give me hope that there could be a possibility of improvement for up to a year post injury. I could wait, though a year was still eight months away. God was still teaching me the very valuable lesson of learning to wait on Him. He would be with me and I would go on believing. I wasn't going to sweat the small stuff. I had physical strength and lung function that needed to be restored before I would need my voice anyway.

To tell you the truth, I was beginning to feel like "my warranty had run out" (To quote my brother-in-law, Remer). It seemed like every time I turned around another CT scan was ordered, another chest x-ray had to be done, or another lab had to be drawn. I had always been so healthy and active. Now it seemed a different part of me was falling apart on a continuous downhill spiral. I was ready to hear some good news. I wondered how long this walk in a dry, barren land was going to take. I was trying to learn my lessons well by staying in contact with God. I listened for any word of direction, but instead of direction He just told me to "Keep walking."

So that was exactly what I did. I walked through each day as if it were a normal routine, even though it wasn't. I tried to use every opportunity to share what God had done and was doing in my life, whether it was in therapy, a doctor's office, or a hospital waiting room. I survived the heat of the desert by keeping my eyes fixed on my Lord and His promises. He was the One who would help me keep walking and whenever He felt I was ready, together we would head towards the mountaintop. He was the One who would give me water when I was thirsty and shade when I needed to rest.

Obviously, there were lessons that He still needed to teach me and since I wasn't prepared or strong enough to start climbing yet, I kept walking. I didn't know the destination or the provision, I just had to follow. One day I would see His purpose in my suffering. In the Psalms I read that in my afflictions I would learn His statutes and in Jeremiah that I was chosen in the "furnace of affliction." He was still refining me and I would keep waiting.

In March of 2006, I began Outpatient Cardio-Pulmonary Rehabilitation. It was a divine appointment for several reasons. One reason was my nurse. Immediately we connected on a spiritual level as sisters in Christ. We shared similar circumstances in our lives where God had allowed us to witness His power and healing as well as His pruning process. We were both writing a book, though she was much farther along than me. At that point, mine was just pages of notes and accumulated thoughts. God used her as an instrument of instruction and she was a lot of help in getting me on the right track.

She was also a great rehab nurse. Trudy helped me to accept that my life was going to be different, but that it was not over. Part of my recovery involved a change in lifestyle. During the course of my therapy, I came to see myself as she saw me - a respiratory patient with a need to adjust my activity to accommodate a decreased lung capacity that limited my stamina and endurance. I learned how to breathe and how to push myself only as far as my lungs would support me. It was the beginning of a realization that my condition might very well be a "disability." That doesn't mean that I gave up hope for improvement. It means I accepted whatever it was that God intended for my life, as long as He allowed me to bring honor and glory to Him. This was a landmark in my recovery and a necessary step on my journey through a barren land. I was struggling to become the best I could "physically and spiritually" be.

Trudy encouraged me to start journaling and since I could now use a pen and a computer, I thought this was as good a time as any to start putting my thoughts on paper in a more organized fashion. In my heart, I felt that my story was not over as God continued to open my eyes and show me how He was working on my behalf.

I would like to share with you some of my earliest entries in my journal so you can get a better picture of my humanness and transparency. As I pour out my heart to God, you will see that my heart's desire was to grow in my relationship with

Him and this occurred because I sought Him. He came to me and He answered my prayer to know Him more. I was beginning to understand that life is not about a destination. We will never arrive until we enter glory. It is instead, a journey, one that will lead us through all kinds of learning experiences. It is our response to these experiences that molds us into the "image of God."

Excerpts from my Journal
April 15, 2006:

Today is a beautiful, sunny spring day. While sitting on my back porch sipping my morning coffee, my eyes are drawn to the wonders of nature. The grass is beginning to turn green, the trees are budding, and a few volunteer flowers are beginning to place some color on the canvas of our yard. I watch as the squirrels play and jump from the tall pines. I listen to the birds chirping as they flee from branch to branch running from our barking dog, Abbey.

I begin to marvel at the process of God's re-creation. It's something I have never taken much time to enjoy before. I realize now how much I have missed. The sky is so blue and the cool breeze is refreshing. Why have I not taken the time to be alone with God in this beautiful setting? Why have I taken for granted His gift of beauty? He created all of this for my enjoyment and I have allowed the "busy-ness" of life to distract me.

I see my life in much the same way. This spring is a re-creation for me as well. The old me has been withered and barren for so long, yet each day brings a little improvement. I am like the tiny bulb that is trying to push its way through the dry, hard ground. For many months, I have felt buried, yet protected from the cold of winter. Like the bud, I have received nutrients from the soil and sunlight from above. All this has been preparation for my time to bloom. Eventually, if I remain patient, my leaves will start to unfold and push their way upward and out into the world. Day after day as the "Son" shines on me, I will grow and reach heavenward. For everything there is a season and I believe that this is my season for rebirth.

Springtime is a season of not only rebirth, but of resurrection. Is it not a wonder that God chose to resurrect His Son during this time of year? Now He is bringing me back to life. This season I will produce a much better harvest because of my pruning. His shears have cut deep into my soul as He discarded the branches that were dead and barren. With His love, He has nurtured me. With skill, He has grafted me so securely into the vine that my connection will never weaken. With the water of life, He has nourished me. He propped me up so that my leaves would point towards heaven and not fall to earth to wither and die. The soil he prepared by ministering to me of His truth and grace and now that nourishment has become a longing in my heart to serve Him in His purpose, not my own. My life is a much slower pace. In many ways it has remained dormant. I know that it takes time to grow strong. It also takes exposure. Thank you Heavenly Father, for exposing me to your love, your mercy, and your grace. It is my prayer that you will use my life to produce abundant fruit for Your kingdom; that You, and You alone, may be glorified. Renew a right spirit in me and grow me deeper and deeper into the vine, which is my Lord Jesus. I love You, Lord.

It was near the end of my six weeks of therapy that I had gained enough confidence and strength to drive. I had now been home from the hospital for six months. I felt like a teenager who just got her license. It was a short trip to therapy, but I was driving alone, finally! It was great not having to depend on someone else, let alone feeling like such a bother. I was finally getting somewhere. On a good day, I would stop for a quick errand.

One thing that continued to plague me was the chronic fatigue. It was associated with activity, which was also associated with shortness of breath. It took so little to exhaust me and I don't mean just being a little tired. I mean fatigue that made my legs quiver, my head swim, and my heart race. It was an overwhelming weakness that kept me close to home in fear of getting too fatigued to drive back.

I also had extreme muscle weakness and stiffness in the mornings or after sitting in one position for a while. This made it difficult to walk and affected my balance. If I laid in one position too long during the night, I could hardly roll over. Most mornings, I awakened feeling more tired than when I had gone to bed. I found myself either unable to get to sleep or awakening many times during the night.

I had mentioned this several times to my doctor. In response, she decided to check my oxygen saturations during sleep to see if my lungs were adequately oxygenating

I wore a monitor that night which was picked up the next morning. By the end of that day, I had received a phone call for delivery of oxygen to my home. I was told that while sleeping, my oxygen saturation had dropped into the low eighties (Normal is around ninety-six). Saturations this low mean that the body is not receiving enough oxygen, which can create restlessness and fatigue. I thought to myself, this is crazy! I am supposed to be getting better. Now I am going to be attached to an oxygen tank! When the monstrosity arrived, I hardly said a word. I think I was still in shock. When the deliverer asked where to place it, I pointed to a corner of my bedroom where I supposed it would be appropriate to leave this thing for a few days. I paid very little attention to his instructions because I kept saying to myself, "This is not going to be for long!"

April 19, 2006

My prayer today is that You continue to keep me grateful for where I am in my recovery. Please don't let me lose hope, for tests have now revealed a need for oxygen. Is this a setback or is this a sign that You continue to work Your healing power on my lungs? I pray, dear Father, that You will help me to accept this new change and that You will continue to use my illness as a means of bringing glory to You.

Sitting here in the darkness of night I promise that no matter how this earthly body feels, I will continue to praise You for the opportunities You give me each day to share my story. It's not about me, but rather about You. Let my light shine that others might see You, I pray.

During this process Lord, there have been days that I have fallen prey to discouragement. I pray that You will keep me from these thoughts by keeping my eyes fixed on You.

Help me to trust You for finances. Help me to walk in faith and belief that You are in control. In my weakness, there is so little I can do. Busy my hands with things that bring glory to You. Busy my mind with words of comfort and reassurance that I am going to come through this dry barren land. Busy my heart with a passion to be all that You want me to be. I love You, Lord.

April 21, 2006

I found some more promises in Your word today, Lord. Psalm 26:11, "...but as for me, I will walk in mine integrity: redeem me, and be merciful unto me. My foot standeth in an even place: in the congregations will I bless the Lord."

Psalm 35:18, "I will praise thee among much people."

Psalm 30:5, "...weeping may endure for a night, but joy cometh in the morning."

I am passionately seeking You. I long to be continually in Your presence. I never want to forget my encounter with You and our walk together. Keep me close Lord, as I learn of You. For years I missed out on a relationship with You because I didn't open Your love letter enough. I didn't take the time to enjoy Your gifts of breath and life, and I spent too little time telling others about You because I needed to know more of You myself. Forgive me Lord, and continue to work Your miracles in my life. I love You, my Lord.

May 1, 2006

I had a restless night last night for various reasons; like the constant click, click of the oxygen machine, the coolness of the night, and our dog Abbey who insists on cuddling up next to me. Most of all, it was my thoughts concerning this seemingly unending desert experience. Sometimes I feel as if I have fallen into a deep hole. The outside world seems to keep moving, only my world has stopped.

Why do I wrestle with thoughts of tomorrow when I know that God is with me and I know He has His reasons? Some things are not meant for me to understand. Sometimes I wonder why He has given me a mind to think, when I would be more useful to Him as a robot that He could program to do His will. I know it's because He lovingly gives me choices so that I will choose to follow Him.

Lord, I do choose to follow You. I thank You for giving me a mind to think and choose "Your" way. Having so much time on my hands to think has helped me to realize what is most important in life...it is my relationship with You. You have removed from my life the things that I thought were necessary in order to show me that You are my only necessity.

Every day I long to hear Your voice saying, "Okay Karen, your preparation is complete. Now go do what I have told you to do!" Sometimes I listen for Your voice so intently, only to be met with silence. Why do I feel embarrassed by silence and feel I need to fill in the void? For when I am silent, You speak.

It has been months since my illness. I see little improvement. In fact, there are times when it seems I grow weaker and more short of breath since I am no longer taking the Prednisone. It would be easy to give in to feelings of loneliness, uselessness, or depression, but I have thus far and will continue to trust You, my Heavenly Father, for grace to bear whatever it takes to bring me to Your place of usefulness. In my desert, You are preparing me, perfecting me, teaching me, and refining me. I know You are there, even though You are silent. It is my longing to hear Your voice that keeps me continually seeking You. As I sit in my chair, there is such peace. It has become my place of worship, praise, and communing with You.

I mailed a letter to Women of Faith today. I don't really know why. I guess because it was at one of their conferences that God placed a burden on my heart to help people who are hurting or who just need a word of encouragement and hope. I don't know why God chose me. I am not a speaker. I am very critical of myself and I battle with maintaining my self-esteem. I am not a theologian or great teacher and there is so much of God's word that I yearn to know more about myself. God didn't need my excuses; He just wanted my humble heart.

Lord, keep me humble and grateful to You for all things. Having to endure the uncertainty and inconsistency has removed any pride that may have remained since my "Close Encounter" with You. I will never forget my promise to You. From my bed in ICU, I told You that if You chose to leave me here on earth, I would live the rest of my life serving You, even if that meant in a full-time capacity. You told me to use my story to help others grow in their own relationship with You. This is my desire.

I don't know when my race will end. I pray for strength to endure it, belief to conquer it, and power to overcome anything that threatens to throw me off course.

I am Yours, Lord. Do with my life as you please. Just make sure that whatever I do brings You honor and glory. Hide me behind Your cross. I am Your servant.

Forgive me for being impatient at times. Forgive me for being weary. Forgive me when I am low in spirits. I know that You will raise me up at the appropriate time. Though Satan may tempt me with discouragement, fight that battle for me and give me the courage to continue in Your name. I am so grateful to You for loving me enough to draw me closer to You. I love You, Lord.

May 6, 2006

I saw my pulmonologist today and got some good news. The condition of my lungs is stable. She remains concerned about the shortness of breath and feels that the damage to my vocal cord may be contributing. Otherwise, I still work on regaining my strength.

I read some great information today in a book about Moses. God revealed to me that I am here in this desert: *First* - by His appointment, *Secondly* - in His keeping, *Thirdly* - under His training, and *Fourthly* - for His time. Moses was a servant of God who didn't feel capable of answering God's call, but he obeyed anyway. God had said, "Answer my call and I will use you." His response was, "Here I am Lord, send me…use me." Like Moses, I want God to use me too.

Yesterday, I could sense emotions that were coming straight from Satan himself. Things like: fear of my loss of control, loss of usefulness, loss of gifts, and feeling that God had forgotten me and left me behind because I was too much work. I also felt I was losing precious time and opportunities.

I felt pangs of guilt over not being able to add to our income and the mounting medical bills that my illness had created.

Today God has shown me that He is perfecting these things in me for my good and His eternal use. He has a purpose for not taking them away.

Psalm 17:8 says, "Hide me under the shadow of Thy wings." This is where I want to be, Lord. I want to be under your wings as you lift me to great heights and allow me to soar above my emotions, my trials, and my disabilities. Though I do not know how long this dry, barren desert experience will last, I know that You will protect me, guide me, and provide for me during my journey.

Today I needed to hear from You, and You weakened my body to keep me in Your space and unable to attend therapy. Tomorrow will be another day. I will go on, my past I will leave behind me. I accept Your mercy and Your grace as I wait for my burning bush. You have my availability. You have slowed me down long enough to seek Your face. You have removed from my life things that were obstructing my view of Your plan. I am unworthy of your love, but I accept it and embrace it, as I seek to do Your will.

I know You have a plan and I accept my part as Your instrument to carry out that plan. Help me to have ears to hear, hands to work, feet to move, and a heart to respond to You. It's not my reputation at stake here, it's Yours. My life is not about me, it is about what You can do through me. You work the miracles as I burn with passion to serve You.

I realize that it is okay if I don't have all the answers, perfection, abilities, courage, or details. All I need is You. I love you, Lord. Forgive me for growing weary of waiting to see progress in my life. I need for You to either do something that will bring a breakthrough in my circumstances or give me a fresh anointing to wait. I trust You, Lord, to answer my prayer and I want You to know that whatever Your answer may be, I love You. I accept Your will always. In Jeremiah 30:17 you tell me, "For I will restore health to you and heal you of your wounds, says the Lord." In Hebrews 10:23 Your word says, "He who promised is reliable and faithful to His word." I believe Your word.

May 9, 2006

I will not retreat from battle. I will not look for shortcuts. I will believe in You! My circumstances create my dependence on You. My dependence on You creates patience as I wait to hear from You. My patience creates wisdom as I learn Your ways. James 1:2-5 tells me, "When all kinds of trials crowd your lives, my brothers, don't resist them as intruders, but welcome them as friends. Realize that they come to test your faith and to produce in you the quality of endurance."

Yes Lord, the endurance that I will need to finish my race. Thank you, Lord, for your reassurance. I love You, Lord.

Today I wrote the poem, "Faith to Finish." One day I will include it in my book.

Today is the two year anniversary of my daddy's transition to Heaven. I miss him so much, but I rest in peace knowing that he is in Heaven waiting for all of us to join him.

I wonder if he stood at the gates of Heaven watching what was going on with me when I was near death. I wonder if he was continuously asking God, "Is she coming yet, is she coming yet?" I could picture him doing just that!

Daddy, I hope you are as anxious to see me as I am to see you. But until the day I am with you again, God is taking care of me and evidently He is not finished with me yet. I don't know if you can hear me, but I know Jesus can. So Jesus, will you tell Daddy how much I love him today and how much I miss him?

May 13, 2006

I am sitting on my back porch having my quiet time. I am continuing to read from the book about Moses. I realize why God placed this book in my hands at this important time in my journey. His timing is always perfect.

Here is how I relate: God led me out of Egypt, a land of haste, prosperity, possibility, and provision and placed me in the desert so that I could hear His voice and so He could lead me into a land of promise. I just pray that it doesn't take me forty years to learn my lessons, as it did the Israelites! "Teach me Lord."

I have been looking for my burning bush, but now I realize that it surrounded me and my bed in ICU. It was during my tenth day on life support that the Holy Spirit gave me my orders to speak and write. It was during this time that He asked me for my complete surrender to do His will. In His presence, I stood on "holy ground," just like Moses.

It was at this time that He surrounded me with peace and protection. By then, I had become a precious commodity. God had invested a lot of time and work in me and I knew that He would make sure to lead me out of the valley. I had not been so sure until He said, "This is what I want you to do." How could I have felt anything but peace? When God's presence, in the form of His Holy Spirit filled my room, when His voice spoke soft, but sure, when He comforted me through the valley, His love was confirmed in my heart and I knew that Satan himself could not touch me.

God knew that it would take a burning bush experience to get me to see Him for who He is. It wasn't that I was ignoring Him, by any means. I was just blinded by other things. I was working so hard to "make things happen" that I wasn't taking the time to see "what was happening."

As I write these words today, I feel that God is about to reveal to me an unknown territory. It may or may not be my promised land and it may or may not be filled with giants. Either way, I will follow Him all the way. I love You, Lord.

I decided today to write a poem for those who had cared for me over the past months. I will send it as my note of thanks.

God's Servant's
by Karen Faith McGowan

Words cannot express my true appreciation
For your kindness and acts of self-less dedication.
You gave of your time, your love and your devotion,
Some of you even rubbed my feet with lotion.

Quiet conversations about life and health
The insight you gave to me goes far beyond wealth.
For you see, it was during my journey that God really
spoke to me
And gave to me my purpose for all eternity.

You are a special part of the plan God has for me.
You gave me insight, support, and encouragement,
And by my side I know you will always be.

God provides special people in our lives to help us along
when we get stuck.
You are that special person, for when I am down you raise
me up.

When I stand upon the mountaintop overlooking my past,
I will see your face in my mind's eye
And remember that our friendship will always last.

Though you thought you were serving me and indeed
you were,
You were also serving our Lord and Master,
And this should give your heart a stir.
For God used you as a vessel that you poured out on me,
And I am so very grateful that God's servant you will
always be.
You are my friend, my brother and sister in Christ,

May 14, 2006

Today is Mother's Day. I find myself with mixed emotions. I am having difficulty breathing today, probably some from emotions and some from the heat, but in my heart, I cannot help but be grateful for life.

Today my husband's sister Harriet is hanging in the balance between life and death. Her bout with cancer, which began only a few months ago, is about to claim her life. She was stricken suddenly with pain and hemorrhage just four weeks after I came home from the hospital. Now I am getting better, and she is about to die. Why does God work the way that He does? I know that's not for me to question.

I have only fond memories of Harriet. Her gentle, quiet spirit, her love of crystal, her ability to cook, and most of all the way she and her husband Ernest have always stood by their children through thick and thin. Their love between man and wife has always been an example for Charles and I to follow. I never heard a harsh word or word of criticism, but always total support.

Not only have they supported their own children, but they have always been there to support the rest of the family as well. They were always at wedding, funerals, and visiting the sick.

Harriet is already in a coma, but so was I. I knew that she could hear me so I told her how much I loved her. I am sure that she is talking with God at this very moment as He prepares her for her transition from life to eternity. I know of the peace in the valley and I pray that she has found that peace already. It is a peace that only God can give.

Please be with her Lord and be with me. Help me to have the strength to be an encourager for my husband's family. They have always been there to support and encourage me.

May 15, 2006

We were awakened by a phone call at 12:20 this morning. Harriet is now with her Lord. My mind races back to the familiar faces that stood at the foot of my bed in the early morning on my first day off of the ventilator. Harriet and Ernest had driven for two hours to come visit me and because I was then off of the ventilator, they were allowed to enter the ICU, even though it was not during a visiting hour. For the first time in three weeks I was able to talk to them. I remember telling them how special they were to me and how much I had always admired them. I am so glad I took advantage of the opportunity to let her know how special she was in my eyes.

The Lord giveth and the Lord taketh away. God's plan for Harriett's life and my life were obviously different. Why God chooses to take some and leave some behind is a mystery to our finite minds. If for no other reason, God was ready to have her in Heaven with Him. As for me, He still has work for me to do. There are tasks that must be completed before my race is finished.

Lord, help me be strong for my husband and his family. I will need Your strength to get through the coming days and the trips out of town. With you I can do all things. I must!

May 17, 2006

As I sat in the chapel today listening to the eulogy for Harriet, I couldn't help but wonder what my service would have been like. I wasn't trying to be selfish, just curious of what things people would find important to say about me.

I had always told my husband that when I died I wanted him to "place me and my sewing machine in my piano and then bury me." At that time in my life, that pretty much told the story of who I was.

But truthfully, the only real thing that has ever mattered to me was that God would use my life to make a difference for eternity. I wondered if that was what others had seen. I wondered if they had seen His light in my life and if that light had been a beacon of hope and encouragement to them. I hoped that through my music, God had ministered peace and joy to hearts and that through the words of the songs I had sung over the years, He had touched wounded warriors and drawn people closer to Himself.

If this had been my service, I wouldn't have had a long list of titles, accomplishments, or successes. Those things never mattered to me anyway. My greatest honor would be to have my children say that I had been a blessing in their lives and hopefully, that they were proud to call me, "Mother."

I would have wanted mine to be a joyous occasion, filled with lots of music such as; "It Is Well With My Soul," "Amazing Grace," or "How Great Thou Art." Oh, and I would have wanted them to play the recording I made for my family for Christmas in 2005, especially the song, "I Bowed On My Knees and Cried Holy."

I would have wanted my friends and family to tell about fond memories and even laughter from great times we had shared together. I would have wanted the minister to share the salvation message, but after that, I would have liked my friends and family to speak openly about how God had touched their lives through me so that God received all the recognition. I would have wanted their words to help others see that the life we live speaks so much louder than the words we say. I hope this is the testimony I would have left behind. I would not have wanted anyone to be sad for me. Instead, I would have wanted everyone to be excited about meeting me in Heaven. I would have wanted my poem, "Faith to Finish" to be read so that everyone could praise God that He had allowed me to walk by faith to my finish line.

Because my life now had a different meaning, I thought about those whose lives would be changed because of hearing or reading my story about a "Close Encounter" with God. Would it have caused them to want to seek Him as a personal Savior, a Friend, and Guide? I wondered how many would accept His gift of love. This would be my greatest eulogy. It is my reason for living and it will be my reward in Heaven. What a celebration that will be!

It's ironic how God has moved my focus from preoccupation with sickness to "How can my situation help others?" As my health has improved somewhat, I have realized that there is a much larger purpose for my suffering and that it extends beyond my immediate circle of friends and family. There is a world that needs to hear a message of healing and restoration, both physically and spiritually. God in His mercy had allowed me to be sick in order to help others heal.

Thank you, Lord, for removing my desire for selfish recognition and for giving me a desire to bring "You" recognition. I searched a lifetime for a reason for my existence and You allowed me to find my purpose, which is "Your" purpose. You have performed a plan that was set in motion before I was ever born...before my parents ever named me, "Faith." My middle name has become a part of me that is bigger than my life itself. It is the part of me that permanently connects me with You. I love you, Lord.

Harriet's race is over, but her memory will linger in our hearts forever. God bless you, my sister. This is not my good-bye it is my farewell, until I see you again in Heaven.

I know You will take care of her Lord, she is precious.

May 20, 2006

When I think I have been through all I need to go through, it is time for me to think again. When I think I have arrived, I have only just begun.

This is God's lesson for me today (I Corinthians 10:6).

Reasons I can see God is allowing me to wander in a dry barren land:

To test me
To humble me

208

To learn what is in my heart
To learn what is most important to me
To spend time with me
To know if I am willing to keep His commandments
To stretch my belief
To develop my faith
To plant my feet on solid ground

The events I can expect in the desert are:

Abundance – God will supply all my needs – even in the desert (I look up)
His Promises – He has promised, we can expect Him to answer (I look ahead)
Disappointment – To strengthen my faith in His deliverance (I look down)
Letting Go – In my humanity I will be tempted to look back (I look forward)
Provision – Trusting God to give me what I need, when I need it, and in just the right amount (I look around)

My promise from God today: Exodus 15:26, "And He said, if you will give earnest heed to the voice of the Lord your God, and do what is right in His sight, and give ear to His commandments, and keep all His statues, I will put none of the diseases on you which I have put on the Egyptians; for I, the Lord, am your healer." Praise God! Yes, You are My Healer.

If we would just take heed to His promises, God will provide for us, guide us, lead us, and protect us as well as "heal" us. Oh, we of little faith (including me sometimes), that we should perish because of our unbelief!

Thank You, Lord, for teaching me today about what to expect in the desert. Now I will know what to look for.

June 14, 2006 – A Letter to My Children

Today is my fifty-third birthday. Life truly is a vapor, as the scriptures say. I have been so blessed in my lifetime. My focus today is not on me; it is instead, on my children, Paul and Nathan, because I am so blessed to have another birthday to celebrate with them. If there was such a day as "Children's Day," I guess this would be it. But since that occasion does not exist (at least not that I am aware of), I will just make this my special day to remember the two of you.

First of all, I want you to know how much I love you both and how proud I am of you and the wonderful men you have become; despite my failures and shortcomings as your mother. God is such a loving God and He takes up where we leave off. We do the best with the knowledge we have, but He makes up for what we don't have.

I feel that my life has been so blessed at every stage of your growth, from birth to adulthood. It's me who celebrates the joy of being "your Mom." I am so grateful to God for allowing me the privilege of bearing this title.

Forgive me for the times I was impatient, for the times I raised my voice, and the times I spoke instead of listening. Forgive me for not always having my priorities in check: like taking more walks in the park, more bikes rides, more pitching ball, or visiting more art museums.

If I could turn back time, I would spend more hours on the floor helping you with puzzles or setting up racetracks. I would read more books and sing you more songs. I would gaze into your perfect little faces, listen intently to your questions, and pay more attention to your little stories about playmates, school, or your dreams.

If I could turn back time I would pray with you more. I would ask God for more discernment and wisdom so that I could teach you and train you better how to walk in His precepts. I would rethink the process of discipline, help you to see the error of your ways, and help you to see that all sin has a consequence.

I would also make sure you understood that regardless of what you do that might displease God, He loves you unconditionally, just like me! Nothing could ever separate you from my love, and so it is with the love of God. Don't ever forget that! He will always be standing with open arms to welcome you back, no matter how far away you may drift from His will. There is no sin so great that would cause God not to love you and there is nothing you could ever do to cause me not to love you either. NOTHING! Our sins fail to please Him and they grieve His heart and separate our fellowship "with" Him, but they never separate us "from" Him. I am so grateful that both of you have sealed your destination of an eternal home in Heaven by accepting Christ as your Savior. This means we will be eternally together.

I had a reality check on December 18, 2005. The wake up call was a "Close Encounter" with God Himself. I know you must have felt His presence in the room, as I did, and I know that He was there to give you comfort too. I pray that the experience strengthened your faith in Him to deliver you, no matter how difficult your trials may be. I hope you learned that when our difficulties come, and they will, it is not meant to punish us or condemn us, but rather to strengthen us and grow us into the vessel of service God created us to be. The lost and unsaved are victims of their circumstances, but as God's children, we are victorious.

While lying in ICU, I couldn't help but think of how Christ must have felt as He hung on the cross. Rejected, bruised, forsaken, and separated. I felt a million miles away from you, though I could feel your kisses upon my cheek. It was so painful to know that you were hurting and this time Mommy couldn't kiss your boo-boo and make it better. I couldn't console your broken hearts. I couldn't wipe away your tears or give you a hug. I couldn't speak the words that I so wanted to say to you that would have encouraged you. For the first time in your lives, I couldn't say "Merry Christmas" or "Happy

New Year." But God knows best. If you could have heard my voice, you might not have been so inclined to listen for His.

I want you to know that I am not perfect (I am sure you know that already) and I am humbled and reminded of this fact every day, especially over the last six months of my life. I know that God has a reason. I know that He is preparing me for my next assignment. He has given me a sneak preview and now I am awaiting the curtain call. How blessed I am.

I may not be the same Mom in a lot of ways, but in God's eyes, I am a better Mom, a better person, a better child of God. In my weakness, He is made strong and in Him, I am made whole because my soul has been restored. I am much more useful to God healed in my spirit than I was when I was healthy in my body.

God is preparing me to finish my race, but you both have a race to run of your own. I pray that God has allowed my experience to help you grow in your faith so that it will be strong enough to carry you through the storms of your own lives, to your finish line, and on to your eternal home.

I pray that through my experience, you have learned what it means to have patience and what it means to wait on God. I pray that you have learned that He will provide all your needs, just as He has provided mine. Most of all, I pray that you will draw closer to Him in your relationship. Get to know Him intimately as your Heavenly Father, His Son, and His Holy Spirit. Each person of God has a very important part to play in your lives.

God has left me here to help you finish well. I hope that one day when my days on earth are over, you will be able to feel me worthy and that you will "Rise up and call me blessed."

I love you both with all my heart. The best legacy I could leave you with is the example of a life walked by faith. A "Faith to Finish."

God bless you forever, Mom

For months, I had been homebound and able to attend only a few services at church. I so appreciate pastors who share their Sunday morning services via telecast, but nothing takes the place of being able to fellowship with God's people. For my heart, nothing takes the place of being able to minister to them on the piano.

A good friend of mine had asked me if I would like to play the piano for her church on Father's Day, June 18th. It had been six months to the day since my illness began. I was so excited about the prospect of doing something that was "normal" for me. Though it was only for one Sunday service, it was easing me back into life as I had known it. I felt I could handle it with God's help. I prepared by getting plenty of rest and lots of oxygen.

I got up that Sunday morning thrilled at the possibility of ministering in music to a congregation again. After my usual cup of coffee, I headed to the bathroom to start getting ready. I was still requiring supervision in and out of the shower. I informed Charles of where I was headed so he could listen out for me.

The Cardio-Pulmonary therapy had helped me build stamina, but my balance was still poor. As I stepped into the bathroom, I suddenly lost my balance. With nothing close by to grab, I fell to the floor. It was the thud and the moaning that brought Charles running to help me. I don't know which one of us was crying the hardest. Immediately, I knew my arm was severely broken because it was so displaced. It looked like a stair step. Though I was sobbing from the intense pain, I asked Charles to first call Nancy's husband, who was the music director of the church I was to play for that morning. I knew that I would not be playing the piano that day for sure! I was broken-hearted to disappoint them, but I was also very disappointed myself. I had so looked forward to the opportunity and now I was unable to fulfill my obligation. In my humanness, I couldn't understand why God kept allowing my barren land to get dryer and dryer. About the time I thought He was going to bring a spring shower and dampen the dry land, there came another storm. This one didn't bring any rain, only PAIN! So here we go, back to the hospital again! Charles called our son, Paul to help him get me in and out of the car.

I was so willing to serve God and yet, now another piece of me was broken. Many years ago, I remember saying, "If I were to lose my voice and the use of my hands I would be useless to God." Hmm, do you think He might have been trying to prove me wrong? Do you think He might have been trying to show me that I might be broken, but not destroyed? I couldn't help but wonder how much more of me I might lose!

My arm was broken alright, in two places! I went to surgery and received three nails in my wrist to hold the bones stationary. It was the only way the doctor could give me hope of a near normal function in my arm. I had already told him that I played the piano and that he needed to do whatever to fix it. He said he would do his best. What he didn't tell me was how painful those three nails were going to be!

I lay on the gurney in the emergency room awaiting surgery and pondered God's reasoning behind this (another) injury to my person. Now I had less lungs, no voice to sing or speak with, and a broken arm that may never play the piano again. I said, "God, are you sure You want me to speak, sing and glorify You through music because my abilities are becoming very limited?"

It's hard to not to get in the flesh when things are falling apart. It is, however, easy to let Satan discourage you and cause you to doubt God's plan. No, I will be honest, I didn't understand God's wisdom and I didn't understand how all this could possibly be for my good, but I still had faith in Him. Through my tears I trusted Him. In my prayers I trusted Him to again give me grace and mercy to bear another burden and to accept His plan. It was a detour in my race, that's all.

June 18, 2006

Lord, I know You are in control. I trust Your plan for me, though I don't understand it. Here lies another challenge and another test of my faith in You to provide. It is another test of my endurance. Here lies another chance to let others see that when the "call" is great, so will be the challenges that You use to prepare us. Give me the strength to endure the pain and may all the honor and glory go to You. Help me to overcome yet another test of my faith.

My voice and my hands are such essential parts of me. What can I do for You now, with one hand and a weak voice? As always, I love You, Lord. I know You will show me the way.

June 19, 2006

Today I am back to having sitters. I am in such pain that nothing controls the throbbing in my left arm, not even the pain killers. My fingers are so swollen they are immobile. There is no way to rest comfortably. The pain is nauseating. I can hardly think to write this entry. I just want You to know, I need You, Lord.

June 23, 2006

I am staying by myself today for the first time since I broke my arm. Hubby is worried, I am not. It is time for me to again try to stand on my own. I know God has a reason for keeping me in this holding pattern. There has been nothing but painful, sleepless nights since my injury, but finally I found a combination of pain killers that at least numbs the pain for an hour or so.

Lord, I pray that You use me as an example to those around me. They are the "crowd of witnesses" that is monitoring my reaction to difficulty, pain, and suffering. Help them to see that no matter what I go through, You are bigger than any problem and that You

215

give me the strength to make each step, each day of my life. Help me be still and know You are God as I wait on You. Let my life be a light that shines forth faith, humility, patience and courage.

June 27, 2006

Lord, give me patience to bear the incapacity of this broken part of me. I pray that I will regain full use of my arm and hand so that I will again play the piano to honor you. This is my prayer continuously. I know that my greatest challenges are meant to take me to a higher level. I am so ready to move up, Lord. Help me be patient until You know that I am prepared.

July 11, 2006

Four weeks after my injury, with my arm still in a cast and while still on pain meds, I spoke at a ladies meeting at a local church. It was an opportunity I was not going to pass up because it meant that I was fulfilling the commandment God had given me. It was my first public appearance to speak as God's voice of victory. It was also my first opportunity to show these women what a miracle looked like. I knew I needed experience in the are of public speaking and these ladies were mostly friends so I knew they would be very forgiving. It was awesome to share what God had done and continued to do in my life. I was blessed and I pray that they were too.

For six weeks, I was in a cast. It was six weeks and three days of constant, agonizing pain. It never left completely and grew in intensity between pain meds. Again I was unable to drive and found myself confined to home, stuck in my chair, and in solitude. God sure does like being alone with me!

Finally, the cast was off and for the next two and a half months I was in therapy again. This time it was to regain function of what was initially a non-functioning arm and hand. I was so determined that I would play the piano again that even while my arm was still in a cast, I would often attempt to move my stiff, practically immobile fingers over the keys, considering it a form of therapy. It's another part of me that is healed and functions, but will never be the same as it was before.

Believe it or not, there are two good things that became of the day I broke my arm. The first is that I was left with three nail scars to remind me everyday that no matter how bad things may seem, Jesus suffered so much more. Thus, my scars help me to get through my trials.

Another good thing is that for some reason, maybe the screaming and moaning I did from all the pain, the volume in my voice increased a little. That was truly a blessing. I was finally able to squeak out a little bit of a tune, but, of course, only behind closed doors!

In August, I spoke at another local church. It amazed me how God prepared my testimony to minister to those who attended. There were two couples there who needed encouragement and hope after recently enduring a layoff. Charles and I could associate with what they were going through and we were eager to let them know that there is life after layoff, especially for those who are trusting in God's plan.

Also in August, I returned to our home church to share my testimony to a Ladies ministry meeting. God continued to provide opportunities for me in the public setting, but I also made it a point to share the story of my "Close Encounter" everywhere I went.

September 7, 2006

I had appointments with both my pulmonologist and my primary physician today. Everything remained stable, but not improved. My mind is so ready to go on with my life, but my body continues to suffer from chronic fatigue that is

217

exacerbated by shortness of breath. I was looking for some glimmer of hope that an underlying cause may be present, could be diagnosed, and hopefully cured, or treated. Nothing surfaced. Both physicians agreed, as they had told me many times before, that I should give recovery a full year. I am into my ninth month. I will keep pressing on.

My primary physician told me that I would never be physically capable of working again as a floor nurse. I have mixed emotions about this. I love caring for people and being a nurse was one way I had of giving back. But I also know that working in the hospital presents opportunities to be exposed to infections that may trigger another attack of the disease that had already claimed a third of my lungs. If I were to be in contact with the same pathogen that caused my first attack, it would be likely that I would find myself back on life-support or in Heaven. My career as a nurse seems to be another thing I will have to let go of. I know that if God is permanently closing this door, He will open another one. I will continue to wait on Him.

I must keep moving forward. I cannot dwell on my past. My life is not over, in fact, in many ways, it has just begun. I don't want to get addicted to dysfunction. I will find ways to pour myself into others as much as I possibly can.

Lord, I know that if I just keep walking through this desert, one day I will reach the other side. Keep me safe, provide for me, lead me, and give me grace to press on. I know that the harder it is to wait, the more valuable the wait will be. I also trust You that the more struggles I endure, greater will be the prize. I don't want to be just mediocre. I long to go higher with You. I love You, Lord.

September 20, 2006

I paid a visit to the thoracic surgeon today. It was the first time he had seen me since ICU and he had never seen me before that time. Needless to say, he was quite shocked to see the "real me," instead of the person who was near death when he took over my case. He was so pleased that I had recovered as much as I had. I wanted to make the appointment with him because I wanted to thank him in person. He was the doctor who initiated the change in treatment that was influential in saving my life. Most of all, I wanted to thank Him for giving God the glory for my healing, instead of taking all the credit himself. It was he who had said, "God knows that doctors still need to see a miracle every now and then." I think so too!

I know God is my Healer, but I do believe He used my doctors and the knowledge He had given them. It was awesome to hear so many of them give God the glory. It is even more awesome to know that God chose me to be His miracle.

Lord, this is what it is all about... spreading the news of Your power and Your healing and letting others see a miracle that You performed. It's about letting them see that there is a grateful heart behind this circumstance. It is my heart, the heart of Your servant. I don't want to be a saved soul with a wasted life. I want to live a fruitful life. Give me opportunities to share what You have done for me. I love You, Lord.

The next few months were fairly uneventful as far as recovery. I continued to put forth the effort to exercise by walking as much as I could. I worked at trying to lose the extra weight I had gained over the last year, but it was difficult. My decreased lung capacity, weakness, and limited stamina made it difficult to exercise. I ate a well balanced diet to build up my immune system. I tried every juice and potion that was suggested to me, in hopes that something would increase my energy. Nothing worked.

September 27, 2006

I find that I am preaching to myself today for today has been a trying one. Not because of any particular occurrence,

219

but because of the battlefield in my mind. It has been another day on the roller coaster ride of mixed emotions. These episodes are fewer and farther apart, but every now and then, the ugly face of discouragement will make its presence known.

Today I read a verse that brought me a lot of comfort. Sometimes I feel so useless in the eyes of man, but I know that am never useless in the mighty hands of God.

Thank you for speaking to me from Your word today, Lord. In I Peter 5:10 Your word says, "after you have suffered a little while, the God of all grace will Himself complete and make you what you ought to be, establish and ground you securely and strengthen and settle you."

I am learning to walk in your purpose. Everyday I find that I am placing myself on the alter so that You can alter all that I am. You are making me who I ought to be, not who I thought I was. You are grounding me and on most days, You are settling me. Today is one of those days when I need You to plant my feet firmly on the Rock.

Lord, give me the strength and wisdom to endure the suffering and the battles that rage within my mind. I have Your promise to use my suffering to complete me so that You can use me. Help me to focus only on You. I know that if I am to grow strong, I must pick up something heavy. This has been evidenced to me by the burdens of the last nine months. At times they have been so heavy to bear that without Your strength, I would have surely fallen. I am continuously learning to depend on You to help me carry them. More and more, I am learning to cast them at Your feet. I can see that You are making me stronger and more dependent on You. For that I thank You.

Contrary to popular belief, getting better is not a decision you make and all of a sudden you jump out of bed and say, "It's over!" It has taken time for my body to heal, my heart to heal, and my soul to be restored.

It has required me to learn to live with changes in my body such as stiff joints, decreased energy, weight gain, and shortness of breath. For all these months I have trusted You as I wondered how You would put my life back together again.

Some days, it is hard to fight excuses and I am often tempted to compare myself to the person I used to be. I lack motivation and desire. Daily routines become drudgery. The one thing I have to look forward to is seeing how You will turn my ashes into beauty. Forgive me, Lord, for my faults, failures, and shortcomings. How can I make excuses when You have taken such special care of me?

I sleep very little and when I do, it is interrupted by bad dreams and memories. I pray that You will replace these dreams with visions of my future. I never want to forget my "Close Encounter" with You, Lord, for it is a precious reminder of who I was and who I am becoming. I long for the day when I feel like myself again. The only way I find escape from this drug induced battlefield in my mind is to come into Your presence. It is there that I find the peace that I need so desperately and there that I find fullness of joy.

Lord, I am ready for a comeback. Prepare me physically, mentally, and spiritually as only You can do. I thank You that I am alive. Only a loving, omniscient, omnipresent God could bless me as You have done. I don't ever want to miss Your perfect plan for my life. You have given me a new life, a new direction, and a new opportunity to discover Your ways and Your eternal purpose.

Thank you God for my husband who seems to think his quietness will consume my sorrow and make things better. He suffers in silence with me. He has been so patient with me and I know it has been hard living with a person whose emotions are up and down and who is sometimes different from day to day or hour to hour. Help him to continue to be patient as You work Your will and way in my life. Help him to see that I am not getting bitter, I am getting better.

He is consumed with protecting me and sheltering me from illness or injury. When he said "For better or for worse" he probably didn't think the worse would be this bad! Thank you for the mate you have given me. I love You, Lord.

October 2, 2006

I need to make some decisions about my business and I need Your help, Lord. I am not capable of maintaining my obligations. I carry around feelings of guilt and inadequacy in this area of my life and I feel that the energy I spend on these thoughts would be better used in other ways. I want every minute of my life to be fruitful for You. I don't ever want to feel like I am out there on my own again. I don't ever want to take control of my life again. I don't want to be the one who thinks she has to figure things out and put all the pieces together. I want You to do that for me. I thank You that now I am willing to allow You to do just that. No more hands on for me. I am a Christ follower; willing to go wherever you lead me and do whatever You say.

I could spend my time obsessing over my title and my career in business, but I know there are details of my life that are more important at this time and they are my health and my fellowship with You. I will trust You with the details. I know that You will open the doors that need opening and I trust You slam those that need to be closed. By doing so, I know that You will keep me moving in the right direction.

I trust You to use people, events, and all circumstances to move me ultimately toward fulfilling

Your will for my life. In the process of doing Your will, may I become more like Christ every day.

Lord, You are my everything. In You, I lack nothing. I have not lost anything in this desert journey. Instead, I have gained everything in the joy of Your presence. You didn't teach me how to be sick, You taught me how to be a survivor and a conqueror. You have taught me to walk by faith, not by sight. You have connected me with people who needed an answer to the question, "How do I make it through a desert experience?" You used me to give hope, as I found my own hope in You.

Writing in my journal has kept me connected to You. As I look back on its pages, I see how You have continued to answer my prayers. You have guided my thoughts and enabled me to chronicle events in my life that have given meaning to this journey and to what You were doing in my life. My writing is not an egotistical attempt to be praised in the eyes of the world. Documenting my thoughts is an obligation and act of obedience. In anticipation, I look forward to the day when I witness what You will do with my feeble attempts to convey Your love to me through this faith journey. I love you, Lord.

October 22, 2006

I spoke at another church today. It was wonderful to have another opportunity to share what God has done and continues to do for me.

Lord, I am amazed at how You remove my fears and give me boldness and God-confidence to do things far beyond my limitations. I pray that the seeds I sowed today will determine how far You take me tomorrow. May you reap a bountiful harvest from my effort to magnify You.

Paul said in Philippians 3:10, "My determined purpose is that I may know Him."

So it is with my passion to know You, Lord, more than life itself. I long for more open doors. Help me not get overcommitted to things which have no significance in Your eternal purpose because this only leads to under-satisfaction. Thank you for moving me from whining to dining on the feast of Your love. I try, I fail. I trust, You succeed. I am resting and abiding in You until every time You say, "Go!"

You continue to work on me as You chip away the unnecessary things that hold me back. Keep me humble as I stand against the blows of the chisel, knowing that each strike draws me closer to becoming Your masterpiece.

Lord, help me to keep pushing against the immovable stones. I want to grow stronger and I want to build muscle that will carry me through the last leg of my race. As an athlete in the race of life, I realize that I must push beyond my limits, endure the pain, and retrain my mental thoughts to win this race. I am victorious by Your grace. I love You, Lord.

November 8, 2006

Lord, today I pray that you clothe me with Your Holy Spirit. Allow Him to make a difference through me. As He imparts love, may He give me opportunities to serve. As He gives me opportunities, may I find hope. As I find hope, may I also find the liberty to be used by You in ways that will touch others with Your love. Let there be a living interaction between the Holy Spirit and me, that I may make a difference in a life today.

I John 2:16-17 was my verse for today. It says, "The man who does the will of God lives forever." Lord, how I live is so much more important to me than how long I live. I will live for You.

Father, forgive me for often ignoring the simple blessings of my life. Pardon me for the sin of selfish living and fill me with the knowledge of the privilege

224

and potential of belonging to You. Reveal Your purpose again to me and give me the grace to pursue it with all my heart.

I know that life wasn't meant to be easy. I realize that the mountains will sometimes be high and many times as I reach the top, I will find myself at the bottom of the next big mountain. Help me to see that when I find myself promoted to the next level in my spiritual growth, I will merely be at the bottom of a higher level. I accept my challenge because I know that regardless of the climb, Your hand will be there to guide me, protect me, and cheer me on.

One day I will stand before You, Lord. The pain of struggling uphill will pass. It is then that I will have reached the eternal mountaintop and there I will find a mansion that You have prepared for me.

Holy Spirit, fill me today. Empower me and keep me walking uphill. I love You, Lord.

November 22, 2006

You continue to amaze me Lord. You lead me, guide me, and open my eyes to things about You and You give me reassurance of Your call. I am totally and utterly amazed that You would choose me, but knowing that I have been set apart, also leaves me with a huge responsibility. Sometimes this scares me, but I know that whatever You bring me to, You will also bring me through.

I know that You are still preparing me. I am cautious not to move ahead of You. I am longing for You to fill me with Your fresh power, Your fresh faith, and Your fresh fire.

I am watching as You work in the lives of those around me. Through Your eyes, I am beginning to see how You heal broken hearts, mend broken relationships, and humble Your people.

225

Father, please don't let pride get in my way. Keep me humble, kind, tender, and loving towards others, even those who reject me. Help me have a forgiving heart, without grudge or malice. There are battles that I need You to fight for me. There are those who don't understand my decisions, my motives, or Your call. Open their eyes to the fact that my life is in Your hands. Have Thine own way in my life.

A friend sent me a card that ministered to my heart. This is my prayer to You today:

God of life, I reach out to You for help! On my own, I cannot walk through the days and I need You to hold me up and keep me from fainting. Renew me in Your strength. Breathe Your hope into my spirit that I might believe that my heavy heart will again run and even rise up and fly on eagles' wings. Let the light of Your healing love shine into the deep hurt and the dark places in my heart. In Your name I pray, Amen. (author unknown) I love you Lord.

December 1, 2006

Today I wrote a letter. It was to a person who holds a position of significance and honor in my life. However, our relationship has been hindered for many years because of the sin of unforgiveness. I have done this many times, but with less conviction than today. The Holy Spirit has been really dealing with my heart over the importance of making sure that not only have I asked for forgiveness, but that I have also forgiven. I want to obey Him. The last thing I want is a bitter, unforgiving heart to stand in the way of my service for Him.

There has been a root of rejection between us for many years. For whatever reasons it exists, I have no control. The thing I do have control over is my decision to love "unconditionally."

I had to let this person know that I no longer hold them accountable for my happiness or my need for acceptance. I will stand accountable to God for any bitterness or resentment that may have resided in my heart and I have asked Him to remove any trace of it. I pray for this person daily and I love her, unconditionally.

Lord, You have shown me so many things during this process. I feel I must write them down; to recorded them not only on paper, but forever in my heart.

Lesson #1:

You have taught me that though apologies can be made, we are not in control of whether or not they are accepted. Our role, as Your child, is to be obedient as You work through our efforts to change hearts and mend relationships.

Lesson #2

You have shown me that harboring bitterness, anger, resentment, or unforgiveness in my heart does more damage to me than to the other person involved. It is a form of self-punishment. It separates me from becoming all that You want me to be and it interferes with our fellowship. Nothing in this life is worth that. In Ephesians 4:32 You teach me, "Be kind to one another, tender-hearted, forgiving each other, just as God in Christ also has forgiven you."

Lesson #3

You have taught me the meaning of forgiveness: it is the willingness to give up the feelings that are harbored against someone who has hurt you, regardless of how serious or painful the act may have been. Forgiveness means that I forgive the wrong, I forgive the wrongdoer, and I give up my need for retaliation because You are the One who fights my battles for me.

Lesson #4

The sin of unforgiveness is, of course, the opposite. In Ephesians 4:31, Paul associates unforgiveness with bitterness, wrath, anger, clamor, slander, and malice. It is so hard for me to understand why someone would choose the negative emotions of unforgiveness over tenderness, gentleness, and a forgiving heart. The sin of unforgiveness destroys peace and joy and it is a "cancer" that eats away at the joy that is found in a relationship with You. It could also be likened to a poison that chokes out every godly trait that You have placed within us.

Lesson #5:

An unforgiving heart focuses and clings to the past, refusing to offer others what God has offered us, "forgiving each other, just as God in Christ also has forgiven you."

Lesson #6:

I have learned that unforgiveness is a self-inflicted pain that I choose whether or not I allow it to be placed upon me. Blaming someone else for my misery only becomes a form of self-sabotage that creates a bondage of chains and strongholds.

Lesson #7:

You have used Your word as a mirror that has exposed my inner need to forgive and to ask for forgiveness. In the mirror, I have seen that my unforgiveness created acts of pride and rebellion against You because these things kept me from accomplishing all that You wanted to do in my life.

Lesson #8

In Matthew 6:15, I read, "If you do not forgive others, then your Father will not forgive your transgressions." I realized that forgiveness had to start with me. It is my heart and my decisions that I will stand accountable for when I stand before You. I want You to forgive me of my transgressions and I ask for any unforgiveness in my heart to be removed.

Lesson #9:

I have learned that the apology is not nearly so important as the forgiveness. It makes the person who is asking for forgiveness feel better because they are obeying, but it does not restore the relationship until it is accepted and forgiveness is given. In Matthew 18:22, the Bible says that we are to forgive, "seventy times seven." I have no control over the acceptance of my apology, but I do have control over my willingness to forgive. Forgiveness is a by-product of the victim.

Lesson #10:

A very important lesson that I have learned is that a consequence of unforgiveness is unanswered prayer. I want to be a witness of Your power and grace manifested through answered prayer in my life. I want to continue to grow in my relationship with You and if it were for that reason alone it would be enough for me to always forgive. I want my witness to be testimony of the power of forgiveness, for You have forgiven me. I don't want my relationships with others affected by signs of unforgiveness such as: stress, anxiety, depression, and resentment.

Lesson #11

You have taught me how to deal with an unforgiving spirit:

1. to take it seriously
2. to assume responsibility for my decisions and my actions
3. to recognize that unforgiveness is a sin against God
4. to confess my sin to God
5. to let go of any anger and discard it
6. to begin praying for the other person
7. to ask for their forgiveness
8. to find ways to show my love to them
9. to refuse to bring up what has been forgiven ever again

Lesson #12

You have taught me how I am to know that I have forgiven.

1. when my feelings towards the other person have changed

2. *when my feelings turn into genuine concern for the other person*

I leave the rest in Your hands. Only You, Lord, can remove hatred and bitterness from the souls of man. Only You can mend a broken relationship and restore fellowship.

Lord, You know that it is my desire to offer You a vessel that You can use. Anything standing in the way of this I give to You, including my sin of unforgiveness. I ask You to remove anything that would prevent fruitfulness in my life. Sever the root that feeds anything, but love.

I can't help but regret the years that have passed and the opportunities that have been missed in my relationship with this person, but I can also say that out of the pain of rejection has come my understanding of Your unconditional love because You were also rejected by men yet, You forgave.

You give to me such amazing love. How can it be that You, my God, would die for me? In search of understanding what it means to be loved unconditionally, I found Your love and a relationship with You. I praise Your name for revealing this to me. Though my earthy father is in Heaven with You, You have shown me that You are the Father to the fatherless. You have taught me what it means to not only accept Your unconditional love, but to also be able to give it away. You have taught me that to forgive is to show love.

Bless my efforts and work in the hearts of those whom I love, dear Jesus. I love You, Lord.

December 22, 2006

I had an appointment with my pulmonologist today. It was one year to the date of my hospitalization. I had been told to give my recovery a full year and now it was time to come to the realization of where I stood physically. Little had changed

230

as far as my stamina, endurance, strength, or shortness of breath. I continued to use oxygen at night and occasionally during the day, if warranted by overexertion. There had been some improvement over the last few months, but overall, it seemed I had reached a plateau.

My life was a vicious circle of activity, shortness of breath, and rest. Sometimes it was hard to tell which one came first. I had learned to listen to my body when it was telling me to stop. I had learned to rest when I needed to recover from shortness of breath and I had learned to prioritize my activities and plan for energy needs.

God had been so good to me. The fibrosis in my lungs as a result of the inflammation had claimed about one third of my lungs. However, this amount was still less significant than had been expected. At one point, there had been mention of a lung transplant, but this no longer seemed to be a consideration. That was really good news.

It was discovered that I had some residual damage to the valves in my heart from the inflammation, but that was also something they had anticipated and the effects were less than had been expected.

My voice had improved, but was still affected by fatigue, shortness of breath, and weakness. I could sing one song at a time, if I was rested and if my lungs were pumped full of oxygen. This was enough to encourage me that one day I would be able to sing even more. I couldn't say that I sang with self-confidence anymore because I never knew what was going to come out of my mouth. I just trusted God to expand my lungs and take control of my damaged vocal cord. Therefore, I sang in God-confidence. I liked to say that I had learned to sing with my heart, instead of my head. I still didn't have the energy to participate in the choir, but it felt good to be able to join in congregational singing during worship. Once I had actually sung a solo.

My life consisted of intermittent activity combined with rest. But, at least I could function and I could maintain simple activities of daily living, only at a snail pace compared to my previous lifestyle.

I was getting better use of my left arm and playing the piano was part of my therapy to regain function in my wrist. I lost some extension in my fingers, but since I have extra long fingers anyway, I could still reach an octave with only occasional missed keys. Considering the initial prognosis of my fracture, I was happy to be able to play at all. God was continuing to restore my soul as He gave me back pieces of my life that had been perfected for His glory, not my own.

I guess you could say that I was learning to live with my disabilities and how to make the most of my capabilities. The last thing I would ever do is give up after all God had done for me. There were still days of discouragement and setbacks, but with prayer and God's help, I would always be able to pick myself back up and keep going.

My doctors encouraged me to live my life as free of stress as possible and to be cautious of being around illness or infections. In their opinion, moderation was the key. I will admit that it was a little disturbing to hear them say, "Permanently and totally disabled." Maybe to do man's work, but not the Lord's. God has proven to me over the last year that He gives me the strength to do the things He has called me to do, even though sometimes that is all I can do. I might be disabled, but I am not unable!

In many ways I was taking better care of myself than prior to my illness and that was a good thing. Because I was determined to lose the extra pounds that medication and inactivity had blessed me with, I had started to eat a better variety of nutritional foods and I determined to get as much exercise as my body would tolerate. At the advice of my physician, I joined a yoga class at a senior center and found that I could handle the exertion, as long as I rested when I got home. Most of the time, I could keep up with the eighty year olds. The exercise began to improve my balance. That was another good thing because it's kind of embarrassing to be witnessing for the Lord and look like you are staggering!

I learned to stop when I was feeling tired and that it was not a sin to take a nap if I needed to recover from overexerting. It was better to be down for a couple of hours than a couple of days. I was going to do my part in keeping my remaining lung tissue as healthy as possible. God would do the rest.

I never doubted God's ability to heal me. I never doubted His plan and that He would bring it to fruition. I never doubted that regardless of a disability, He had the ability to use me for His kingdom purposes. He continues to sustain me and for that reason, I give Him praise. Thank you, Lord.

December 22, 2006

A year has passed. Oh God, how You have provided for us and taken care of us. You have sustained me, strengthened me, and raised me up to a higher level spiritually. You have allowed me to accept the things I cannot change and You have given me the will to keep pressing on.

I have ceased to think about uncertainties. My first year is up. Now I can work on learning to live with the "certainties." I am moving forward with what I know is true and leaving the rest to You. In obedience to You, I am keeping myself busy with finishing the book and I have started a card ministry within our church family. This is giving me an opportunity to encourage those who are going through difficulties because I, too, have been encouraged. You have allowed me to have credibility in the "Been there done that" category. Father, You have allowed me to bless others because I, myself, have been blessed. Thank you, Lord, for loving me through the suffering, through the dry, barren land, and through the valley of Your silence. I love you, my Lord.

I have offered to volunteer at a hospice hospital by being a story-teller. Basically, this means putting a patient's last

233

thoughts down on paper in letter form for their family to cherish after they are gone. Many times, it is hard for people to say the things they want to say to their loved ones, but easier for them to say them to a stranger. Sometimes, I just go by to play the piano, including requests from the terminal patients as well as the staff.

I can't do all things, but I can do something. If God's people would just realize that it doesn't take huge efforts to bless another person. A kind word or a smile goes a long way and a note of encouragement brightens a day. We are God's hands, whether He chooses to use them to cook a meal, clean a house, play a piano or write a book.

Everything I do continues to be scheduled around rest breaks to allow time for recovery and prevent exhaustion. But since God has given me lots of time on my hands, that is easy to do.

God has blessed me with talents and abilities. I know that He will hold me accountable for their use. To whom much is given, much is required. I have a lot of work to do.

Even with disabilities, I can be the arms of God to hold those who needed His touch and I can be His hands to write a simple note to let a brother or sister in Christ know that I care. I can speak at every opportunity to share what God's love has meant to me and I can sing, even if I only have enough breath to get through one song at a time. I can spend time in prayer and communication with God; lifting up the names of those who need to feel His touch.

However, my number one priority will be to obey God by spending my life discipling others. I long for them to develop their own personal, intimate relationship with Him. Ultimately, I pray that God will use me to help them learn to walk by faith and not by sight.

Lord, I relinquish all my hopes and dreams in order to serve You. In sweet abandon, I have given up all the things that I thought made me who I was and I have placed them at Your feet. You have turned many of these things around to use them for Your glory. You have placed my feet on solid ground and You have given me a new direction and new vision. I know that when I was settling for my own dreams, I was settling for too little. You have proven to me that You can take little and make it much.

I don't worry anymore, for worry is a lack of faith. I have faith because faith means I lack worry. I have confidence in You to do Your work through me.

You have freed me from the chains of my past and I no longer let other people determine my value. Thank You for allowing me to be able to break away from their expectations. I am "Justified" by Your grace through salvation; I am "Sanctified" by the renewing of the Holy Spirit; and I will be "Glorified" one day when I see You in Heaven. Thank You for showing me who I am, "I am Yours."

What You have begun in me, I know You will finish. Help me to enjoy who I am on the way to who I am becoming. I know You are still working on me and I still need a lot of help. I pray that You never let me lose hope, for I am Your servant, Lord. I love You, Lord.

December 25th, 2006

I am alone in my chair at 1:00 in the morning, except for You, Lord, my pen, and my thoughts. I have learned to treasure the nights that I sit in anticipation of hearing from You. This chair has become my place of refuge, a place where I get alone with You.

Every day is a one year anniversary now. One year ago yesterday, I was placed on a ventilator. One year ago today, my family spent Christmas Day in the waiting room of an ICU.

But that is past and this is now. I had a wonderful day today. It was kind of quiet since we celebrated Christmas with our children last evening. Today,

235

Charles and I ate leftovers and rested. You have blessed me with life and abilities. You have blessed me with so many things, but, other than your Son, there is no greater gift that You could ever give me than to be right where I am at this very moment, alone with You!

Today Charles and I reflected on Your goodness and our gratefulness to You for life, breath, and opportunity. My heart is so grateful for all the things that You have brought us through this year. What an incredible journey! Most of all, I look forward to the great things You have planned for us in the coming year. I love you Lord, with all my heart and all my soul.

January 7, 2007

It was a warm winter afternoon in Augusta, Georgia. As Charles and I sat on our porch sipping some wonderful Pumpkin Spice coffee, we began making plans for a summer garden. It was a strange, but good feeling to be making plans for the future. For over a year now, our plans had consisted of doctor's appointments, tests, therapy, and recovery. We had rarely thought past the day or the week. Now, we were making plans for the spring and summer. This was a new thought and it was wonderful not to be so consumed with "me and my health."

It was wonderful to see life in the future again. This doesn't mean that I don't intend to still keep trusting God on a day-to-day basis because I know that none of us are promised tomorrow. But it does mean that God was allowing me to see visions of a tomorrow and hope for the unveiling of His plans for my many tomorrows. In His word He says, "Without a vision the people perish." For so long my vision has been obscured by issues concerning my health. Today is a beautiful day and a reason for a new beginning.

Lord, I will put my trust in You today and every day of my life. I trust You with my today and I trust You with my tomorrow. I am learning to lean on You

236

more and more and I am finding more power than I ever dreamed. I love you, Lord.

January 8, 2007

Today is the one year anniversary of my coming home from the hospital. Lord, I will make it my effort to make this year one of significance. My goal is to finish writing the book You gave me instructions to write, "Faith to Finish" and as You continue to lead, possibly the second, "Finding Faith to Finish." You have given me the faith to endure and the perseverance to overcome. When some people look at me they may see a weakened outer shell, but this is just my earthly body. Inside me is a soul that is strong in faith. It is a part of me that might not be visible at first glance, but I pray that how I live my life proves to You how much I love You and how much I love others.

Some may see an arm that healed crooked and is scarred by three nails. Some may consider me weak and frail. Others may hear my voice and say, "There is no way God could use her to speak or to sing."

I know that I can do all things through the power of Your Holy Spirit. I will depend on Him to guide me and teach me the plan that You have for the remainder of my life.

I put my faith in You and You alone. Until the day that You make me whole in Heaven, I will serve You in the body that I have. I praise Your Name for You have been so good to me. There will be no more pity parties because no one ever came but me anyway. I choose joy, and I pray that You will offer me ways to display it to others in a mighty way.

There is no request from You that is too big, Lord. I will do whatever it takes to follow You. I forsake all else and fix my mind on Your ways and Your thoughts. You are My Lord, My Savior, and My Guide. I honor You with every fiber of my being. I am nothing without You, but with You, I have the power of the Holy Spirit within me and I can do all things. Hide me behind Your cross forever, Lord, and let Your light shine through me to this dark and sin-sick world.

I know that You measure my faith in You not by how I stand in times of peace and comfort, but rather in how I stand in times of challenge. I pray that You have found me worthy. I pray that I will continue to fight the good fight; armed with the breastplate of righteousness and the shield of faith. I would rather live with my physical limitations and be in Your will, than to have all the praise of man. I know that my trials are just channels for Your grace and that You bestow Your blessings even in the midst of my most difficult hardships. You did not give me a spirit of timidity, "but a spirit of power, of love, and self-discipline" (II Timothy 1:7).

You have promised Your bountiful blessings for those who trust in You. I go to the ocean with a bucket, Lord, not a spoon. I want to experience all that You have created for me. It is with great anticipation that I wait on tomorrow. Together we will walk. Together we will accomplish Your will for my life.

One day, I asked you for Your blessing and You heard me. Your answer came with a refining process. I asked You again and You pruned from my life the unnecessary things that were standing in my way. I asked You again and You blessed me with the greatest honor anyone could receive and that was to be in Your presence. I asked You again and You gave me a desert - a dry barren land - where You revealed to me every aspect of Your person and where You allowed me to experience unfamiliar emotions so that I would understand these emotions in others. In Your silence, You taught me to wait on You. I ask You now, Lord, to be with me as I continue to seek Your face and live in Your statutes. I love You, Lord.

If someone had told me on December 17, 2005 (the night before my illness struck) that the way I lived and the decisions I made over the next eighteen days would determine the rest of my life, would I have done things any differently? No, absolutely not! Would I have wanted God to rearrange the circumstances so that things would have been easier for me to bear? Again, absolutely not!

As difficult as it has been, God knew what it would take to bring me to my knees. He worked my challenges and my trials into my good. He also knew what it would take to turn my eyes toward Heaven and off my circumstances. With a humble heart, I praise God for the refiner's fire. I praise Him that in love, He placed me in the furnace, melted me, and then molded me into a worthy vessel. I am, and I will be forever willing to give up everything in order to follow Him, even my life! It took an ending to create a new beginning. It is the beginning of a new race, a life now lived in obedience to God.

Lord, I give You my promise:

"I thank Jesus Christ our Lord, who has given me strength, that He considered me faithful, appointing me to His service" (I Timothy 1:12).

"My lips shall greatly rejoice when I sing unto Thee and my soul, which thou hast redeemed" (Psalm 71:23).

"My lips shall utter praise, when Thou hast taught me Thy statues" (Psalm 119:171).

"Let my soul live, and it shall praise thee" (Psalm 119:175).

"While I live will I praise thee Lord" (Psalm 146:2).

When You turned on the life support, You turned on my attention. My eyes are fixed on You, forever. I trusted You through my darkest days and I want to finish my race still trusting You. I am a Lazarus come forth; awakened from the dead and risen to walk in the newness of life.

You have shown me that Your grace is sufficient for me and Your power is made perfect in my weakness.

"Therefore I will boast all the more gladly about my weaknesses, so that Christ's power may rest on me. That is why, for Christ's sake, I delight in weaknesses, in insults, in hardships, in persecution, in difficulties. For when I am weak, then I am strong"
(II Corinthians 12:9-10).

In my weakness, I tap into Your divine resources, by faith. In my weakness, you have heightened the sensitivity of my need for a relationship with You. I know that I would never have realized my full capability as long as I continued to say, "I" can handle this. Lord, "I can't" handle this or anything else without You.

I am honored to be Your servant and I am privileged to be a vessel You chose to use. I am humbled to know that You love me so much that You chose me to walk this journey with You. My greatest desire is that my life will glorify You, God, and that I exalt Your name by my walk, my talk, my work, my will, and my ways. I pray that I keep my input greater than my upkeep so that my output won't be my downfall when I stand before You in Heaven. I love You, Lord.

Medical odds are irrelevant when compared to the unfathomable love and power of God Almighty. When I think of the alternatives, anything was possible from death to complete recovery. I knew that God could and would restore my health, if that was His will, but until that time, I had to learn to be patient and wait on Him. I am still waiting. Since God gives me a choice, I would rather be weak and close to

Him, than strong and running the other way. As long as He keeps me humble and dependent on Him, I will know that He is enjoying my company enough to keep working on me.

God's word tells me that "As a man thinketh, so is he." I choose to think on things above and I cling to my faith in God because I know He has a plan in motion for the rest of my life. If not, He would have taken me home to Heaven. Instead, He left me here on earth for a reason – His eternal purpose; to win souls and disciple others.

If I had to do it all over again, I would gladly walk with Him through the valley of the shadow of death because I felt His peace there. I would trudge through the valley of emotions that haunted me during the dark hours of night. As I wandered in a dry barren land, I would refuse to allow my emotions to become a stronghold. Instead, I would allow their existence to be the very thing that catapulted me into the arms of God. In my hour of need, I would not let the threats of Satan discourage me. I would let God fight that battle for me. I would trust Him when I couldn't see my way and I would keep walking towards my finish line, as I am now, with my gaze towards Heaven; until God says it is time for my race to be over. And finally, I would look forward to hearing Him say, "Well done My faithful servant. "Oh yes, Lord... because of You, "I'd Do It All Over Again."

My Friend,

Trials are non-discriminate. Whether you are weak or strong, it doesn't matter. They come in all sizes. They can attempt to destroy a person of strong faith or spare a weaker person resigned to failure. Trials do not come with a special grading system. The value of each one is based on our attitude and the valuable lesson God is able to teach us in the process.

Trials are not a reflection of who we are, our title, or our occupation. God is not interested in prestige. He is only interested in purpose. He doesn't choose us by our qualifications; He qualifies us after the call. He is looking for a willing heart that wants to serve Him. He has already gifted you with the necessary talents; all He needs is your availability to use them for His purpose, not your own.

Trials also have nothing to do with your worthiness. You could never deserve or do anything to earn God's love. It is freely offered and freely given. You will never do anything that would cause you to lose God's love.

Trials have nothing to do with your fear or faith. Funny how these two play off of each other. You have a choice. You can approach your trials in fear and miss the power of God on your life, or you can choose to walk in faith and watch Him work all manner of miracles.

As ridiculous as it may sound, God wants us to rejoice in our trials because it is in our darkest valleys that He is able to manifest His love towards us and reveal Himself to a dying world through us. Your trials are made for you, just as a Holy God designed them to be.

Life is a challenging race and the outcome is based on our attitude to believe God, to have faith no matter what happens, and to keep running our race, not "around" our trials, but "through" them. In you, God has placed a certain measure of faith. If you want to build your faith into the measure that will carry you to the finish line, get to know Him more. This is the way you will find the "Faith to Finish" your race.

Chapter 4

Lessons I Learned in the Desert

As I sit down to write this last chapter, I am faced with the realization that it has been me, the writer, who has learned the most from this endeavor. How amazing it has been to have the Holy Spirit lead, guide, and direct me as I penned each word. I thank Him for teaching me to be attentive to His voice.

I have attempted to capture my experience and give you a glimpse of what it was like to have an encounter with my Heavenly Father, His Son, Jesus, and the Holy Spirit. I have emptied my soul in order to share with you who I was, in order for you to understand who I have become. I have shared with you what it was like to walk through a dry, barren land in search of a word from God while He taught me patience and dependence on Him for my every need.

I have done my best to tell you how much God loves you. I have shared with you the joy of being in His presence and how much He wants to have an intimate relationship with you.

In all honesty, truthfulness, and transparency I have emptied my cup so that you could enjoy the greatness of God. It is my prayer that every word has brought glory and honor to Him and not to me. I was just a willing and ready vessel; a messenger relaying a message of love to you, from God.

In my study on the Trinity of God and through my times of reflection and prayer in preparation for the remainder of this book and handbook, I have realized that this encounter was just my "introduction" to God the Father, God the Son, and God the Holy Spirit.

My "Close Encounter" with Him was my "burning bush" experience. However, it was while walking through the dry, barren land that I learned many things about myself and about how God works. I even learned the reason for His silence.

My favorite lessons were:
* His teachings were made clear to me through my sufferings.
* H is conduct is of truth and integrity.
* His purpose for my life is revealed through my faith in Him.
* He is patient with me.
* His unconditional love always has my best interest at heart.
* He pursues. His perseverance teaches me to wait on Him.
* He gives me the grace to endure persecution and rejection. It is because in this I learned the importance of looking heavenward, even during times when I was rejected. I also learned to love those who reject me with an unconditional love and heart of forgiveness.
* Finally, to appreciate His sufferings. There has never been another human being who suffered like our Lord Jesus Christ and He did it all for you and me.

While at my "burning bush," I received enlightenment and instruction. However, it has been during the many months following my illness that God has chosen to teach me His ways. By doing so, He humbled me and developed the pure heart that was already surrendered to His will. In ICU, God showed me enough of Himself to let me know He was there as My Father, who is the Great Physician; My Savior, who suffered and gave His life for me; and the Holy Spirit, my Comforter and Guide, who lives inside of me. He is the One who guides and directs my actions and my choices. He is the One who protected me when I was totally helpless.

One would think that my time of greatest need would have been while I was connected to life-sustaining machines. Instead, my times of greatest need have been in the many months of recovery when God was often silent. It was during these months that I had to accept that my life was going to be different than I had known it. It was during these months that I had to search for usefulness, though in my heart I knew I had a purpose. That is what sustained me. All the extraneous things of life took second place to my obedience. It has been a long walk through the dry, barren land, but God has "raised me up" as He proved His promises in my life.

I have spent months preparing the story about "a miracle," while God has spent months preparing "me" for a miracle...the miracle of His transforming love.

Over the last year and a half I have often been asked, "Do you believe that God is going to heal you?" I was often confused by this question, wondering if my continuing to press on, despite my disabilities, expressed to them a lack of faith in God to heal me. So many times I wanted to say, "Do you not see that He has already healed me because He has restored my soul?"

Yes, I had faith that God would heal me. The day I opened my eyes from a coma, I knew that He had. You see, to "heal" me didn't necessarily mean to make my body whole again. What God promised was that in the valley, He would **restore my soul** and He did so by showing me who He is and by calling me according to His purpose.

I can now complete this chapter knowing that my story will continue. If one day God chooses to make my body as it was, I will praise His name all the more for yet, another miracle. Either way, the miracle of my restoration is far more valuable to me than a body with imperfections. I know that God can use me either way and I rest in His presence and power in my life.

The thing about a desert experience is that we are not to plant a garden there. We are to search for the good in the experience as we are passing through, we are to look for God's provision during our stay, and we are to learn our lessons well. After all, God is teaching and preparing us for the next level in our spiritual walk with Him...the climb up the next mountain!

God's Miracle

Psalm 119 says, "It is good that I have been afflicted, for therein have I learned thy statutes." I feel especially blessed to have been chosen as one of God's students. To the world I may not be the Karen that they once knew, but to God I am the person He was creating me to be. I thank Him for my affliction, for truly this has been where I have grown closer to Him.

In His classroom, I have learned to view my life differently:

*The world sees a disability, but I see my ability to do what He has called me to do. Sometimes it's no more, but it's never any less.

*The world sees my weakness, but I know that in my weakness He is made strong.

*The world lacks understanding, but I enjoy wisdom from God.

*The world questions "Why you," but I say, "Why not me, or you?"

*The world is fearful of the outcome, but I walk in peace.

*The world doubts my self confidence, but I walk in God confidence.

*The world lacks faith, but I know God will supply all my needs.

*The world might think correction, but I know it's a "call."

*The world is seeking, but I have found what they are looking for

*The world lends a deaf ear, but I have heard His voice.

*The world sees a need for oxygen, but God is all the breath I need.

*The world says "Your life is over," but I say, "It is just beginning."

*The world hears a voice that is weakened, but I use it to sing praises unto the Lord

*The world waits for an answer, but I wait on the Lord.

*The world may weep in sadness for me, but weeping only endures for a night. My "joy comes in the morning" (Psalm 30:5).

During my walk through the desert, I was not alone. When there was only one set of footprints in the sand, it wasn't because I was walking alone; it was because God was carrying me.

The day I awakened from an eleven day coma was the day God took me down from His lap and helped me to stand on dry land. He released me from the bondage of chains that had held me fast. Gone were the unnecessary things in my life in order to make room, for the necessary ones. After He had made room on my schedule, He gave me my list of things to do.

I knew at the moment of my surrender that He had been waiting patiently for me to realize my need to walk in His purpose, not my own. My race was not over, by any means, and by God's grace I would find the faith to finish. The best part was yet to come.

When my feet touched dry land, I had no idea where I was going. I asked God often for directions because I sure didn't want to be left in the desert for long. Most of the time, He was silent, but continued to provide all my needs. All I knew to do was to keep walking; though, at times, my feet burned and my mouth was so dry. I often prayed for a shower of rain or even a cloud to shelter me. Instead of sending the things I thought I needed, God sent "the Light." I had no idea what I would find in the desert. Surely somewhere there was an oasis where I could rest my weary soul! I just kept hearing God say, *"Wait on the Lord: be of good courage, and he shall strengthen Thine heart; wait I say, on the Lord" (Psalm 27:14).*

One of the hardest things we will ever have to do is wait patiently on the Lord. In my weakened condition, I had no other option. For the first time in my life, I didn't have the strength to run ahead of Him. I couldn't even keep up with Him. I just had to be still and listen as He taught me the valuable lessons of depending on Him. No longer was my life about my agenda. I was working from God's date book.

The Holy Spirit was my Comforter and my Guide while I was in a coma and it was He who walked with me through the bitter last days of discomfort and uncertainty of life. In the desert, it has been the Holy Spirit who has guided me through the many difficult decisions about my life; through the treatments, through the financial burdens from medical bills, and the hard task of letting go of things that I loved.

The encounter I had with God was just the beginning of our deeper, more intimate relationship – a relationship that came to fruition during my walk through the desert and continues to grow still today. It was in the desert that His promises came true and I learned to trust Him more.

There have been so many lessons learned. The most important one being - that it took a detour through the desert for God to draw me even closer to Himself. It has been in the desert that He allowed me time to heal and be loved. The things I learned while in this place created an ending to my story. This is where our relationship has truly grown and it has been where I have learned to depend on Him for every detail of my life.

In the desert, I sought for comfort and He brought soothing peace to my soul. I sought for peace and He quieted my spirit. In my solitude, I sought His presence and He was there. When He was silent, I listened. In my weakness, I learned to let Him fight my battles for me.

My desire was to be more like Christ. Therefore, God taught me humility. The things I couldn't see through my eyes, He helped me to see through His eyes. I prayed for wisdom and He gave it to me. I prayed for grace to bear my burdens and found that His yoke is easy and His burden light.

There have been so many sleepless nights, too many to count. But I now enjoy knowing that this is when God speaks to me most. When I awaken with a thought, it's because I need to get up and write it down. When a name comes to my mind, I know it's because I need to pray specifically for that person and at that moment.

When I had no voice to sing, He gave me a song in my heart. When I couldn't play the piano due to a broken arm, I felt like a part of me had been severed. But when the cast was removed, I saw three nail scars to remind me forever of the cross and what Christ did for me at Calvary. When I couldn't understand His ways I learned to trust Him. When I was rejected, He replaced the emptiness with His love.

How do you write an end to a story that has no end? Growing in my relationship with God will be an ongoing process until the day He returns or either calls me home. I trust Him by faith to be my Guide until my race is over and my time here on earth is done. Until either of these times come, I will serve the Lord.

The 23ʳᵈ Psalm

I don't think there is any portion of scripture that has meant more to me during my illness and recovery than Psalm 23. I suppose that is because I lived every word.

I want to share with you how real these verses have been to me and how God has proven Himself so true and faithful. It has been through the many months of rehabilitation and recovery (in the desert) that everything I knew about God; every attribute, every promise, and every word has been experienced. Through His grace and mercy, I have witnessed a healing no physician could touch. It was the healing of my soul.

"The Lord is my Shepherd" - We have a *relationship*.

"I shall not want" - He *supplies* all my needs.

"He maketh me to lie down in green pastures" – He gives me *rest*.

249

"He leadeth me beside the still waters" – He brings me peace.

"He restoreth my soul" – He *healed* my broken heart.

"He leadeth me in the paths of righteousness" – He is my Teacher.

"For His name sake" – He gave my life *purpose* and direction as I waited on Him.

"Yea, though I walk through the valley of the shadow of death" – He *tested* my faith.

"I will fear no evil" – He *protected* me from my enemies.

"For Thou art with me" – God was *faithful.* He promised to never leave or forsake me, and He never did.

"Thy rod and Thy staff they comfort me" – I found *security* in knowing that He was working all things for my good because I love Him and because I am called according to His purposes, not my own.

"Thou preparest a table before me in the presence of my enemies" – God fought my battles for me and protected my heart from pain. This gave me *hope.*

"Thou anointest my head with oil" – I *believed* in God's power to heal me. All it takes is a touch from His hand.

"My cup runneth over" – He filled my heart with pleasures forevermore. He answered my prayer and gave me a story. My tears He replaced with joy. My heart is full of rejoicing for His *abundant* blessings and His provision.

"Surely goodness and mercy shall follow me all the days of my life" – What a *blessing* to know that God is always looking

out for me, guiding my steps, and clearing my path of obedience to Him.

"And I will dwell in the house of the Lord" – He has *promised* me a home in Heaven; a reward for my faithfulness.

"Forever" - I will spend *eternity* praising Him for loving me enough to choose me and set me apart for His service.

I know that God loves me. He is constantly perfecting me for His glory. He chose me to spend eighteen days of constant togetherness with Him, plus months of countless, sleepless nights and quiet days in prayer. He wanted me to get to know Him more, and I did. I still am!

Despite the mounds of medical bills, the many hours of therapy, appointments, Cat scans, x-rays and labs, God has always made a way. I am learning to spend my time serving Him in other ways than what I was accustomed to. Before I do anything, I always try to ask myself, "Is what I'm doing bringing glory to God and will it in some way further His kingdom?" If it doesn't, then it is not important to me.

It is possible that you have also had a "Close Encounter" with God. If so, you know the passion that I feel about walking with Him. It is also possible that you have never met Him and because of that fact, you fail to know Him as your Savior. If this is true, then you have yet to realize the joy of a relationship with Him. God loves you, just as much as He loves me. He wants you to know Him as: the God, who reigns; the Son, who intercedes; and the Holy Spirit, who enables.

You might say Karen, "How do I find "good" in my difficult circumstances?" My best answer to you would be to trust God, knowing that He is always in control and He always allows what is best for us. He allows our testing to help us grow stronger in our faith. The more faith we have, the harder the test. Why does He do this? It's because He loves us enough to want to fellowship with us on a continual

251

basis. He loves us enough to draw us closer to His heart and sometimes, that takes a trial.

The way we handle our trials tells Him how much we love Him. He wants us to view them as ways to show forth His glory and He does this through you and me. He wants us to grow in our relationship with Him and to be more like His Son, Jesus Christ. He allows our difficulties to prove His love towards us. As we seek Him, we find all that we need I Thessalonians 5:16-18 tells us to, *"...rejoice always, pray without ceasing, in everything give thanks, for this is God's will for you in Christ Jesus."*

I want to ask you a question. If you were told that you had twelve hours to live, what would be your focus? If that question doesn't give you an eternal goal, such as making sure your heart is right with God or reaching as many people for Christ as you possibly could, then you may need to re-evaluate your life's purpose and align it with God's. You may need to let go of some things that are keeping you from passionately pursuing a relationship with God. If you step out in faith, you can walk on water...but if you hang on to the boat, you will miss God's best for your life.

A sign of spiritual maturity is when we can look on our difficulties and give thanks. Becoming spiritually mature takes a lifetime. We will never reach full maturity because there is no way we could ever know all there is to know about God. What God asks for is that we continue to pursue Him, that we seek Him, and that we have faith in Him to help us finish the race He has set before us.

#1 - When we thank God in difficult circumstances it keeps us aware of His presence. It reminds us that He never leaves us or forsakes us. Isn't it sad that we often fail to call on Him until we are facing a difficulty. He created us for fellowship with Him. He longs to talk to you everyday all day, not just in times of need.

#2 - When we thank Him for trials, we begin to search for His purpose in the trials. As our attention is focused on what His purpose might be, a sense of strength and wholeness develops and we become motivated to be more submissive to His will. When we are thankful, we will keep our eyes open and our hearts attentive to His direction.

#3 - When we thank Him for trials, our faith and trust grow and develop and we are enabled to rejoice, even midst our hardships.

#4 - When we thank God during our trials, it gives us a more powerful witness and brings glory and honor to God.
God is glorified when we rejoice in our trials and trust Him to lead us through them.

#5 - When we thank God in trials, we realize how much He really loves us because if He didn't love and care for us, He wouldn't take the time to refine us and purify us.

#6 - When we thank God in trials, we are placing our will and our attention on Him, rather than on ourselves. Learn to get yourself out of the way!

#7 - When we thank God for our trials, it demonstrates a humble spirit. There are two character qualities that I admire so much about Christ: His humble spirit and His genuineness. He humbled Himself so much that He left His home in Heaven to come to earth and dwell among men. He and God are "One," yet He bore the burden of all our sins in order to provide a way of salvation. He did all this out of His love for man, yet, it was man who crucified Him on a cross.

God knows my prayer. It is to keep me humble and obedient. If my disabilities are what it takes to be what and where He wants me to be, then so be it. I am still so blessed because I am healed by His stripes.

God longs for you to know Him personally and passionately. All you have to do is seek Him because then you will find Him. Enjoy the journey as you grow to love Him more and more and be sure to take the time to smell the roses along the way because they don't allow them in ICU!

Conclusion

The Race

This book is based on Hebrews 12:1-2. The fact that the scriptures compare our lives to a race is a good one. You see, we have a clear **path** mapped out for us (Jeremiah 29:11). We are surrounded by a crowd of on-lookers, **spectators** who are cheering us on (Hebrews 12:1). We have a **finish line** (II Timothy 4:7). We have **obstacles** (John 16:33) and we are working towards a **prize** (I Corinthians 9:24).

In order to truly understand our role in the race, we must consider the things that might hinder our success. God's word calls these things encumbrances and entanglements. What exactly do these words mean? It is something that slows our progression in the race or weighs us down. Think of the marathon runners. Would you expect to see them wearing a backpack filled with unnecessary items? Of course not! A good runner has prepared himself for the race by eliminating any excess body weight. He also considers the weight of his clothing, including his running shoes. The slightest encumbrance will hinder his speed, making his run tougher and slower. These things are taken into consideration if the runner wants to win the race or even finish it.

Any entanglement is exactly what you would think. It is something that tangles the runner up, such as vines in the path or a loose rope. The runner knows that if he gets caught up, he will need to stop and untangle himself, but then he would lose valuable time. On the other hand, he cannot run with his feet tied together either. He might lose some time, but he will surely finish, if he takes the time to rid himself of the encumbrances and entanglements.

Many times while running my race, I have had to take the time to stop and untangle myself from things like guilt, regret, fear, doubt, and unforgiveness so that I could continue and finish my race. My prayer is that you have a desire to build your faith and finish your race and that you may have taken the time during the reading of this book to free yourself from entanglements that are hindering the progression in your race.

We all get tied up at some time in our spiritual life. We often call these things burdens. Jesus never intended for us to run our race while carrying a heavy, burdensome load. He came to carry our burdens for us and to free our paths from destruction.

What burdens are you carrying that you need to give to Jesus? What vines are tripping you up and preventing you from moving forward towards the finish line? I encourage you to get rid of them; they are only slowing you down!

By now, you should have a pretty good grasp on why the scriptures compare our lives to a race. By now, you may be finding yourself standing at a place where two paths meet. This is a defining moment. Choose the world's way and struggle or choose God's way and find rest.

Have you been moving in the wrong direction, not realizing the importance of looking unto Jesus, the author and finisher of your faith? Have you been aimlessly wandering, trying to decide which way to go? Are you now ready to make a decision to choose the path of least resistance and allow God to have His will and way in your life? If so, Calvary is a picture of the crossroad you face.

At the foot of the cross, I am reminded that "I am crucified with Christ: nevertheless I live; yet not I, but Christ liveth in me: and the life which I now live in the flesh I live by the faith of the Son of God, who loved me and gave himself for me."

In a matter of four hours, my life changed forever! For some people, it's a split second. Whose team are you running for? It may be that it is time for you to change coaches!

You may need a place to begin again. Salvation is free and it is eternal, but maybe your crossroad has led you to a point of asking for forgiveness of sin and a fresh, new start in your race. God is a God of new beginnings. Draw a line to separate yourself from your past and move forward towards your future with Christ Jesus. Let go of the past and take hold of the future. God doesn't want us discouraged and looking at all the things that are wrong with us. He wants us looking at all the things that are right with Him. He is not looking for a perfect, world class runner. He is looking for a heart that is surrendered to Him. God can make miracles out of messes! No matter how deep the pit is that you are in, God's arm is long enough to reach in and pull you out.

The Lord's mercy and loving kindness never fail and they are new every morning. God knows what He is getting when you give yourself to Him. After all, He created you. He knows what parts of you He wants to use. Are you willing to give them to Him? Isaiah 43:19 says, "Behold I am doing a new thing." God loves to give us a new start. The prodigal son knew that he had made a series of bad choices in his life, but he also knew that he wanted to go back to his father, even if he had to work as a slave. Can you imagine the surprise he felt when his father ran to greet him and then planned a celebration in honor of his return?

God will do the same thing for you. He has given us a wonderful promise of new life in Christ. He will lift you up and give you a new beginning. Look, He stands at the crest of the hill, waiting with open arms to greet you. You will soon find Him running to meet you right where you are and He will give you a life of hope and future blessings. Jesus knows where you have been, He knows where you are, and He knows where you are going.

Of course, there is always the possibility that we will get off-track, but know that any discipline from God is framed with His eternal love. God has the power to enable us and help us maintain a heart completely devoted to the One who is able to keep us from falling all the days of our life (Jude1:24).

When you are running down life's road trying to do your best and still everything seems to be crashing down around you, open your eyes. Your limited perspective may be the one thing blinding you from the One who is walking beside you. It would be a shame to never see Him.

When we follow Jesus, it doesn't take long to realize that doors don't just fly open in front of us. But every open door signifies that someone has already walked through it. That someone is Jesus Christ, who prepares the way. God is always opening doors for us. Each one is an opportunity to share what He has done in your life. There are no coincidences with God. Everything is a divine appointment. The question is, will you walk through the door to a new beginning or will you keep to your present path because it feels comfortable?

Make sure your priorities are in the right place. There is nothing worth stepping out of God's will to obtain it.

God's work leaves little room for self-imposed boundaries because God knows no boundaries. Nothing is too big for God to accomplish. Take for instance, the Great Commission. Jesus left twelve disciples with a job of evangelizing the world. Now, over two thousand years later, look what they have accomplished! All God is asking of us is to reach our corner of the world. The same fuel that fed the disciples belief and gave them the strength to persevere is available to each and every one of us, through the power of the Holy Spirit. Do you find that motivating? As a child of God, you have the power of the Holy Spirit living within you. There is no job too big for you to do. Are you beginning to get a greater vision of what God could do with your willing heart?

I want you to stop for a moment and examine your spiritual location in the race. Are you like Abraham who trusted God? Are you like the prodigal son, feasting on a pig trough, instead of God's blessings? Are you like the children of Israel, griping and complaining, even though God has provided for you and rescued you from sin's slavery? Or, are you feasting at the Father's table? Wherever you are, get up and finish your race!

The legacy you leave behind may or may not be remembered by historians, but it certainly will be remembered by God. He will recall every step you took towards obedience. He will recall how many times you got up when you fell. He will remember your acts of love and He will remember your holiness. The greatest legacy you could leave behind is to love the Lord, your God, with all your heart.

When was the last time you felt the presence of God in your life; not just there because He is everywhere, but intimately abiding within you, controlling your submissive will? God is calling you into a relationship with Him. He is calling you to lay your burdens down, pick up your cross, and follow Him. He is calling you to run your race, by faith, and He is calling you to a life of service. His call is always followed by His promise to go with you and to give you the faith to finish your race. Ability is not about what you can accomplish. It is about what He can accomplish through you. Ephesians 3:20-21 admonishes believers that God is "Him who is able to do far more abundantly beyond all that we ask or think, according to the power that works within us, to Him be the glory."

I don't know about you, but I don't want my family and friends to stand over my grave wondering where I stood in my relationship with God. I want my life to be the evidence of a heart surrendered to Him. I want them to know with full assurance that I didn't just follow Christ to the very end of my race; I chased after Him because I longed to be near Him. I want them to have the assurance that we will meet again in Heaven and that for all eternity we will walk the streets of Heaven together. I want them to know where they will find me when they get there because I will be sitting at the feet of Jesus. I don't want them to mourn a loss, I want them to celebrate a gain. My greatest joy would be to know that they picked up my place in the race, grabbed hold of the baton, and passed it on.

I pray that the footprints I leave behind will lead others to Christ and that they will take their place in the race and finish well. When you listen to a speaker or read a book, what gives the speaker or writer their credibility? It is their personal testimony. No one can dispute what God has done in your life. I pray that God has added the credibility to my story that you

259

needed to make it believable. I pray that I have validated your trust in me. I have shared with you my intimate experience, in hopes that you might also learn of God's desire to have a relationship with you.

I am not perfect, nor will I ever be. As I have said before, I am not a Bible scholar or theologian nor do I hold any degree from seminary. I am a sinner, saved by grace. My intent has never been to preach to you, judge you, or condemn you. It is my prayer, however, that the Holy Spirit will use every word to convince you of God's unconditional love and convict your heart of your need for His salvation. His desire is to fill you with His presence and His longing is to have an intimate relationship with you. Every word in this book has been written in love and with a desire to help you grow in the grace and knowledge of your Heavenly Father, your Lord and Savior, and His precious Holy Spirit.

There is a position in the race just for you. God has equipped you for it. No one else will be able to complete this part of the race like you can. The course has been prepared just for you, obstacles and all. How well will you run?

God knows that you have already endured setbacks, tragedy, failure, weakness, disappointment and/or pain, but we must not let these things defeat us. Those who finish their race well, refuse to give up, let up, shut up, or give in.

When you think you have given all you've got, ask God for a second wind. When you fall, listen for His voice because He will be telling you to, "Get up and finish your race!" You will hear Him applauding you for continuing to run, not because you are winning. He will be applauding you for finding the faith to finish your race, in your relationship with Him.

Dear Heavenly Father,

I live my life for no other than You; not for applause, not for notoriety, not for fame or fortune. It is to one day hear You say, "Well done, good and faithful servant." I live not for Your approval because You have already given that to me. Instead, I live my life by faith to do Your will.

I am sure that there will be times when Satan will tempt me and try to discourage me because he loves to steal, kill and destroy. People will let me down. They will misinterpret my efforts and they won't see my real motives. I am sure they will criticize me too. But that's when I will remind myself that I am not running for them, I am running for You.

As I press on, I realize that I will not be relying solely on my own strength and efforts to win my race. Isaiah 40:31 says, "Those who wait for the Lord will gain new strength; they will mount up with wings as eagles, they will run and not get weary, they will walk and not faint." God, You are my enabler. Sometimes I will soar and other times, I will need to rest. Resting in You, I will find the strength to "keep on keeping on" no matter what obstacles lie in my way. I know that what You expect of me is to keep running towards the prize and that I will be blamed only for not pressing on and for finding myself content with anything short of the prize.

I must keep running to finish my race, not out of fear, but because I don't expect Your Almightiness to cover my unwillingness. I will put forth the effort, water the seeds, fertilize the soil, and wait for the harvest. I will run till the end. When I fall, I will get up, and I will finish the race.

You set a mark of excellence at the end of my race and then you invited me to a higher calling. I have accepted the challenge, I have prepared for the race, I have my running gear on and I am waiting for the signal to start. You trained me in a desert, but You supplied all my needs there. You lightened my load, and You made me more fit for the race. You have encouraged me all through my training, and I am grateful for having the number one coach - the Holy Spirit.

The road appears long and narrow and I can only see to the first bend, but You have taught me to keep my eyes fixed on eternity.

I know that I will feel the chip of Your chisel until the day I walk into Heaven, but the hands that hold the chisel are nail-pierced and tender and the masterpiece in progress "me." You will continue Lord, because You love me, not because you are punishing me. Because You loved me to death, You have also loved me to life...eternal life.

How much was I a part of my surviving? I believe a main ingredient was my faith in You; a faith that was enough to keep me trusting in You through dark times, silent times, and the mountaintop encounters with You. It was my faith that sustained me when medical science was at a loss for direction. It is my faith that ties me to a promise I made to You in ICU. I told You that my life belonged to You and that I would spend the rest of my life running with patience while preparing to cross the finish line into my Heavenly home and I would do it obeying You. It is my faith that thanks you over and over again for giving me a second chance. It is my faith that keeps my eyes on eternity, knowing that there is no greater place to be. It was and is my faith that continues to say to You, "wherever you want me to go, whatever You want me to do, I will do it." Consider the willingness of my heart, Lord, and use me I pray.

Affliction did not make me less alive, it made me more alive. I will live a better life, I will enjoy my days with relentless passion, and I will have a determination to make my last days on earth my best days on earth. My life will be more complete, fulfilling, and rewarding because of affliction. Therefore I will be a better wife, mother, sister, and friend. For that, I am grateful to You.

I believe You have placed within each of our hearts a miracle. I have the power to do things more abundantly than I can imagine when I tap into the power of the Holy Spirit that lives within my heart.

It is impossible to experience an encounter with You and not be changed. I accept this change and welcome the final preparation for my entry into Glory. My life has been changed by a "God-experience," not a "religious experience."

Resuming parts of a normal life means progress. The only reason I look back is to see how far I have come. To give You less than my best, would be accepting defeat. You have never demanded my perfection. I give You "my best" and no less.

"I have fought a good fight, I have finished my course, I have kept the faith" (II Timothy 4:7). Until the day I see Your face, I will praise Your name here on earth. And for eternity I will shout with a new voice, I love You Lord.

I thank You for who You are. I thank You for teaching me to appreciate who I am. I thank you for breath and life. I am blessed because You love me with an overflowing, unconditional love. You are more than I deserve and all that I need.

Help me to always be grateful, humble, and striving to follow in Your will. Keep my mind clear that I may hear Your voice. Keep my eyes on You that I may follow. Give me wisdom to accept all things and help me to walk as a Christ follower.

I know that when I can't find the words to pray, You listen to my heart. Fill me so that I may pour myself out and bless others. Keep me strong, that I may help the weak. Keep me uplifted that I may encourage those who are struggling. Help me not to misjudge, but rather to understand.

I pray for those who don't know You as their personal Savior and I pray that before this day is over, they will accept You so that they too will know the joy of having a relationship with You.

I thank you for allowing the Holy Spirit to illumine me and fill me. Thank you for the fact that He will always be with me.

For those who are troubled, Lord, I pray that every eye that reads and every ear that hears will learn that there is no problem, no circumstance, and no situation greater than You are. You are bigger than all our problems, fears, or any mountain we have to climb.

In Your holy and precious name I pray, Amen

Closing

I pray that you have gained insight into the power and majesty of God as you were introduced to Him as Father, Son and Holy Spirit.

I pray that as you began to experience the story of how God showed His love to me, His transforming love also began to speak to your heart. I pray that you found yourself loving Him more. When this happens you will find yourself in the midst of a deeper, richer, more passionate, more intimate relationship with God.

The call to love God with all your heart and all your mind is to experience God's grace, which is His unmerited favor. His grace will enable you to receive from Him a new sense of His presence in your life. It will give you strength for what He calls you to do. Best of all, it will give you joy as you walk with Him, rely on Him, and trust in Him day by day.

How could you help but love the One who gives your life purpose and direction, who enables you to achieve its purpose, and then promises you a reward for doing so? His greatest reward is eternal life in Heaven. It is granted to you because you accepted Christ as your Savior, you worshipped and brought glory to your Heavenly Father by the life you lived, and you walked in obedience to the Holy Spirit.

Finally, I pray that you begin to run your race with a faith that will give you the endurance you will need to finish. Every challenge presents His opportunity to increase your faith. Your faith will come by hearing and your hearing, by the word of God. Listen, for He will speak to you. May you find yourself always in preparation for the race. By seeking God's face, reading His word, and by listening to the guidance of the Holy Spirit you will walk, even run in newness of life.

If you give up, give in or quit the race, the pain will last forever. You must never quit. Finding the will to go on brings our reward. Would you rather live with regret or defeat? Being a winner doesn't mean you will be the first to cross the finish line. A winner is the person who crosses the finish line, even though they may be battered and worn from the race.

How will you run your race? Will you take hold of the baton which is God's message of salvation and pass it on to the next person, or will you say, "Life is too hard" and lay it down? Will you accept it, but never reach out to offer it to another runner because you are too busy? Will you allow Satan to steal your confidence to run the race well? Do you feel that God's training ground is too rigorous? Are you willing to cross valleys, forge rivers, and climb mountains? Do you find yourself at the starting gate ready for your instructions to "Go?"

So what do we do? Where do we go from here? How do we find the strength to keep running? It is by realizing that greater is He who is within us, than he that is in the world. Running reveals our weaknesses, but faith reveals our innermost strength.

The crowd is cheering you on…they believe in you as God believes in you. They have prepared you for the race by sharing the gift of salvation, but the decision to take the first step towards building a relationship with God is up to you. The decision to walk a life of obedience is up to you.

This is a new race. The end you cannot see. Are you questioning the obstacles, the detours, maybe the injuries from falling? A victorious finish awaits you through a belief in what you cannot see…your faith to finish. God will hold your hand all the way.

He did not create you to leave you in some black hole of despair. He created you for eternal fellowship with Him in Heaven. The cumulative events in your life were orchestrated by God for His purpose, in order to reveal to you, "your purpose." Your Heavenly Father has prepared the way for you.

If you know Him, get to know Him more. You and I can never know Him enough and we will never regret our commitment to seek Him with all our heart.

I pray that I have succeeded in hiding myself behind the cross so that you could see Christ. To God be all honor, glory, and praise for the things He has done!

If you are wondering how to begin your race, it starts with accepting Christ as your Savior; believing that He came to earth to die on a cross in order to redeem you from sin and that He was buried, yet rose again to sit at the right hand of His Father to intercede on your behalf.

In John 3:16 we read, *"For God so loved the world, that He gave His only begotten Son, that whosoever believeth in him should not perish, but have everlasting life."*

I would like to ask you a simple question. If today you were to find yourself one step away from crossing your finish line, do you know where you would spend eternity? If you are not positively certain that it would be in Heaven, this could be the day of your salvation and the beginning of your relationship with God. All it takes is stepping out in faith.

Step One:
Realize that you are a sinner by nature of mankind.
"For all have sinned, and come short of the glory of God" (Romans 3:23).

Step Two:
There are wages to our sin, and there is a way to forgiveness.
"For the wages of sin is death; but the gift of God is eternal life through Jesus Christ our Lord" (Romans 6:23).
"Verily, verily I say unto thee, Except a man be born again, he cannot see the kingdom of God" (John 3:3).
"Jesus saith unto him, I am the way, the truth, and the life; no man cometh unto the Father, but by me" (John 14:6).
"That if thou shalt confess with thy mouth the Lord Jesus, and shalt believe in Thine heart that God hath raised Him from the dead, thou shalt be saved. For with the heart man believeth unto righteousness; and with the mouth confession is made unto salvation" (Romans 10:9-10).

"Behold, I stand at the door, and knock; if any man hear my voice, and open the door, I will come in to him, and will sup with him and he with me." (Revelation 3:20).

Step Three:
Answer these questions:
1. Do you believe that you are a sinner?
2. Do you want forgiveness for your sins?
3. Do you believe that Jesus died on a cross for your sins and rose again?
4. Are you willing to surrender to Christ and His will for your life?
5. Are you ready to open the door of your heart and ask Jesus to come in?

If you answered yes to these questions, please pray the following prayer with me:

Heavenly Father, I realize that I am a sinner. I ask you to forgive me of my sins. I believe that You sent Your Son, Jesus, to die on a cross for my sins and that He rose again. I ask you to come into my heart, and become Lord of my life. This I ask of You, Father, in the name of Jesus I pray. Amen

If you prayed this prayer and meant it with all your heart, I welcome you into the family of God. I encourage you to live your life in obedience to Him because there is no greater joy! May God's grace abound in your life as you begin the journey. I will see you in Heaven!

I want to leave you with these words of encouragement from *Revelations 7:14-17.*

In the end, God will cause you to stand among those…*"who have come out of the great tribulation; they have washed their robes and made them white in the blood of the Lamb. Therefore, they are before the throne of God and serve Him day and night in His temple; and*

He who sits on the throne will spread His tent over them. Never again will they hunger; never again will they thirst. The sun will not beat upon them, nor any scorching heat. For the Lamb at the center of the throne will be their shepherd; He will lead them to springs of living water. And God will wipe away every tear from their eyes"

God works in mysterious ways
His miracles to perform.

Nothing would please me more than to know of your decision to accept Christ as your Savior or to hear how God has spoken to your heart through this book.

I encourage you to read and study my second book, "Finding Faith to Finish." In it, I discuss aspects of my life that God used to draw me into a deeper, more intimate relationship with Him.

In order for me to disciple you, I must teach you and give you a tool that will help you pass on what you have learned. Thus, it is written in handbook form. May it be a resource that you will return to over and over again as you spread the gospel of Jesus Christ. It is His commandment (Matthew 28:16-20).

This book would be a great addition to any church library. As a handbook, it can be used for personal or group Bible study. Just think what God can do with one person who is ablaze for His glory. If He can use me, He can use you too!

For book ordering information or to schedule a speaking engagement, please contact:

Karen Faith McGowan – "Faith to Finish"
PO Box 204534 Augusta, Georgia 30917-4534
FTF@knology.net   **706-449-2863**

Psalm 30
"My Testimony"

"I will extol thee, O Lord; for thou hast lifted me
up,
O Lord my God, I cried unto thee, and thou hast
healed me.
O Lord, thou hast brought up my soul from the
grave: thou hast kept
me alive,
weeping may endure for a night, but joy cometh in
the morning.
I shall never be moved
Lord, by thy favor thou hast made my mountain to
stand strong:
thou didst hide thy face, and I was troubled.
I cried to thee, O Lord; and unto the Lord I made
supplication.
Hear, O Lord, and have mercy upon me: Lord, be
thou my helper.
Thou hast turned for me my mourning into
dancing: thou hast put off my sackcloth, and
girded me with gladness;
To the end that my glory may sing praise to thee,
and not be silent. O Lord my God, I will give thanks
unto thee for ever."

Faith to Finish

By:

Karen Faith McGowan – January 2006

Lord grant me the wisdom to depend on You;
Help me be patient as You see me through.

Trials surround me, anxiety beyond end;
Please, Holy Spirit, on me descend.

Open my eyes to Your plan for me;
Fix them on You, then through them, let me see.

Your purpose, my desire is submission to You,
Mold me, fill me; I am Your vessel, Your will to do.

You are "I Am," without You I am nothing.
My life is Yours. Take it and make it something.

I have no desire for earth's wealth or gain,
But I press towards the prize, the high calling of the One who
was slain.

I know not the path of the race You have chosen for me to run,
But when I cross the finish line, I long to hear You say, "Well
done."

It takes courage to walk daily by Your side and to trust in
You by faith;
Strip me of the sins that hold me back; humble me with
whatever it takes.

Help me conquer the hurdles and pass all the tests.
Life is not about winning. It's about who serves their best.

Forget bronze or silver, I'll go for the gold.
Refine me, purify me, mold me, and make me whole.

And whenever my faith in the outcome starts to diminish,
Open my eyes, fill me with Your strength, and give me the
"Faith to Finish."

About the Author

Karen is a native of Augusta, Georgia. She now resides in nearby Martinez with her husband of thirty-seven years, Charles, and their dog, Abbey.

Karen and Charles have two sons: Paul, who is married to Suzanne, and Nathan who is married to Sharon.

Karen believes that throughout the many seasons of her life, God has used her place in the world as her "mission field" and that every part of her life's journey, the good times as well as the bad, has only deepened her relationship with God.

God has blessed her with many talents and she has spent her life using them to help others. Besides being a devoted wife and mother, she has been a Registered Nurse, a professional seamstress who designed and created wedding gowns, and a business owner who held the position of Sales Director.

Music is also one of her many gifts and she says, "Music connects me with God. When I sing, it's as if I am singing only to my Heavenly Father and my song comes from a heart of adoration. When I am playing the piano, my hands become my instrument of praise. My music is not a performance, it is my ministry." Karen began her ministry in music at the young age of thirteen and she has spent the following forty plus years serving God as church pianist and soloist.

"The difference in my singing today, versus prior to my illness, is that I used to sing with my head in self-confidence and now I sing with my heart in God-confidence. Out of all the fulfilling things that I have done in my life, my greatest accomplishment has been reaching my present level of spiritual maturity. I accepted Christ at the age of five and my desire has always been to seek and do His will. Nothing in my life matters more to me than the relationship I have with my Heavenly Father, Holy God."

Karen enjoys helping others grow personally, emotionally, and spiritually. She shares her definition of success as: "Knowing God and walking in obedience to His will. To me, there is no greater ambition."

When asked to describe herself she says, "I am very introspective, transparent, truthful, and honest. I am confident that I can do all things through Christ who strengthens me, but that without Him I can do nothing. I know who I am in Christ, and I know that He loves me unconditionally. My desire is to introduce others to Him and then to help them grow in their relationship with Him; discipling them as Christ commanded us to do. I believe that it is only in the relationship that we have with God that we find the "Faith to Finish" our race and the peace that comes from enjoying the journey."

"As a candle lights the darkest room, so does the testimony of one who has walked in the shadow of death, but like Job, rose from the ashes to tell her story. Thank you, Karen, for sharing. You have enriched, encouraged, and inspired us to stay at the feet of Jesus."
Jeanne Gibson